Practices of Ephemera Modern England

CW01567114

This collection is the first to historicise the term ephemera [obscured] ings for early modern England and considers its relationship to time, matter, and place. It asks: how do we conceive of ephemera in a period before it was routinely employed (from the eighteenth century) to describe ostensibly disposable print? In the sixteenth and seventeenth centuries – when objects and texts were rapidly proliferating – the term began to acquire its modern association with transitoriness. But contributors to this volume show how ephemera were also integrally related to wider social and cultural ecosystems. Chapters explore those ecosystems and think about the papers and artefacts that shaped homes, streets, and cities or towns and their attendant preservation, loss, or transformation. The studies here, therefore, look beyond static records to think about moments of process and transmutation and accordingly get closer to early modern experiences, identities, and practices.

Callan Davies works across early modern literary, cultural, and theatre history. He's part of the Box Office Bears project (researching animal sports in early modern England), as well as the Middling Culture (www.middlingculture. com) team examining early modern status, creativity, writing, and material culture, and the Before Shakespeare team (www.beforeshakespeare.com). His book, *What is a Playhouse? England at Play, 1520–1620*, is an accessible account of the playhouse across early modern England (Routledge 2022). He is the editor of the Curtain playhouse records for *Records of Early English Drama's Records of Early English Drama REED London Online* and author of *Strangeness in Jacobean Drama* (Routledge, 2020) as well as articles across literature and history journals.

Hannah Lilley is an Independent Scholar, previously of the University of Birmingham. She is interested in the material culture of early modern scribal practice.

Catherine Richardson is Professor of Early Modern Studies and Director of the Institute of Cultural and Creative Industries at the University of Kent. She studies early modern material culture, and has written books on *Domestic Life and Domestic Tragedy in Early Modern England* (Manchester, 2006), *Shakespeare and Material Culture* (Oxford University Press, 2011), and, with Tara Hamling, *A Day at Home in Early Modern England, The Materiality of Domestic Life*, 1500–1700 (Yale 2017). She has edited *Arden of Faversham* for Arden Early Modern Drama, and is PI on the AHRC project 'The Cultural Lives of the Middling Sort': https://research.kent.ac.uk/middling-culture/

Material Readings in Early Modern Culture

Series editor: James Daybell, Plymouth University, UK and Adam Smyth, Balliol College, University of Oxford, UK

The series provides a forum for studies that consider the material forms of texts as part of an investigation into the culture of early modern England. The editors invite proposals of a multi- or interdisciplinary nature, and particularly welcome proposals that combine archival research with an attention to theoretical models that might illuminate the reading, writing, and making of texts, as well as projects that take innovative approaches to the study of material texts, both in terms of the kinds of primary materials under investigation, and in terms of methodologies. What are the questions that have yet to be asked about writing in its various possible embodied forms? Are there varieties of materiality that are critically neglected? How does form mediate and negotiate content? In what ways do the physical features of texts inform how they are read, interpreted and situated?

Reading Mathematics in Early Modern Europe
Studies in the Production, Collection, and Use of Mathematical Books
Edited by Philip Beeley, Yelda Nasifoglu and Benjamin Wardhaugh

Elizabethan Diplomacy and Epistolary Culture
Elizabeth R. Williamson

The Circulation of Poetry in Manuscript in Early Modern England
Arthur F. Marotti

Playbooks and their Readers in Early Modern England
Hannah August

Practices of Ephemera in Early Modern England
Edited by Callan Davies, Hannah Lilley and Catherine Richardson

For more information on this series, please visit: https://www. routledge.com/Material-Readings-in-Early-Modern-Culture/book-series/ASHSER2222

Practices of Ephemera in Early Modern England

Edited by
Callan Davies, Hannah Lilley
and Catherine Richardson

Routledge
Taylor & Francis Group

NEW YORK AND LONDON

First published 2023
by Routledge
605 Third Avenue, New York, NY 10158

and by Routledge
4 Park Square, Milton Park, Abingdon, Oxon, OX14 4RN

Routledge is an imprint of the Taylor & Francis Group, an informa business

ISBN: 978-0-367-52836-2 (hbk)
ISBN: 978-1-032-43139-0 (pbk)
ISBN: 978-1-003-05858-8 (ebk)

DOI: 10.4324/9781003058588

Typeset in Sabon
by codeMantra

Contents

Figures

Acknowledgements

Chief thanks go to the collaborators, who have made this book a reality and who enthusiastically ran with the collection's collaborative ethos. These chapters were drafted and finalised over the course of several coronavirus lockdowns and a radical change in both personal and professional lives across the world over the past two years. Such events have made the notion of "ephemera" disconcertingly topical. We accordingly looked to find new ways to engage in generative conversation around the subject of the book – our digital "draft parties" in the summer of 2021 were enjoyable exercises in academic exchange, and contributors took forward this spirit of cross-pollination in their approach to chapter-writing. The editors send a thank you to each other: the collaborative approach of this venture has not only lightened and brightened the editorial process but also opened up the volume's possibilities. Finally, thanks to Sarah Wasserman, who kindly offered sage advice on a draft of the introduction, and the series editors, Adam Smyth and James Daybell, for suggesting the idea of the volume in the first place.

Biographies

Robert Bearman, formerly Head of Archives and Local Studies at the Shakespeare Birthplace Trust in Stratford-upon-Avon, is the author of *Shakespeare in the Stratford Records* (1994) and *Shakespeare's Money: how much did he make and what this did mean* (2016). He has edited Volume 6 of the *Minutes and Accounts of the Stratford-upon-Avon Corporation, 1599–1609*, and has prepared for publication a further volume covering the years 1610–1620. His other published articles and essays mainly concern Shakespearean biography in the context of Shakespeare's native town.

Bruce Boehrer is Bertram H. Davis Professor of English at Florida State University. He is the author or editor of eight books and former editor of the *Journal for Early Modern Cultural Studies.*

Callan Davies works across early modern literary, cultural, and theatre history. He's part of the Box Office Bears project (researching animal sports in early modern England), as well as the Middling Culture (www.middlingculture.com) team examining early modern status, creativity, writing, and material culture, and the Before Shakespeare team (www.beforeshakespeare.com). His book, *What is a Playhouse? England at Play, 1520–1620*, is an accessible account of the playhouse across early modern England (Routledge 2022). He is the editor of the Curtain playhouse records for Records of Early English Drama's *Records of Early English Drama REED London Online* and author of *Strangeness in Jacobean Drama* (Routledge, 2020) as well as articles across literature and history journals.

Megan Heffernan is Associate Professor of English at DePaul University and the author of *Making the Miscellany: Poetry, Print, and the History of the Book in Early Modern England* (University of Pennsylvania, 2021). She is at work on a new monograph on lyric form and the history of book conservation and care.

Katherine Hunt is Lecturer in Sixteenth- and Seventeenth-Century Literature at the University of East Anglia. Her work is concerned with the relationship between writing and material culture in early modern England and Europe, and how these interactions affect us in the present. She is completing a monograph, *The Brazen World: Brass and the Making of English Renaissance Literature*, which asks how the technologies and processes of making in bronze and brass helped to shape writing in the early modern period.

Elaine Leong is a Lecturer of History at University College London. Her research is centred on medical and scientific knowledge transfer and production, with a particular focus on gender and the everyday. She is the author of *Recipes and Everyday Knowledge: Medicine, Science and the Household in Early Modern England* and the editor of a number of essay volumes and journal special issues, most recently *Working with Paper: Gendered Practices in the History of Knowledge* (Pittsburgh, 2019) and "Learning by the Book: Manuals and Handbooks in the History Science" (*BJHS Themes*, 2020).

Michael Lewis is Head of Portable Antiquities and Treasure at the British Museum managing the Portable Antiquities Scheme – a project to record archaeological finds made by the public – and oversees the administration of the Treasure Act 1996 – by which the most important archaeological finds are acquired by museums. He is also Visiting Professor in Archaeology (University of Reading), Research Associate (University of York), and Honorary Research Fellow (Birkbeck). Michael is an (archaeological) small finds expert, specialising (principally) in medieval finds associated with religion and everyday life.

Hannah Lilley is an Independent Scholar, previously of the University of Birmingham. She is interested in the material culture of early modern scribal practice.

Jemima Matthews is a Lecturer in Early Modern English Literature at King's College London. She is currently completing her monograph *Habitat and Habitation: The River Thames 1550–1650* for publication. She has published on Shakespeare and site-specific performances at Whitehall. Her research explores the relationship between early modern literature and early modern literary geography.

Anna Reynolds is a Lecturer in English at the University of St Andrews. She works on the intersection of material practices and imaginative thought in early modern England, attending, in particular, to the physical biography of paper and the metaphorical life of books, loose sheets, and textual fragments. She is currently preparing her first monograph, *Privy Tokens: Waste Paper in Early Modern England*, and has published an article on early modern encounters with binding waste in *The Journal of the Northern Renaissance* (2017).

She is co-editor of the volume *The Paper Trade in Early Modern Europe* (Brill, 2020) and has chapters forthcoming on waste and material texts in *The Oxford Handbook to the History of the Book in Early Modern England* and *The Oxford Handbook of Early Modern Women's Writing in English*. With Adam Smyth (University of Oxford) and Megan Heffernan (DePaul University), she is designing an open-access, online database of early modern printed waste paper.

Catherine Richardson is Professor of Early Modern Studies and Director of the Institute of Cultural and Creative Industries at the University of Kent. She studies early modern material culture, and has written books on *Domestic Life and Domestic Tragedy in Early Modern England* (Manchester, 2006), *Shakespeare and Material Culture* (Oxford University Press, 2011), and, with Tara Hamling, *A Day at Home in Early Modern England, The Materiality of Domestic Life, 1500–1700* (Yale 2017). She has edited *Arden of Faversham* for Arden Early Modern Drama, and is PI on the AHRC project 'The Cultural Lives of the Middling Sort': https://research.kent.ac.uk/middling-culture/

Helen Smith is Professor of English Literature at the University of York, UK. She is the author of *Grossly Material Things: Women and Book Production in Early Modern England* (2012) and co-editor of *Renaissance Paratexts* (2011), *The Oxford Handbook of the Bible in Early Modern England* (2015), and *Conversions: Gender and Religious Change in Early Modern Europe* (2017). Her current monograph project is an ambitious account of early modern matter and its shifting forms. With JT Welsch, Helen is the co-founder of Thin Ice Press.

William Tullett is Associate Professor in Sensory History at Anglia Ruskin University in Cambridge. His main research interests, on which he has published several articles, are the histories of smell and sound in the early modern and modern world. His first book was *Smell in Eighteenth-Century England: A Social Sense* (Oxford University Press, 2019), and he is currently preparing further books on the history of smell and an online "Encyclopaedia of Smell History and Heritage" as part of the EU Horizon-2020 funded project "Odeuropa."

Alison Wiggins is Reader in English Language and Manuscripts at the University of Glasgow. She was AHRC Leadership Fellow during 2017–2019 (*Archives and Writing Lives*). Her monograph *Bess of Hardwick's Letters: Language, Materiality, and Early Modern Epistolary Culture* was published for the series *Material Readings in Early Modern Culture* (Routledge 2017, paperback 2019; AHRC Project

Reference AH/F01308/1). She is currently co-editing with Andrew Prescott the volume *Archives: Power, Truth, & Fiction* for the Oxford University Press Series *21st Century Approaches to Literature.* She has collaborated on projects with the National Trust, Chatsworth House Archives, The National Archives, The Bodleian Library, and the National Library of Scotland.

Introduction/Spawning

Callan Davies, Hannah Lilley and
Catherine Richardson

> The trifles of each how'rs vain exercise,
> Toys that should be *Ephemera* indeed
> Dying the same day they were born and bred.
> *Clarastella together with poems occasional,*
> *elegies, epigrams, satyrs,* Robert Heath (1650)

How do we historicise the 'trifles' of everyday life – the distinction between what lasts and what does not – and understand what was regarded as *ephemeral* in early modern England? The chapters that form
this volume seek to frame early modern ephemerality as part of social
and cultural ecosystems – from the familiar categories of paper things
and insects that are thought of as *ephemera,* to the less familiar sense-
scapes, practices, bodies, and wider world of temporary or metamorphosing things that might also be considered part of this category. This
volume draws out early modern conceptualisations of time, fleetingness,
and the value of things, through writings that consider the term *ephemera* and through ephemeral material. The chapters are grouped sugges-
tively to map out early modern perspectives on the subject. Section 1
looks at how the concept evolves during the sixteenth and seventeenth
centuries through the explosion of printed and handwritten writings
produced during this period, forcing early modern individuals to consider what could be kept and what could be discarded, and the value of
the discourses circulating at local and national levels. Section 2 considers ephemeral objects and practices, and how early modern people got
to grips with the fleeting and the eternal as categories of time through
things and writing. Section 3 turns its attention to the ephemeral environment of early modern London: the scents, goods, paper, and people
that populated a landscape buzzing with things that died the day they
were born, either literally or in the attention of the beholder. Linking
these chapters are ideas of insect lives representing notions of quality,
quantity, and reproduction, a sense of ephemera's temporalities, and the
implications for early modern studies of seeking after ephemeral evidence of various kinds. We try, in other words, to pin ephemera down
in time.

DOI: 10.4324/9781003058588-1

Across the sixteenth to the eighteenth centuries, the word was starting to develop its modern meanings of transitoriness. Originally mainly used to describe the kind of fever that lasted only for a day, it was also tied up with descriptions of natural history phenomena (for instance it was the name of a fish "which ariseth in the Sea water euen as the Bubble doth, where as much raine is. Whome *Iorach* in his Booke *de Animalibus* reporteth after thrée houres of the day to die" [Maplet 85]). More broadly, the way the natural world was seen to function shaped the meanings of the ephemeral. Eighteenth-century writers, for instance, "understood smell as an endless stream of atoms – or effluvia – constantly exhaling from all and any objects" (Tullett 212), turning the making of tea into a fight against time to trap its virtues before they could evaporate. The ephemeral was tied up with the texture of everyday life. Robert Heath's poem, quoted above, goes on to explore the status of insignificant things "of so smal concern or moment," and to ask who would record them in their diary: "As what he wore, thought, laugh't at, where he walkt,/ When farted, where he pist, with whom he talkt" (Heath 3).

If the evanescent nature of the natural world was thought-provoking, then this was also a period in which material things became notably less lasting. Cheap print, breakable pottery, and new types of less durable cloth were produced in unprecedented quantities, and the presence of things whose materials, design, or function gave them a deliberately short shelf-life brought about a fundamental change in the way people regarded the objects through which their identity was negotiated. Conversely, although the movement towards a disposable culture was noteworthy, the fundamental relationship between material and form was still palpably different from our own. Buildings were taken down and rebuilt elsewhere, windows and panelling were considered moveable goods to be taken with one when one moved house, and a whole range of furnishings, dining, cooking, and sleeping objects and clothing, bedding, and napery were given between the generations in wills and deeds of gift, sometimes multiple times, and then remade repeatedly into other things until they became worn, while there was still any material left. Tying the material to the natural world, this was a preserving culture, in which salt, sugar, and vinegar ensured that perishables would be available in the kitchen even in the winter months.

Outside the house, the chapters in this volume pick up on other significant contexts within which the ephemeral was understood. Trade routes produced "a set of new entangled histories about maritime ephemera" (Matthews 174), moving things and people around the world. On the land, urbanism and population growth invited comparison with the prodigious breeding of insects and necessitated increased record-keeping to keep track of the births, marriages, deaths, taxes, and misdeeds of men and women. Things sprang up all over the place in early modern England, and the sense of growth and multitude put pressure on ephemeral metaphors. In slower timescales, on differently urgent subjects, "humanist scholarship was concerned with what could be made of the fragments that had survived from the antique," and "humanist imitation was also, always, concerned with remaking new knowledge from these fragments" (Hunt 113). Across the period we consider here, ephemeral print took a firmer shape as "literary trifling, figured as frantic and swarming and brief," easily and clearly contrasted against "literary attainment, figured as calm and unique and durable" (Boehrer 61). And behind all of these concerns, the need to live and die well, to fix sights beyond the daily to the eternal, provided the outer layer of the onion of concerns over durability, fixity, and accountability. This was therefore a culture that looked beyond the tangible and with an eye to the eternal: life beyond death and the possibility of achieving everlasting salvation or damnation. These possibilities gave another dimension to the term *ephemera* and metaphors of things that lasted only a day, which made writers consider their own "existence as an exercise in momentariness" (Smith 163). Thinking about the ephemeral alongside the lasting allowed early modern individuals to conceptualise a time beyond that which they could perceive.

The essays that follow deal in various types of smallness, lightness, or brevity. In reading through them, you will discover multiple tiny scraps of paper – "sweet-wrapper-sized squares written with sums being worked out" (Wiggins 84); pieces pasted into the bindings of later volumes, or folded around gifts of money; the page of an almanac's calendar, twisted into a cornet for spice and painted balanced on upturned oyster shells at the bottom of a still life. But you will also find butterflies, mayflies, dayflies, and moths with their essential qualities of "flyness": "plurality, swarming, confusion of kinds, summer heat, moisture, daintiness, flimsiness, novelty, triviality, extreme brevity, and sudden putrefaction" (Boehrer 46). Such small things briefly occupy a spot in the world – on their way from one use to another, one state to another – somewhere between creation and destruction. Some of them are still physically present for us to study now, others in an altered form, either as a textual or pictorial record of material presence or an archaeological trace of translated matter; all of them demand skills of careful analysis (our own piecing together), or of practice research, to comprehend their ephemeral qualities.

The twist of paper and the insect reflect two essential strands of analysis that run through the volume, the textual and the biological, or the human-made and the natural. The interplay between them is key to understanding the value for early modern studies of attending to ephemera. But the picture is more complicated than single-use, brief, and insignificant things. Over the couple of years of meetings, discussions, and writing through Covid lockdowns via which this volume has come together, we have glimpsed a considerably more complex landscape. Some clear definitions emerge from the chapters: ink is "transitory" in the sense that it "does not survive as a liquid, whose natural components … decayed over time, and for which the process of making was an ephemeral practice"; its ingredients are ephemeral "in the sense that they were used in large quantities across multiple contexts to generate consumables like inks, dyes, and beer, but (apart from the iron ore from which copperas was drawn) had a short lifespan" (Lilley 134). But the subjects treated here also reveal that the material qualities of an object are only one of the aspects that define its duration. There were, for instance, lasting forms of attention that were paid to ephemeral things, and repeated uses that made them central to social practice; they reveal paradoxes such as paper's almost opposing qualities of disposability and durability, which made it both the most lasting and least expensive aspect of letter-writing (Wiggins).

A particularly significant aspect of ephemerality across several essays is the way things bore evidence of the close contact they had with one another: the constant circulation of eighteenth-century objects "allowed them to build up a tactile, olfactory, and visual patina as they accumulated matter from the city around them … soaking up the … qualities of tobacco, brandy, rose wood, or shit" (Tullett 215). Texts moved across oceans, where they "rubbed against all manner of substances including spices, tobacco, pies, meat, and skin," or exhibited "passing phenomena" from a voyage on their surfaces, "such as various changes in light, air, salt, ink composition" (Matthews 177). Objects also, of course, interacted with humans, who sometimes appear far more ephemeral than the materials with which they engage, and with the places in which they were kept at the time and have been kept since: bindings lurking in archives "wearing each other down, eating away at the very texts they were once meant to preserve" (Heffernan 21). Powder for fireworks was subject to a test in the period, which "involved placing it on white paper, firing it, and then seeing whether it left 'sooty' marks and a 'noisesome' smell" (Tullett 219). The process points us towards ephemeral paper and its contact with the raw materials of an ephemeral show, potentially leaving a mark which, not lasting in itself, attests to a brief event of assay – ephemerality is not merely inherent in things but is contingent on material, use, and timescale.

As it appears in these examples, the ephemeral is one aspect of or element in an ecosystem. Anna Reynolds points out that early moderns "were sensitive to the ways in which their books were made up of diverse sorts of matter, inhabited varied environments, and progressed along the stages of a life cycle" (34) – they had a tendency to appreciate the different parts of which individual objects were constituted and were sensitive to their various durabilities. But they also understood how different things might function together as groups of more or less long-lasting items – distinct paper types with various "relationships with ephemerality" (Wiggins 87); the way "the eternal simultaneously appears in and through the ephemeral, which cradles it and gives it presence, making it perceptible to time-bound beings" (Boehrer 49). Enduring things may have been framed as more noticeable than ephemeral ones and understood in relation to them, but the lasting and the brief are also visible as part of a wider, mutually-supportive plan of action in which, for instance, slips of paper related to books of recipes, or "ephemeral encounters shored up more durable habits and forms of commercial knowledge" (Tullett 214). Epistemologically, it is the interplay between durable and ephemeral things and practices, abstract elements and their material manifestation, that makes knowledge transferrable across space and time.

Throughout these chapters, we see, prominently, the locations where these ecosystems operated. There are playhouses and bear-bating arenas, ships, muniment rooms, and cabinets of curiosity. Some are intended to guard against the passage of time, drawing a "physical barrier against ephemerality" which has since proved in many ways illusory; some function as "a storehouse composed of materials, resources, and ephemera with various life cycles and ephemeral to different degrees and under different conditions" (Matthews 182), where the receptacle is in itself a key term in the distribution of ephemeral qualities that allows them to operate in relation to one another. The fate and the scale of these receptacles often determine what survives directly to the present day, and therefore what constitutes the archive with which we work.

If the ecosystem is one clear way of thinking that emerges from the chapters, then the lifecycle is the other. Here, the focus is pulled back to reveal that the distinction between brevity and longevity is only one of perspective: Bruce Boehrer quotes Cicero: "contrast our longest lifetime with eternity: we shall be found almost in the same category of short-lived beings" as the fly (44). In this period of reuse, recycling showed knowledge of and respect for the changing material possibilities of current forms. Katherine Hunt, for instance, recounts the impact of bronze's ephemeral potential, as a metal that can be endlessly recycled. The fate of Sejanus' statue, "the face that was number two in the whole world" later "turned into little jugs, basins, frying pans, and chamber pots" (120), shows both a metamorphic inventiveness and a hierarchy of forms – public statue to quotidian pot – which is heavily moralised. There are questions here about what brevity of form means: does it mean "unworthy of prolonged attention," or that the object's purpose is served, like the ubiquitous almanac which, at the end of the year, moves into quotidian use as a cover for mustard pots, for example? It is the endurance of form that eclipses the brevity of use, and the short articles on individual objects below show things in use, reuse, discarded and then reconstructed, tracing a lifecycle that brings them right up to the present.

Callan Davies follows the apples used in the early modern playhouse from growth, through various types of ludic use, to destruction of the fruit itself and translations into archaeological remains as pips and textual remains as description. Hannah Lilley, using Joyce and Gillespie's ideas about itineraries as complex biographies ("strings of places where objects come to rest or are active, the routes through which things circulate, and the means by which they are moved" without beginning or end [129]), traces the constituent elements of ink from the business of North African merchants and the hands of slaves, to middling and elite English households. Like William Tullett's perfumes, these things set off very long trains of thought and association across time and space, taking in things absent and present in material, textual, and imaginative form. The decisive moments in these trajectories include the decisions about preservation that were taken between the early modern period and our own. Robert Bearman's description of "destruction schedules … based on a pyramid view that some of the records at the bottom can be dispensed with if a more refined digest exists at a higher level" (66) both provides a less positive definition of ephemera as excrescence – the parts of an archive that can be done without – and offers insight into what has been and could still be lost: the lived experience of decision-making (such as votes for and against an election result, for example) or the personalities and intentions visible in drafts whose ambitions are eventually scaled back in final documents. Certainly, the volume does not exhaust early modern concepts of ephemerality, nor does it address all the contemporary categories of brevity, but we hope it gestures revealingly to the value historical study of brief lives might bring.

Histories of Ephemera: Pre-Modern to Modern

The ephemeral lifespans and ecosystems of this collection offer context for later, more dictionary-defined ideas of ephemera. Studies of the subject have opened a range of theoretical approaches with which to comprehend both historical negotiations with fleetingness and today's investment in what does and does not last (an urgent subject amid mounting concerns over the climate emergency and unrest about structural injustices under late capitalism). Sianne Ngai has recognised the importance of the twentieth-century gimmick – an "aesthetically suspicious object" often regarded as a "'contrivance', an ambiguous term equally applicable to ideas, techniques, and things" (1). Gimmicks are designed to save labour and time but are also regarded as "working too hard"; these concepts or objects, therefore, indicate a fundamental "uncertainty about value and time" (1). Much the same can be said about the practices of ephemera that form this volume. If contrived gimmicks represent something of the late capitalist mindset, then the paper, insects, toys, trifles, and statues discussed here speak to a developing early modern category spanning ideas, techniques, and things. Ngai emphasises that gimmicks are not merely objects but are also mindsets and processes. The discussions in this volume take a similar attitude and accordingly give insight into premodern attitudes toward disappearance and durability and the daily practices that shaped these notions. What results is a longer history of *the ephemeral* than has been explored to date – one with a relationship to the twentieth-century gimmick but equally distinct. Ephemera's paradoxical place between transience and survival links the late medieval to the late capitalist, and the concept repeatedly raises questions about both value and time. Yet ephemerality is always culturally contingent, and accordingly different periods within the history of ephemera have different attitudes towards, vocabularies for, and understandings of it.

The surge of interest in contemporary experiences of ephemerality across "ideas, techniques, and things" has much to do with pressing ecological and social crises – of the environment, race, class, and gender. Sarah Wasserman's study of post-war American literature sets out a helpful theoretical model. "Things are not simply absent or present," Wasserman observes, "but somehow both" (2). Attending to "transient things" can thereby "remind us to look askance at heroic and punctual – often masculinist – narratives of origins and ends" and to "interrogate the whiteness of the material turn" (36). Indeed, "it is often in the detail, the discard, and the disappearing object" that "concerns with ethnicity, class, and minority status reside" (36). While such concerns have a particular social charge in the twentieth- and twenty-first-century United States, the early modern period was equally a catalyst for race-making discourses and colonial endeavours. It is therefore no surprise that ethnicity, class, and minority status are key concerns for this volume – whether in Lilley's travelling ink ingredients or in issues of access and education underwriting the archive and the cultural patrimony held by lasting monuments (Bearman; Wiggins; Ketelaar).

Contemporary reimaginings of the politics of ephemera extend to a radical embracing of its inherent changeability. Caitlyn DeSilvey has celebrated the shifts and transmutation of buildings, objects, and landscapes as part of a push within heritage studies to accept and adopt decay: "it is possible to perform remembrance through transience, although this may require a willingness to find value in alternative material forms" (5). The ephemera discussed in this volume attend both to preservation and to DeSilvey's call to embrace physical change. Both Anna Reynolds's and Megan Heffernan's understanding of the shifting but serious value of early modern ephemera depends upon the ability of temporary objects and texts to mutate and endure in new forms. Their readings of early modern texts prompt reconsideration of the way memory works within and through cultural institutions like libraries, museums, or personal archives. All the chapters here encourage us to think beyond the static artefact towards the fluid and the fungible.

Twentieth-century concerns with the politics and practices as well as the aesthetics of ephemera have roots in a much longer historical enthusiasm for printed or documentary ephemera. Anne Garner's survey of ephemera scholarship observes a gradual move "towards a more logical historiography," which "agrees on the elusiveness of the category" and its "instability [...] at different moments of consumption, collection, and conservation over time" (259). Indeed, historians have long looked to the concept as key to understanding past practices and life experiences. "In the reconstruction of the past," Asa Briggs contended, "everything is grist to the historian's mill, and what was thrown away is at least as useful as what was deliberately preserved" (9). Briggs's sense of intentional and unintentional archives is central to Bearman's institutional history of ephemera, in which accident and happenstance underpin documentary preservation.

The twentieth-century historian Maurice Rickards was a crucial early pioneer of the history of ephemera. His *Encyclopedia of Ephemera* offers an A to Z of the different (chiefly textual) forms in which collectors, curators, and historians might find objects of interest. For Rickards, ephemera referred to all those "minor transient documents of everyday life" (*Collecting Printed Ephemera* 7). The nature of the term "minor" has perhaps been contested by some recent analyses of such forms – overturning long-held value judgements – but Rickards' career demonstrates how the obdurate survival of documents against their inherent or perceived transience opened up the study of the past, and his lifetime of work pioneered "serious study of ephemera" (v). When the late Rickards's encyclopaedia was edited by Michael Twyman, he pointed out how its variety of manuscript and printed matter represents "the very lifeblood of literate societies" and offers a reader everything from graphic design to business history (1) – a practice he terms "ephemerology" (see "The Long Term").

The burgeoning of ephemera studies also generated a range of institutional bodies and archives that matched the academic pursuit. Rickards founded the Society of Ephemera (UK) in 1975, which continues to draw together libraries, museums, and universities as well as dealers and private members. Such societies exist across the world, including in Rickards's former department, at the University of Reading, which is home to a Centre for Ephemera Studies that now contains Rickards's own extensive collection. Ephemera Societies operate in Australia and the USA, and there are numerous specific library collections, ranging from American Advertising to British printed ephemera held at the Bodleian. E. Richard McKinstry sets out the variety of these different institutional repositories or bodies for ephemera in a resource list of items originally created with disposability in mind.

Many longer-standing ephemeral archives, eventually folded into newer bodies, were eighteenth- or nineteenth-century creations, born from an antiquarian interest in quotidian historical flotsam and jetsam. Among the earliest of these belonged to Samuel Pepys, who curated a range of daily documents, from gaming apparatus to ballads. Others followed, however, including John Evelyn (whose collection now belongs to the British Library); founder of the eponymous library at Oxford University, Thomas Bodley; and, later, the University's printer John Johnson (whose collection is now housed at the Bodleian). For Marilyn Butler, these collectors were "early social historians and social scientists," whose passions sat alongside new interests in political economy and natural science (*Mapping Mythologies* 124; see Gillian Russell's discussion, 25). In documenting the granular details of their past and present, these collectors were part of a burgeoning empiricism – one centred on cultural life and artefacts alongside the natural world. The development of such a scientific approach is playfully explored here, for example in Bruce Boehrer's appreciation of the shifting meaning of "flyness" for early moderns – a concept that fluidly ranged between taxonomical, religious, social, and imaginative connotations of ephemera. Boehrer's chapter demonstrates that Butler's language of social science had an ephemeral pre-history that doubtless influenced later antiquarian collectors. For Boehrer, this pre-history was part of a developing creative language and practice in early modern England.

Gillian Russell's recent study identifies such "ephemerologists," (with Johnson exemplary among them) as part of a practice and a field of knowledge built from "forms of print that are ubiquitous and familiar but which occupy a marginal, even buried, place in institutions and disciplinary formations" (3). The significance of this field, for Russell, is its interest in knowledge, culture, and aesthetic experience beyond the codex-form book "The investments of literary studies and bibliography" in such a form,

> as a vehicle for authorial genius and the pre-eminent genres of drama, poetry, and prose fiction, to the extent of subordinating the materiality of the book itself to the intangibility of the 'work', have similarly entailed the marginalisation of ephemera.
>
> (3)

Book historians of the early modern period have recognised the longer history of such non-book printed materials, as well as the significance of transience to book history more broadly. "The history of the early modern book," Adam Smyth explains,

> is also a history of loss and destruction: of print as impermanent; of literature as something that needs to be forgotten; of books that

burn; of reading as an act of throwing away. Most printed texts lived very briefly, and then were gone, forever.

(55–56)

Russell's and Smyth's recognition of the temporality and temporariness of early texts pushes back against potentially pernicious literary myths of universality, timelessness, or monumentalism – often associated with authors valourised by Romantic writers and typically represented by a narrow white, male canon. Chapters here by Hunt and Boehrer explore this tension between a desire for literary or artistic immortality and the fleetingness of one's expressive medium – a tension not lost on early modern writers and makers.

The eighteenth century saw an exponential rise in transitory printed material, and the period has come to shape our understanding of ephemerality. Russell dubs pre-modern textual production "ephemera before 'ephemera'" (8). For Russell, as for many other scholars of the busy print market of the age of Johnson and Defoe, *The Spectator* and the *Tatler*, it was the late seventeenth and early eighteenth centuries that birthed the concept of "ephemera" as it applied to print. Yet the centuries preceding the coffee house and the subscription novel offer a distinct cultural engagement with physical and metaphorical transience. Early modern engagements with paper did not always draw such fine distinctions, and the frequent repurposing of writing materials that punctuate this collection suggest that generic distinctions between codex and slip, account book and ballad sheet, or even flax and paper were less significant than the uses to which they were put and attitudes to them (Calhoun). The idea of the book was still in flux.

In the years under study here, because ephemera was not yet fixed as a *textual* category, the discourse and subjects associated with it ranged across a whole suite of daily practices. Some of these were artistic – poetic, dramatic, or sculptural – while others were borne of practical necessity, such as food or ink recipes. Still more, like commonplacing, fell somewhere in between. It was during these earlier years that the vocabulary of ephemera developed and, with it, a commonly understood sense of its application to various forms of production that extend beyond books. Accordingly, this volume looks not only to the wider "paper continuum" (Russell 15) beyond the codex-book but to other forms of media entirely. Chapters here survey a range of terms through which we can not only recover the daily experience of early moderns but also access debates about aesthetic value, knowledge-making, material reuse, ecological consciousness, and technologies of remembrance and preservation. These include, for instance, "flyness," "accidental" archives, "toy," or "puff." Moreover, as the twenty-first-century theories noted above teach us, ephemera is not limited to materiality at all. It also depends upon process. Performance studies has long recognised the inherent ephemerality of live media (Phelan). The tension between loss and survival at the heart of book history applies equally to acts, actions, or processes understood as ephemeral. Historians of these forms depend upon the "archive" or afterlife of performance – what Barbara Hodgdon calls "scraps, scribbles, drawings and fragments" – to recover "performance as process" (4–5). Similarly, scholars seeking pre-modern sensory experiences recognise the importance of the momentary situation to the nose, tongue, ear, or mouth (Dugan; Smith).

Such evanescent forms help bring us closer to some of the major social and structural changes that occurred during the early modern period. England underwent a profound architectural shift from the mid-sixteenth century onwards, with crucial consequences for everything from archiving to conceptions of privacy (Orlin). The theories of ephemerality mapped here help us chart the changes in the built environment that would have been felt by residents from all walks of life across early modern England. Wiggins' investigation of the Cavendish papers and Bearman's deep dive into the Stratford-upon-Avon Corporation materials, for instance, reveal how notes, jottings, and paperwork shaped the physical world. While the spatial materiality of the past is difficult to recover – perhaps impossible to do so fully – such glimpses suggest how questions of material preservation and fluidity imposed themselves upon everyday lived experience. Architecture and design writing has recently pushed the term "ephemeral" as key to appreciating the "performativity of space" (LaBelle, 159; Karandinou). In this volume, the concept of ephemera extends to a range of reproducible media in a variety of spaces, like objects formed in moulds, across print and handwritten work in the form of ephemerides; this crowding of things and people seen through metaphors of short-lived flies in Boehrer's, Reynolds's and Tullett's chapters points to fears of being lost amongst a burgeoning city population. Matthews argues that Mountfort's *The Launching of the Mary* associates the ephemeral goods traded by the East India Company with the bodies of the workers and their wives, underlining the separation between the company merchants with their lists and tables and the human cost of the trade. The country house and its collections are set alongside the growing early modern city with its shops selling varieties of goods ephemeral or otherwise from farther and farther afield. Ephemera's explosion went hand-in-hand with an ever-larger cohort of middling consumers from the sixteenth century onwards, some of whom sought to preserve some of those things that passed through their hands.

Indeed, early modern individuals often shared, both with later ephemerologist collectors and with later libraries and archives, a desire to preserve what was ostensibly temporary or to repurpose it for another (sometimes equally temporary) lifespan. Across this collection, the very notion of archiving is at issue. These were years when various records – domestic, commercial, ecclesiastical, and political – began to necessitate a range of classification and ordering: part of what Peter Burke identifies as the rise of the "paper state." Yet many of the items within these archives remained themselves subject to change and alteration as "working records" (Griffiths 125). Such observations warrant wider connections to the work of the archive today, not least as it shifts into new media. Indeed, Neil Rhodes and Jonathan Sawday had some time ago, during the dotcom boom, drawn a parallel between early modern technologies of knowledge and modern digital practices in *The Renaissance Computer*. More recently, Wasserman asks, "Can literature help us understand the new forms of transience that are emerging in this digital age?" The question extends to historical ephemera in different media, too, not least that developed in early modern Europe as the understanding of that transience and the language used to describe it were at issue. Megan Heffernan's study of a scrap in the Folger Library recognises the institutional journeys that delineate access to and understanding of ephemera. These matters pertain just as much to the online world, as Wasserman's study makes clear: "even when objects transition from the material to the digital, they can elicit the same sorts of competing desires" (242).

Ultimately, for seekers of early modern ephemera, what survives typically does so against the odds. It is always "untimely matter," in Jonathan Gil Harris's formulation, existing as "polytemporal and multitemporal" objects (3). Many of the examples in this book have something of this quality. They exist beyond what we might now call their planned obsolescence or their deliberate discarding – preserved, curated, or transmogrified into something new. By drawing on challenges and changes specific to the early modern period but acknowledging both physical and imaginative legacies, these chapters lengthen the historical reach of ever-growing ephemera studies, taking it back to the undertheorised period we might playfully call (after Russell) "the ephemeral sixteenth and seventeenth centuries."

Time, Materiality, and Ephemera

Survival and persistence not only link ephemeral materials across periods but situate them, precariously, within the concept of time itself. This volume demonstrates the complexity of ephemera's relationship to time – the tensions between the lasting and the fleeting drawn out in Hunt's brass, Davies' architecturally embedded apple seeds, Tullett's perfume cards and their disappearing scents, and Bearman's documents that were never intended to be kept, against the volumes into which they were digested. Kevin D. Murphy and Sally O'Driscoll draw on this strain in their book on eighteenth-century ephemera, noting there is "an inherent tension in, say, political pamphlets or broadside ballads: materially, they are disposable, yet their content could be worth treasuring" (xii). And, indeed, many of the items described as ephemera in this volume gesture to a world of things that, as Tullett aptly puts it with Lynn Hunt's metaphor about the eighteenth century, were part of the "thickening" spaces of early modern society, experienced on a daily basis as people went about their lives (L. Hunt 86). Printed treasures in our archives like pamphlets and libels, as Reynolds, Tullett, and Boehrer point out, once "buzzed," "flew," "swarmed" and "spawned" in early modern spaces, reaching large audiences and describing a new textual and bodily crowdedness in cities and spaces, which grew from the sixteenth century onwards. Ephemera is fleeting but also simultaneously jostling for a consumer's attention in space.

The way in which the time-limited bodies contrasted with the immaterial, everlasting soul after the body's demise underlines the corruptness of the body and the stuff of life that the soul left behind. The corrupting nature of crowds, print, and objects emerges particularly in Tullett's, Reynolds', and Boehrer's chapters, showing the close connection with rapid material multiplication and questionable morality. The value judgement placed on things deemed ephemera in later periods (as difficult to categorise and unimportant or of a time) means that this category since its conception has had a close connection with the body as divorced from the soul – the material that the immaterial left behind – and so has a post-Reformation quality that makes the spawning of ephemera decidedly early modern. Helen Smith explores this new understanding of the body, its temporariness, and how this contrasted with the immaterial, intangible, imperceptible, and infiniteness of everlasting time in her chapter on commonplacing, where she argues that images of fleeting things, like bubbles, grass or potter's vessels, helped individuals "understand their existence as an exercise in momentariness" and "imagine the possibility of something immaterial, persisting not just to the end of, but beyond, time" (Smith 163). This practice makes the concept of early modern ephemera distinct from the twentieth-century understanding, because sixteenth- and seventeenth-century individuals were encouraged to think about, and prepare for, their earthly demise in a way that made them conscious of the potential lifespan of the material things around them – from charitable gifts to household papers.

Some of the most common derivative terms of ephemera in sixteenth and seventeenth-century print culture were *ephemeris* or *ephemerides*. These terms also gesture to the complicated relationship of the chronological calendar to ways of thinking, organising, and understanding other processes. *Ephemerides* were diaries, but they were also almanacs that tabulated future astronomical events – textually layering up the present and future but also building up a record of the past in the way that habitual diary or almanac keeping encouraged. Their production may have been circumscribed by the day, but the future consumption and treasuring of these objects gave them significance beyond a distinct unit of time; ephemerides were more expansive in their lifetime, from the daily habit of the writer to the preserving culture and consumption of the keeper. Their content, as Smith writes, also encouraged this layered understanding of time, with the temporary placed against the eternal, the material against the immaterial, and the collecting-for-the-future mentality involved in keeping such a record contrasting against the possibility that the writing could be lost or destroyed at any point in the near or distant future.

Ephemeral things and *ephemerides* also force us to consider the attention of the consumer – the owner of Lewis' toy coach who threw it into the Thames, Lilley stirring together her ink ingredients, Davies' apple eaters, Tullett's perfumers and buyers, Smith's readers collecting choice phrases to commonplace. The consumers of ephemera in this volume attend to the fleeting at levels of time that are not necessarily in line with the intended lifespan of the object. Lilley's ink would take days to make in the period and her subject paid close attention to the qualities of his ingredients; playgoers consuming apple snacks would also attend to their significance as objects bought from outside the city, to their rhetorical significance in the performances and to their status as a physical feature of the playhouse. Fleeting things also had the potential to last longer than a day in the mind – like the information contained within Reynolds' pamphlets or Tullett's printed trade cards. Habits of attention were contained within the process through which ephemeral things metamorphosed throughout their lifecycle when their usefulness for a particular purpose was exhausted, and this emerges time and again in the volume: an object with an ephemeral existence in one form might gain a new life in an item intended to be kept for different purposes, like Heffernan's legal documents made bindings. Attention to the material qualities of ephemera by the early modern consumer would cause the no-longer-useful to be reused in needed guises: from bronze statues, to paper cones, to bindings. Ephemera has also been shown to survive in unintended forms – a printed perfume card, or a note to be included in the Stratford-upon-Avon accounts – and absorbed into other objects, like Heffernan's bindings, or crumpled and thrown away like Lewis' toy coach. Ephemera are, then, of the day but also extend beyond it, carried across time in other forms or surviving by accident, one of many texts or things of their kind that once filled spaces and minds.

Time and again in studies of ephemera, those texts placed within this archival category have been celebrated for their usefulness in enhancing our understanding of processes. Martin Andrews has argued that "we can have direct contact with the past through artefacts that were once central to the functioning of society – the etiquette, protocol, private and business life of past centuries and societies" (447). For example, bookmarks that might provide evidence of reading practices, trade cards that gesture to the places, people, and books sold in various places, and ex-libris showing a book's owner (Andrews 434–50). Recording fleeting experiences or collecting ephemeral objects defies the transitory objects' or actions' relationship to time: it treasures a moment for replication or appreciation at future points that might far outlast an object's maker, author, or first collector. Leong's recipe slips record processes that are temporary; their recording, then subsequent archiving, allows the layering of fleeting experiences over time. Small sheets of paper as archival ephemera can allow access to medicinal or culinary experiences whilst also allowing us access to social connections in their sending and sharing. Bearman's Stratford-upon-Avon ephemera give insight into the voting process; Wiggins' sums, bills, and receipts were absorbed into larger volumes of accounts. Documents not made to last in single-sheet-form may once have pejoratively gained the name "ephemera," but in recent studies of everyday life, women's writing and making, writing pertaining to processes and experiences which preserve an ephemeral moment or connection for the future are centrally valuable. Ephemera's insight into processes shows these texts to be "multitemporal," comprised of the moment recorded, the moment of recording, and subsequent recycling, consumption, or study. Early moderns bought, read, handled, made, and experienced ephemeral things in growing numbers at a time when the connections between the material and everlasting were being questioned.

As the subject matter of these chapters suggests, in losing, or failing to pay attention to, ephemera, we risk a partial view of early modern thought, practice, and motivation. Ephemera often take us behind the scenes, to the moment when things happened, as opposed to the formal record of them, and there are oblique glances on identity formation throughout these chapters. Wiggins asks whether wrapping coins as gifts was "a widespread practical use of paper, [or] more of an elite refinement to the culture of deference" (90); Lilley's subject's "identity as a middling, literate man emerges from a web of actions and things attached to his ink making" (129) linking it to the labour of slaves and women copperas pickers. We risk, Bearman argues, hearing only what those who made formal records wanted their audiences to read, if we ignore the faint traces of informal practice to which ephemera often give access. Other histories peer around the corners if we look this way, and adopting their perspective opens up a web of interdependencies – coterminous concerns and social, cultural, and political complexities – that recentres our map of early modern practice.

Several suggestions are made, in the chapters that follow, that looking in this way raises fundamental questions about early modern studies: what constitutes our evidence; what is the nature of our archive? Davies suggests a "reassessment" of "the theatre-historical archive" in which "we look beyond the language of 'survival' and 'loss' and towards an alternative understanding of evidence" (206) – a rebalancing away from the apparently more solid textual parts of the ecosystem. Reynolds suggests that we would "benefit from cultivating an early modern sensibility toward the ecosystems within which our source materials dwell, migrate, and transform," using the long histories of use and reuse to teach us lessons about archival time (27). The work these things did historically and the work they do now ties our agency as archivists, archaeologists and historians of all kinds firmly to the actions of early modern individuals.

A Note on Navigation

This book is structured into three sections, each prefaced by an object study that extends our understanding of ephemera beyond print and text. We would suggest reading chapters in the context of their sections in order to gain a broad perspective on early modern ephemera. The first section provides definitions of ephemera in an early modern context through insects and the archive and is tied together with common themes of multiplication, and rhetorical uses of ephemera and its insect-synonyms in early modern England. The second takes a distinctly thing-based approach to the topic, though statues, ink ingredients, commonplace books, and recipes, extending our definitions of ephemera to encapsulate things that metamorphose, were consumed and survive in shifting forms. The third focuses on London and the distinct nature of ephemera in a space crowded with moving scents, sounds, things, texts, and people. Alternative reading routes could include exploring the object studies as a set of provocations about ephemera, taking those chapters on printed sources (Boehrer; Davies; Hunt; Reynolds; Tullett) together and those on manuscripts together (Bearman; Heffernan; Leong; Lilley; Matthews; Smith; Wiggins) or those that look at fleeting matter (Boehrer; Davies; Hunt; Lilley; Matthews; Reynolds; Tullett; Wiggins) or fluid texts (Bearman; Boehrer; Davies; Heffernan; Leong; Reynolds) as sets. We encourage you to find your own way through this book and would be delighted if you responded creatively to its contents.

Works Cited

Andrews, Martin. "The Importance of Ephemera." *A Companion to the History of the* Book. Eds Simon Eliot and Jonathan Rose. Blackwell, 2007. 434–50.

Bearman, Robert. "What is an 'Ephemeral Archive'? Stratford-upon-Avon, 1550–1650: A Case Study." *Practices of Ephemera in Early Modern England.* Eds Callan Davies, Hannah Lilley, and Catherine Richardson. Routledge, 2023. 65–82.

Boehrer, Bruce. "Time's Flies: Ephemerality in the Early Modern Insect World." *Practices of Ephemera in Early Modern England.* Eds Callan Davies, Hannah Lilley, and Catherine Richardson. Routledge, 2023. 44–64.

Briggs, Asa. "Foreword." *Collecting Printed Ephemera.* By Maurice Rickards. Phaidon, 1988. 1–9.

Burke, Peter. *A Social History of Knowledge from Gutenberg to Diderot.* Oxford UP, 2000.

Butler, Marilyn. *Mapping Mythologies: Countercurrents in Eighteenth-Century British Poetry and Cultural History.* Cambridge UP, 2015.

Calhoun, Joshua, "The Word Made Flax: Cheap Bibles, Textual Corruption, and the Poetics of Paper." *PMLA/ Publications of the modern Language Association of America* 126. 2 (2011): 327–44.

Davies, Callan. "Playing Apples and the Playhouse Archive." *Practices of Ephemera in Early Modern England.* Eds Callan Davies, Hannah Lilley, and Catherine Richardson. Routledge, 2023. 191–209.

DeSilvey, Caitlin. *Curated Decay: Heritage Beyond Saving.* U Minnesota P, 2017.

Dugan, Holly. *The Ephemeral History of Perfume: Scent and Sense in Early Modern England.* John Hopkins UP, 2011.

Garner, Anne. "State of the Discipline: Throwaway History: Towards a Historiography of Ephemera." *Book History* 24.1 (2021): 244–63.

Griffiths, Paul. "Local Arithmetic: Information Cultures in Early Modern England." *Remaking English Society: Social Relations and Social Change in Early Modern England.* Eds Steve Hindle, Alexandra Shepard, and John Walter. Boydell and Brewer, 2013. 113–34.

Harris, Jonathan Gil. *Untimely Matter in the Age of Shakespeare.* U Pennsylvania P, 2008.

Heath, Robert. *Clarastella together with Poems Occasional, Elegies, Epigrams, Satyrs.* London, 1650.

Heffernan, Megan. "Expired Time: Archiving Waste Manuscripts." *Practices of Ephemera in Early Modern England.* Eds Callan Davies, Hannah Lilley, and Catherine Richardson. Routledge, 2023. 21–4.

Hodgdon, Barbara. *Shakespeare, Performance, and the Archive.* Routledge, 2016.

Hunt, Katherine. "More Lasting than Bronze: Statues, Writing, and the Materials of Ephemera in Ben Jonson's *Sejanus His Fall.*" *Practices of Ephemera in Early Modern England.* Eds Callan Davies, Hannah Lilley, and Catherine Richardson. Routledge, 2023. 111–27.

Hunt, Lynn. *Writing History in the Global Era.* Norton, 2015.

Karandinou, Anastasia. *No Matter: Theories and Practices of the Ephemeral in Architecture.* Ashgate, 2013.

Ketelaar, Eric. "Muniments and Monuments: The Dawn of Archives as Cultural Patrimony." *Archive Science* 7 (2007): 343–57.

LaBelle, Brandon. "Street Noise: On the Contours and Politics of Public Sound." *Performance Design.* Eds Dorita Hannah and Olav Harsløf. Museum Tusculanum P, 2008. 159–77.

Leong, Elaine. "Recipes and Paper Knowledge." *Practices of Ephemera in Early Modern England.* Eds Callan Davies, Hannah Lilley, and Catherine Richardson. Routledge, 2023. 105–10.

Lewis, Michael. "Toy Coach from London." *Practices of Ephemera in Early Modern England.* Eds Callan Davies, Hannah Lilley, and Catherine Richardson. Routledge, 2023. 169–72.

Lilley, Hannah. "Uncovering Ephemeral Practices: Itineraries of Black Ink and the Experiments of Thomas Davis." *Practices of Ephemera in Early Modern*

England. Eds Callan Davies, Hannah Lilley, and Catherine Richardson. Routledge, 2023. 128–47.

Maplet, John. *A Greene Forest, or A Naturall Historie*. London, 1567.

Matthews, Jemima. "Maritime Ephemera in Walter Mountfort's *The Launching of the Mary*." *Practices of Ephemera in Early Modern England*. Eds Callan Davies, Hannah Lilley, and Catherine Richardson. Routledge, 2023. 173–90.

McKinstry, E. Richard. "Paper Ephemera: Online Collections and Resources." *College and Research Libraries News* 77.9 (2016): n.p.

Murphy, Kevin and Sally O'Driscoll. *Studies in Ephemera: Text and Image in Eighteenth Century Print*. Bucknell UP, 2013.

Ngai, Sianne. *Theory of the Gimmick: Aesthetic Judgment and Capitalist Form*. Harvard UP, 2020.

Orlin, Lena Cowen. *Locating Privacy in Tudor London*. Oxford UP, 2007.

Phelan, Peggy. *Unmarked: The Politics of Performance*. Routledge, 1993.

Reynolds, Anna. "What do Texts and Insects Have in Common?; or, Ephemerality before Ephemera." *Practices of Ephemera in Early Modern England*. Eds Callan Davies, Hannah Lilley, and Catherine Richardson. Routledge, 2023. 25–43.

Rhodes, Neil and Jonathan Sawday, eds. *The Renaissance Computer: Knowledge Technology in the First Age of Print*. Routledge, 2000.

Rickards, Maurice. *Collecting Printed Ephemera*. Phaidon, 1988.

Russell, Gillian. *The Ephemeral Eighteenth Century: Print, Sociability, and the Cultures of Collecting*. Cambridge UP, 2020.

Smith, Bruce R. *The Acoustic World of Early Modern England: Attending to the O-Factor*. U Chicago P, 1999.

Smith, Helen. "Things That Last: Ephemerality and Endurance in Early Modern England." *Practices of Ephemera in Early Modern England*. Eds Callan Davies, Hannah Lilley, and Catherine Richardson. Routledge, 2023. 148–66.

Smith, Pamela H., Tianna Helena Uchacz, Sophie Pitman, Tillmann Taape, and Colin Debuiche. "The Matter of Ephemeral Art: Craft, Spectacle, and Power in Early Modern Europe." *Renaissance Quarterly* 73.1 (2020): 78–131.

Smyth, Adam. *Material Texts in Early Modern England*. Cambridge UP, 2018.

Tullett, William. "Extensive Ephemera: Perfumer's Trade Cards in Eighteenth-Century England." *Practices of Ephemera in Early Modern England*. Eds Callan Davies, Hannah Lilley, and Catherine Richardson. Routledge, 2023. 210–28.

Twyman, Michael. "Editor's Introduction." *The Encyclopedia of Ephemera: A Guide to the Fragmentary Documents of Everyday Life for the Collector, Curator, and Historian*. By Maurice Rickards. Ed. Michael Twyman, with Sally de Beaumont and Amoret Tanner. Routledge, 2000. v–viii.

———. "The Long Term Significance of Printed Ephemera." *RBM: A Journal of Rare Books, Manuscripts and Cultural Heritage* 9.1 (2008): 19–57.

Wasserman, Sarah. *The Death of Things: Ephemera and the American Novel*. U Minnesota P, 2020.

Wiggins, Alison. "Paper and Elite Ephemerality." *Practices of Ephemera in Early Modern England*. Eds Callan Davies, Hannah Lilley, and Catherine Richardson. Routledge, 2023. 83–102.

Part I
Concepts/Emerging

1 Expired Time

Archiving Waste Manuscripts

Megan Heffernan

The Folger Shakespeare Library's X.d.515 range of call numbers is used for legal manuscripts that were salvaged from other items in the library's collection. As texts with a long history of use and reuse, these documents hold significant lessons about the passage of archival time. Some are large pieces of parchment that once wrapped the boards of folios or smaller portions that had been provisionally stitched around pamphlet collections (X.d.515 28; 7). Some are tiny scraps of paper (2; 6). Some are so faded they can hardly be read (13). What unites the X.d.515 manuscripts is the shifting relation between their status as texts and as objects. At some point in the seventeenth century, these manuscripts stopped being used as legal documents and were repurposed in a range of binding structures, travelling secretly in the nooks and crannies of everything from prose romances to atlases to legal statutes.[1] While they entered the library as hidden parasites in a more prominent campaign of print collecting, those binding structures are not how we access them now.[2] In the mid-twentieth century, these manuscripts once again lost their function as tools to protect other texts. The hybrid books were wearing each other down, eating away at the very texts they were once meant to preserve, so the manuscripts were separated out from the printed books and re-catalogued with their own range of call numbers (see Duroselle-Melish).

One item in this range, X.d.515 (29), is a tattered lease in a seventeenth-century scribal hand. It lays out an agreement between Miles Hobart and Philip Carey over twenty acres known as James Wood, a plot of land in Morley, Yorkshire (see Figure 1.1). The portions of the lease that remain show that, for £69 a year, Carey and his descendants were allowed to harvest timber and undergrowth, but prohibited from razing the woods in order to cultivate the land as tilled or pastured fields. This lease was a document that regulated the passage of time through the management of land. As a legal instrument, it spelled out annual rent payments, as well as the proper stewardship of the woods in order to maintain them for future generations.

At some point, this lease stopped being read or even needed as a record of the agreement it recorded. It lost its value as a text that could

DOI: 10.4324/9781003058588-3

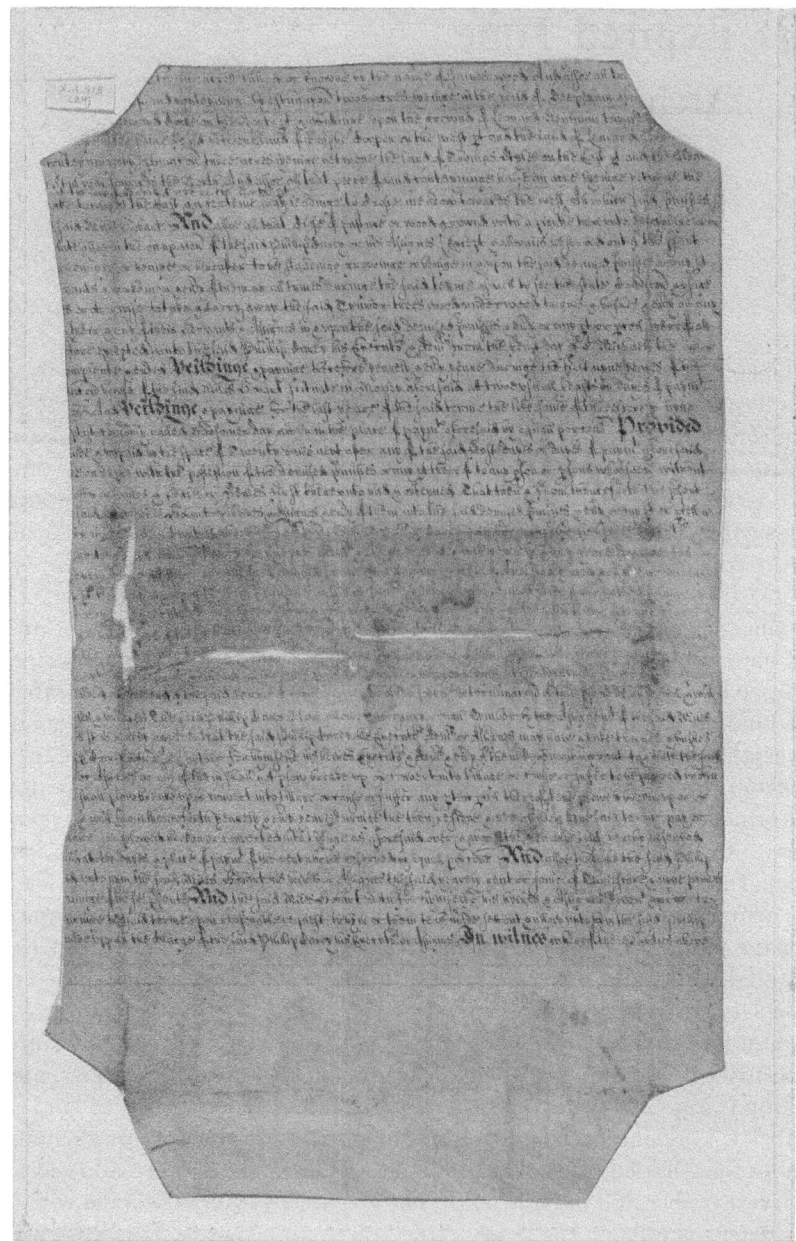

Figure 1.1 Recto of a partially obliterated lease, Folger X.d.515(29). Used by permission of the Folger Shakespeare Library, Washington, under a Creative Commons Attribution-ShareAlike 4.0 International License.

Figure 1.2 The reverse of the lease, with evidence of its later function as a
        binding for a pamphlet collection. Used by permission of the Fol-
        ger Shakespeare Library, Washington, under a Creative Commons
        Attribution-ShareAlike 4.0 International License.

regulate the use of the land, and when we flip it over, we find a whole
other history of preservation (see Figure 1.2). The leftover vellum was
measured, cut, and folded to become the wrapper on a fat collection of
quarto pamphlets. On the spine, there is a list of the multiple texts that
were gathered together to form a composite volume, as well as a label
that was presumably the shelfmark from an earlier library. The ink on
the spine is significantly more faded than the lease, but manipulating the
image by enlarging it and heightening the contrast brings some of the
contents partially into sight. With some squinting, a numbered list of 18
items comes into focus, and with more squinting and zooming some of
the text is legible: a "Gardner" in 17; a "Jane" in 6; a "Coronation Sermon" in 7; "Bishop of Rochester" in 4. Most identifiable is 8, "Meggot,"
probably a reference to Richard Meggott, the Dean of Winchester at his
death in 1692. The outdated lease, an ephemeral piece of a manuscript
that once guarded *against* the destruction of James Wood, was repurposed to protect the godly writing published at a great rate in the late
seventeenth century.

  As an item that repeatedly lived on past the point at which it should
have disappeared, this tattered manuscript urges us to rethink when and
how we define texts as ephemeral. The lease's usefulness was bound by
time, but once it passed its expiration date, it became an object that
guarded a different kind of ephemera, in fact assuring that the printed

sermons would not themselves expire. Of textual waste more generally, Adam Smyth observes that it "complicates or thickens the historicism of the text, since to read waste is to be aware of multiple temporalities" (153). In all these moments of expiration and reuse, not least in the modern re-appraisal of this lease's worth as a document to be catalogued within the library, this manuscript challenges how we read the passage of time. It illustrates the durability of both goods and texts that should have vanished long ago, showing archival time to be closer to a circuit or loop than to the straightforward chronologies of modern catalogues and bibliographies.

Notes

1 The prior relationships between the X.d.515 manuscripts and their printed hosts were not systematically recorded, but I have been able to trace some items back to John Speed's *A Prospect of the Most Famous Parts of the World* (1631), Barnabe Riche's *Riche his Farewell to the Militarie Profession* (1583), *Whole Volume of Statutes* (1587), Augustin Marlorat's *A Catholike Exposition Upon the Revelation of Saint John* (1574), and George Sandys's *A Relation of a Journey* (1627).
2 On the figurative connections between ephemeral texts and insects, see the essays in this section by Anna Reynolds and Bruce Boehrer.

Works Cited

Boehrer, Bruce. "Time's Flies: Ephemerality in the Early Modern Insect World." *Practices of Ephemera in Early Modern England*. Eds Callan Davies, Hannah Lilley, and Catherine Richardson. Routledge, 2023. 44–64.

Duroselle-Melish, Caroline. "Anatomy of a Pamphlet Collection: From Disbinding to Reuniting." *The Papers of the Bibliographical Society of America* 1112 (2017): 185–202.

Reynolds, Anna. "What do Texts and Insects have in Common?; or, Ephemerality before Ephemera." *Practices of Ephemera in Early Modern England*. Eds Callan Davies, Hannah Lilley, and Catherine Richardson. Routledge, 2023. 25–43.

Smyth, Adam. *Material Texts in Early Modern England*. Cambridge UP, 2018.

X.d.515. MSS. Folger Shakespeare Library, Washington DC, USA.

2 What Do Texts and Insects Have in Common?; Or, Ephemerality before Ephemera

Anna Reynolds

In his 1606 *The Art of Drawing*, Henry Peacham advises his readers how best to collect specimens of "flowers, flies and such like ... things of smal moment" (43). When they "walke abroad into the fields," his readers "may gather all manner of flies," finding butterflies "where store of Thistles and Lavender is," and so "may preserve [them] all the yeere, either in close boxes, or sticking them with a pinne severally upon small papers." The objects that Peacham describes are peculiar insect and paper assemblages, made up of a hybrid of notoriously ephemeral matter occupying a temporary structure: small boxes and slips of paper are highly mobile, and pins are especially provisional fixatives. Emblematic of all that is short-lived, flowers and flies are made to endure beyond their natural term; in Peacham's words, "things of smal moment" are "preserve[d] all the yeere." In a series of paradoxes, fleeting matter is collected and stored so as to serve as models for artworks capturing their fleeting nature. Peacham's instructions spell out the extent to which the artistic representation of "flowers, flies, &c" is tied to their temporality: "you may shew your flower, either open and faire in the bud, laden with deawe and wette, wormeaten, the leaves dropt away with overripeness &c" (43). The lack of conjunctions in Peacham's list draws attention to the speed with which the flower progresses between the stages of fullness and decay, and the contraction "&c" suggests the open-ended nature of this process: although a drawing fixes "things of smal moment" in one point in time, it will prompt the viewer to contemplate future moments, just as the fly pinned "upon small papers" is briefly fixed, but will continue to circulate, transform, and decay in its adapted material form.

The material forms and imaginative concerns at stake in Peacham's instructions are the focus of this chapter. It attends to the conjunction of insects and textual objects in the seventeenth-century imagination and so traces the pre-history of the bibliographical category of ephemera (see Garner for an overview of the wide-ranging and always unstable definitions of ephemera proposed since the nineteenth century). As has been established elsewhere in this volume, in its narrowest sense, ephemera refers to either an insect or a fever that lasts a single day (Boehrer; Smith). In the middle of the eighteenth century, a new category of object

DOI: 10.4324/9781003058588-4

was labelled as ephemera when Samuel Johnson described "the papers of the day" as the "*Ephemerae* of learning" (*Rambler* 145). As the scholarship of Paula McDowell and Gillian Russell has demonstrated, Johnson's coinage is part of a broader Augustan concern with the distinction between valuable and worthless literature in a period of rampant, unlicensed textual production. Writers including Jonathan Swift and Alexander Pope worked to distinguish their own literature from the mass of poor-quality, fleeting texts and so, in McDowell's words, constructed "a powerful ideological binary of permanent versus impermanent works" (50). Johnson's labelling of a category of text as ephemera is not, though, derogatory and, in an earlier 1744 essay, he had made the case for the value of "Small Tracts and Fugitive Pieces" ("Essay"). In using the term *ephemerae*, however, Johnson employs the figurative logic of the likes of Swift and Pope. As Russell points out, *ephemerae* supplements "the well-established use of 'grub', as in 'Grub Street'," introducing "the idea of the transience of that life and the 'grubby' papers it was producing" (41–42). In his *Dunciad*, Pope spells out the subtext of Johnson's terminology: this category of texts is "spawn[ed]," taking the form of crawling "embryo[es]" and "maggots half-formed" (I.59–61). This constellation of ideas demonstrates that textual ephemera, in the eighteenth century, were not only "ephemeral" in the sense of its fleeting period of relevance and value: texts were also labelled as ephemera in so far as they resembled insects. In tracing the conceptualisation of transitory texts across the century and a half before Johnson, Swift, and Pope, we will discover that there has always been something inextricably entomological about this bibliographical category.

   This chapter considers the cultural understanding of textual ephemerality in the seventeenth century and how it both shaped and was distinct from its cultural understanding in the century that followed. In particular, it centres on two key aspects identified by scholars of the later period: the first, outlined by Paula McDowell, are the differences between insect and textual ephemera elided by eighteenth-century poets, in which the former is materially short-lived and the latter temporarily valued, but often enduring in its material form (54). The second is the argument, persuasively made by Russell, that the categorisation of certain types of texts as ephemera served to "other" them from the codex form and so from more permanent forms of literature (58). As Russell demonstrates, in the course of the eighteenth century, the book emerged as an enduring object distanced from "transient, disposable, and insignificant" non-codex texts (58). In tracing the imagined correspondence of texts and insects before Pope and Johnson, this chapter demonstrates that, as Russell suggests, earlier writers were less concerned with the distinctions between codex and non-codex textual forms. Instead, seventeenth-century representations of insect-like books focus principally on the material similarity of insect and text – in particular, on the shared metamorphosis of both entities as they progress along the stages of their life cycle, with texts transforming, in many instances, from bound or stitched codices to loose sheets and scraps.[1]

The bibliographical category of ephemera that emerged in the eighteenth century was therefore grounded as much in the transformative potential of all texts as in the transitory relevance and value of a narrower subset. Accordingly, this chapter makes the case that, in the early modern period, ephemerality was understood to be a consequence of material history as much as an idea that denoted an object's temporariness and impermanence. Put differently, ephemerality was not only a matter of temporality or the brevity with which the textual object was understood to exist within time. Instead, the physical endurance and shifting form of much ephemera after their period of perceived relevance, value, and use were central to how ephemerality was conceived in the period. The life cycle of ephemera, we will go on to see, is not always brief, linear, and entropic. Rather, as Jonathan Gil Harris argues of objects more broadly, it is made up of "polychronic matter" that "collate[s] diverse moments in time," often enduring unexpectedly and so exerting a particularly forceful pressure on the imagination (*Untimely* 4, 24). This chapter, then, conceives of ephemera as an unstable category of text perceived as especially likely to be discarded and so transformed, metamorphosing, insect-like, into the altered form of waste. Finally, it makes the case for an "ecosystemic" mode of approaching this entomological matter as it endures in our archives and libraries today. Our literary and historical study of the unexpectedly lengthy histories of many of these supposedly transient objects might be productively informed by the early modern sensitivity to the manner in which texts, again akin to *ephemerae*, or insects, inhabit ecosystems. These networks and environments are ongoing, and we, as researchers, librarians, and archivists, are participants within them. We would, therefore, benefit from cultivating an early modern sensibility toward the ecosystems within which our source materials dwell, migrate, and transform.

Entomological Texts

At what point, then, did books and insects begin to be figuratively linked, and what prompted this metaphorical connection? It is rooted, in part, in the classical formula of instructing one's book to travel to its patron or reader, to "Go litel boke," as Chaucer famously reworks Ovid (l.1786), or in one of Martial's numerous versions of the trope, "frolicsome little book ... fly through the air of heaven. Go, fly; but you would have been safer at home" (Ovid I.i; Chaucer l. 1786; Martial 1.3). These addresses transform into the common instruction or description of books and papers as flying "abroad" in the early modern period, with further elaborations regarding the need for books to "fly" on their "paper wings" (see Lancelot Dawes *4r; George Wither A3r). The material similarity of a book's bifolium, with its two pages resembling spread wings, combines with the rhetorical tendency to grant a text agency as it circulates independent of authorial control. "Milke white paper wings" become the wings of insects more frequently in the seventeenth century, when the volume of texts in circulation was perceived to be escalating uncontrollably (Wither A3r; see also Raymond). Pamphleteers, by the middle of the seventeenth century, readily turned to this zoomorphic simile when attacking opponents. "Since the first Impression of this Book," one controversialist writes, "there is a Butter-fly flown abroad, that makes a fearfull fluttering" (Fisher *2r), and another claims that his counterpart's "printed libels" and "manuscripts ... flye as thick as moths up and down the country" (Higginson A2r). In addition to the similarity between the erratic movement of insects and the apparently uncontrolled circulation of texts, this entomological imagery draws on the symbolic flimsiness and superficiality of insects – particularly butterflies – as well as the widely perceived grossness and foulness of flies more broadly (Dobson 311; Schneider 122). Books and insects were in close literal and figurative proximity, after all, in the often noted, though not wholly accurate, tendency of texts to become food for worms and moths.[2] The "thick" swarming of certain texts is, like that of moths, implicitly destructive (Higginson A2r).

This zoomorphic image of text as insect has much in common with the descriptions of Grub Street pamphlets in the eighteenth century. Pope's "spawn[ing]" embryos and maggots did not, after all, emerge spontaneously; instead, they developed out of the evolving trope outlined above. Notably, though, the seventeenth-century understanding of what insects and texts have in common has less to do with the brevity of either their lives or their value and more to do with the similarities in their material form – in their winged structures, their erratic and far-reaching flight, and their potentially corruptive effect. One particularly striking description of the insect-like nature of certain texts reveals a further material similarity – their shared tendency to metamorphose, or transform, at certain stages in their life cycle. In a 1682 essay, churchman Samuel Stoddon refers to the "petty *Novelties* and *Protean* Modes" that distract from traditional devotional practice (2). These are nothing but "present fashions," "like the spawn of Frogs ... sent out every spring ... which like *Almanacks* or *Insects*, must change their shapes, and expire with the year." These fleeting devotional novelties are disregarded as nothing but "Butter-flies," unimportant, though "the poor *Quaker* thinks it as bad as the plague of Pharoah's flies." In this extended metaphor, Stoddon muddles together a wide range of lowly and fleeting phenomena: frogs, insects, annual calendars, and passing fashions. Implicit is the suggestion that all emerge, or "spawn," spontaneously from gross places such as mud, rotting meat, printshops, and society, and in vast quantities.[3] All of these entities, Stoddon indicates, "expire" after a certain period, here represented by the twelve months marked out by an almanac's calendar, a form of text notorious for turning rapidly out of date.

For Stoddon, "expir[y]" does not mark an end point in the life cycle of the texts, fashions, insects, and amphibians that he describes. Instead, expiry denotes a "change" of "shape," and so the persistence of the expired matter – though in an altered form – is assumed. The reference to insect metamorphosis, here, is clear, particularly in the imaginative progression from changing shapes to butterflies. Stoddon's association of metamorphosis with expiry might seem strange to a modern reader; we understand the process as one of development, in which the mature insect emerges from its larvae state. Throughout most of the seventeenth century, however, the chrysalis was thought to be the carcass of the deceased caterpillar, and the butterfly a separate creature that spontaneously generated from the decaying matter (Jorink 157; for a contemporary explanation of the process see Browne 48). This is why, conterminous with associations of flimsiness and superficiality, butterflies served as emblems of Christ's resurrection and, after the execution of Charles I in 1649, of a Royalist position (Jorink 150; Schneider 89). Stoddon alludes to the interconnected death and birth of certain insects because it reminds him of the life cycle of a notoriously ephemeral text – an almanac. The transformation of an almanac into waste paper was an early modern commonplace: "old" almanacs, "out of date," were "laid aside as useless," "fit for nothing but to cover Mustard pots" (Troughton *5v; *Bradshaws ghost* 11; Bramhall 105). Either discarded after the new year, or sold in bulk once determined unsaleable by the bookseller, old almanacs were frequently encountered in the form of binding waste, wrapping food and spices, and in the privy as toilet paper (Reynolds 353). Almanacs, then, often transformed in shape and appearance as they were dismantled, torn, crumpled, and folded to fit new, non-codex shapes and uses. In 1682, Stoddon readily invoked the metamorphic similarity of butterfly and ephemeral text in just a few words, describing "*Almanacks* or *Insects*" that "must change their shapes, and expire with the year" (2).

In the seventeenth century, then, texts were perceived as being like insects not because they passed rapidly out of existence, but because, after their deaths, they might be reborn in the form of waste paper, akin to a butterfly emerging from a chrysalis. This is far from an annihilation, disintegration, or ending of any sort, and so prompts us to reconsider our assumptions regarding the conception of ephemerality and transitoriness in the period. In Stoddon, ephemerality is closely tied to the "chang[ing]" of "shapes," or transformation of matter. Another, better known meditation on the metamorphosis of "expired" shapes can be found several decades earlier in the mouth of Shakespeare's Danish Prince Hamlet. As Joshua Calhoun notes, Hamlet is "intriguingly attentive to ecology" in his description of Alexander the Great's afterlife (*Nature* 151). Like Stoddon, Hamlet dwells on the way in which forms endure and transform after their death. He asks the gravedigger, "How long will a man lie i' the earth ere he rot," and is informed that they endure for "some eight year or nine year" before being presented with a skull that "has lain in the earth three and twenty years" (5.1.154–57, ll. 163–64). These bones prompt Hamlet's cataloguing of the disintegration and subsequent metamorphosis of corporeal matter from man, to "dust," to "earth," to "loam," and finally to the "clay" that "stop[s]" a "beer-barrel" (5.1.198–202). According to Hamlet, the life cycle of man does not "stop" at either death or the bung of a barrel. Instead, he traces a biography that projects far into the future. The endurance of matter is, then, paradoxically tied to its ephemerality in both *Hamlet* and in the widespread description of certain sorts of texts as insects in the seventeenth century. Stoddon's brief dismissal of butterfly-like "Novelties and Protean modes" suggests, along with Hamlet's graveyard chronology, that waste paper, metamorphosed insects, and human remains might function in much the same way in the early modern imagination. Each has the potential to provoke meditation on both the brevity of life and, seemingly contradictorily, the long history of the transformed matter, be it human, animal, or textual. Though neither human remains, butterflies, nor repurposed paper last indefinitely, they linger for long enough to make a lasting impression on the cultural imagination, and so serve as meaningful reminders and remainders of the complex workings of ephemerality.

Metamorphosis and Matter in Seventeenth-Century Still Life Paintings

In addition to the textual tropes and metaphors explored above, the symbolic similarities between texts and insects are apparent in another cultural realm: in the seventeenth-century still life paintings that depicted all manner of middle- and upper-class domestic objects and settings. This genre, first recognised in Dutch inventories of the same century, contains a vast array of sub-categories – paintings of game, of books, of fruit and flowers, scenes of kitchens, of tables set for breakfast or dessert, and vanitas paintings containing unmistakable emblems of mortality such as skulls and hourglasses (Schneider). Similarities in the content and structure of paintings by Dutch, Flemish, German, and Spanish practitioners suggest a cultural preoccupation with certain objects and themes that, in response to broad intellectual and economic shifts, transcended national boundaries. These shifts ranged from the rapidly increasing wealth of the middling classes, the wider range of foods and commodities available in the wake of global expansion and trade, and, in the artistic sphere, an increasing preoccupation with illusion (Hochstrasser; Grootenboer). In depicting exotic and expensive items, along with more everyday objects such as insects and books, seventeenth-century painters also continued to work within a long history of religious and moral symbolism.

As Svetlana Alpers has argued, it is reductive to equate the complex representational workings of the still life genre to an unambiguous set of moralising emblems or hieroglyphs (229–33). The genre is, however, unmistakably pervaded by a sense of the inevitable transience and decay of the objects represented. Though purchased by the wealthy who likely sought to own both still life paintings and the luxury items depicted within them, these artworks often suggest the fleeting nature of wealth and its trappings. This ethos is most clearly represented within the vanitas sub-genre, but it extends to paintings of fruits and flowers already nibbled or with insects poised menacingly alongside them, paintings of foodstuffs half-eaten and soon spoiled, and of books laid in haphazard bundles, with creased and crumpled pages and bent covers.[4] These book still life paintings are the visual equivalent of the widespread anxiety regarding the uncontrolled proliferation of texts explored above, as well as of the nagging fear that, as Norbert Schneider writes, books were not "permanent, unchanging records of human experiences and knowledge," and instead "reminded" onlookers "of their frailness and transience" (193). This coincidence of objects and ideas is nowhere better represented than in Maria van Oosterwijck's 1668 *Vanitas Still Life* (see Figure 2.1), in which a cluttered table scene contains a butterfly perched on the creased vellum cover of a thick but flimsy book, from which a

Figure 2.1 Maria van Oosterwijck. 1668. *Vanitas Still Life.* Oil on canvas. By permission of the Kunsthistorisches Museum, Vienna.

sheet of paper, perhaps a letter, hangs precariously. Next to the book rests a skull, which appears to hold the binding in its jaw, though the skull is half concealed by an arrangement of richly coloured flowers, on the petals of which perch another butterfly. On the right side of the book is an hourglass and many other objects too numerous to list here.

In these paintings, as in Stoddon's metaphor, texts and insects serve as emblems of much the same processes – of ephemerality and imperma-nence. Again, as in Stoddon's metaphor, the complex nature of ephem-erality is revealed: it is not only characterised by the expiry of a period of time – the life of a human, an insect, or a text – but also by the per-sistence and transformation of expired matter. While some objects in still life paintings, such as hourglasses, emblematise the passage of time, the majority represent temporality by prompting the viewer to consider its full life cycle. When we look on books and flowers, already creased and beginning to wilt, we are cognisant of how they would have looked when crisp and fresh, and how they will look when further decayed. Still life paintings, then, capture the manner in which "things" are consti-tuted of both matter and time, and so are "hybrid, protean assemblages" (Harris *Untimely* 8). Matter, shaped and transformed by time, Harris argues, makes visible the "play of multiple temporal traces" (*Untimely* 8). By depicting assemblages of matter in various states of freshness and decay alongside emblems of temporality, these paintings render the pa-limpsestic nature of things visible in a single moment and manifest the dialogic relationship of past, present, and future. The skull, for instance, is more than a reminder or emblem of death: it is a remainder of the deceased body, a remnant persisting in an altered form. Though frozen in an image at one moment in its biography, the skull simultaneously intermingles a lifetime and an afterlife in the mind of the onlooker.

Similarly, the roughly handled books and loose sheets of paper in many vanitas and book still life paintings would have prompted early modern viewers to consider the long history of texts – transforming from freshly printed or written sheets to pages cast aside and, in many instances, to waste paper. The afterlife of texts as waste is in fact a common feature of one sub-category of the still life genre: the breakfast still life, or *ont-bijtjes* (for an overview, see Vlieghe 219; Schneider 101–19). In Willem Claesz Heda's compositions, such as his 1635 *Still Life with a Gilt Cup* (see Figure 2.2), we look on the disorderly remnants of a meal. A torn loaf of bread, a peeled lemon, and shucked oysters sit on a crumpled, linen tablecloth, alongside glassware and goblets that lay on their sides. Amidst this assemblage, perched on the upturned oyster shells in the bottom left of the frame, sits a cornet of waste paper – a small, conical parcel made from a page of a discarded printed text – containing pep-per or another similarly expensive spice. Columns of red and black text are visible on the cornet, suggesting that it is the page of an almanac's calendar, like those alluded to by Stoddon. The pepper or spice within

Figure 2.2 Willem Claesz Heda. 1635. *Still Life with a Gilt Cup*. Oil on panel. By permission of the Rijksmuseum, Amsterdam.

the waste cornet contributes to the environment of luxury and expense that characterise the *ontbijtjes* and the still life genre more broadly: in a 1627 breakfast still life (*Still Life with a Turkey*) by Pieter Claesz, the waste cornet sits in close proximity to an expensive nautilus cup which, like the pepper or spice the cornet contains, would have been imported from distant parts of the globe (for a discussion of spice in still life, see Hochstrasser 95–100). This tableau of discards and disarray, however, prompts the viewer to question the value and importance of objects depicted, such as the nautilus cup and the spice: vast expense and effort ends in a fleeting, wasteful meal. The paper wrapper itself is far less exotic. It is a flimsy shell that spills out its contents, structurally resembling the oyster shells, peeled lemons, and torn bread that, their insides open to the air, will rapidly spoil. It speaks an emblematic language not dissimilar to the butterfly perched on the cover of Maria van Oosterwijck's flimsy vellum book and the skull that bites it (see Figure 2.1): time passes, things expire, and so matter transforms.

What is more, the sheet of paper that hangs from the bottom of van Oosterwijk's book is only a fold away from becoming a cornet that wraps matter such as spice or pepper: letters, an early modern viewer would have been aware, were particularly vulnerable to reuse in the household as waste. Oosterwijk's vellum book is itself only a further step away from becoming waste: it can be readily disbound and remoulded to fit new, non-codex shapes. The matter that makes up the assemblages of vanitas and *ontbijtjes*, be it skull, flower, butterfly, codex, loose sheet, or waste paper, coalesces past, present, and future in one painted moment. Curling, crumpling, and metamorphosing like the texts that "flye" thickly through the early modern landscape and are prone to changing shape, the pages depicted in these paintings prompt onlookers to meditate on more than the brevity of life: instead we find ourselves thinking on the hybridity of time and matter, and how the ephemeral has the capacity to transform, rather than to disappear, and so often persist as leftovers, remainders, and waste.

Textual Ecosystems

This early modern sensitivity to the insect-like transformation of texts suggests a broader understanding of the correspondence between bibliographical and entomological life cycles: both texts and insects, the entomological texts contained within these similes and paintings suggest, were understood as existing within an ecosystem. An ecosystem is a network of entities that interact with one another within the context of a broader environment. As modern-day readers, it might seem strange for us to conceive of texts as existing within complex networks of living and non-living organisms; early moderns, however, were sensitive to the ways in which their books were made up of diverse sorts of matter, inhabited varied environments, and progressed along the stages of a life cycle. Calhoun has persuasively argued that "texts can never really be disentangled from the ecosystems in which they come to be and in which they will cease to be," outlining the ways in which early modern literature reveals a widespread sensitivity to the plant fibres from which books were made and the environmental conditions within which they endured and decayed (*Nature* 150). By attending to the correspondence between texts and insects in early modern thought, we are able to enrich Calhoun's proposed ecosystemic mode of reading further: in the seventeenth century, we find a widespread ecological sensitivity to the habitat and movement, as well as material make up, of texts. Still life paintings and entomological tropes highlight the sorts of habitats texts occupied in the period, and the ways in which they interacted with other entities in their environment: rather than remaining static in studies and libraries, texts regularly transformed and came to inhabit grocers' shops, kitchens, and privies. Rather than existing in bibliographic isolation, shelved alongside other paper objects and leather bindings, texts rubbed against all manner of substances including spices, tobacco, pies, meat, and skin. To understand the ways in which early moderns read their books and understood textual culture, therefore, we need to think, as they did, ecosystemically and multitemporally: to keep in mind the potential life cycle, transformative matter, and varied habitats of a page, rather than focusing on a single moment in its history.

There is another bibliographical habitat, not mentioned so far, that became prominent in the later seventeenth century and that is crucial for an understanding of the long history of early modern texts. As the seventeenth century progressed, increasing numbers of individuals became preoccupied with removing certain entities from their pre-existing habitats and placing them in new ones, alongside numerous other entities, either of the same category or of an entirely different classification of thing.[5] These collectors were often driven by the desire to gather and display an array of curiosities, such as coins, shells, insects, animals, fossils, feathers, and other objects characterised by rarity and exoticness. Other collectors had narrower fields of interest: as entomology began to flourish as a discipline and scientifically accurate engravings of insects became increasingly in demand, artists and explorers began to collect and trade in insect specimens (Neri; Jorink 166–67). At much the same time, bibliophiles and antiquarians became interested in a specific sort of text – loose sheets, flimsy pamphlets, and occasional documents that would later be labelled as ephemera, either by the likes of Pope and Johnson, or by nineteenth and twentieth-century scholars and archivists (Russell 60–97; Yale). We know that at least two of these "ephemerologists," as Gillian Russell terms them, were intimately familiar with the broader ecosystems and habitats of early modern texts (25). The Oxford-based antiquary Anthony Wood, writing directly onto the loose sheets themselves, records how he salvaged texts from privies and the fate, similar to that represented in breakfast still life paintings, of wrapping tobacco.[6] London shoe-maker John Bagford describes acquiring "Wast fragments," "titles, frontispieces, borders" and "printers' devices" from booksellers' waste, and hunting for similar scraps used as binding waste, "at the endes of oulde Bookes" (qtd in Nickson 52–53). In addition to the shared chronology of the rise of ephemerology and entomology, there is a correspondence between the collecting practices employed by the two emerging disciplines. Wood's and Bagford's collecting habits more than echo the instructions outlined at the beginning of this chapter: "flowers, flies" and textual ephemera, or "things of smal moment," are all easily "gather[ed]" from their natural habitat, if one knows where and when to look, and all may be "preserve[d]" in "close boxes, or sticking them with a pinne severally upon small papers" (Peacham 43). As we will go on to see, the ways in which ephemerologists stored their specimens were not dissimilar to the storage boxes and pins described by Peacham and employed by entomological collectors such as James Petiver (Peck 28).

There is, though, a tendency to perceive both collections and still life paintings as being in some way static. Janice Neri's work on the early modern collection and representation of insects, for instance, sets out a cultural strategy she terms "specimen logic," in which the creatures are decontextualised from "their habitats, environments, and settings" and so prompt their viewers to "imagine them as inhabitants of a timeless space of display" (xiii). Scholars such as Norman Bryson and Harris have employed similar language in their combined analyses of seventeenth-century still life paintings and *wunderkammern*: Bryson describes the "refusal of natural time and of seasonality" in paintings of flowers that "inhabit the same tabular and panoptic space" as cabinets of curiosities (105, 107–08). For Harris, both sorts of assemblage "constitute the object within a freeze-frame of a historical moment" ("The New New" 123).[7] Removed, like Neri's specimens, from the systems within which they exist, collected curios are understood as disconnected from the contexts and networks that grant them meaning, as well as from the natural effects of time that enact change and decay. This line of thought, however, overlooks the palimpsestic nature of both still life paintings and late seventeenth-century collections, like those of Wood and Bagford. As outlined above, still life paintings are in fact sensitive representations of the ecosystems within which entities such as texts, insects, and human remainders exist, expire, and transform. Though depicting a single moment in time, the choice of objects and life stages depicted in these paintings prompt viewers to consider the broader passage of time and the concomitant metamorphosis of matter. The transformative nature of specimens gathered and stored within collections is more self-explanatory: whatever the "logic" or driving force behind the construction of a collection, its contents remain as matter persisting within time, no matter how they are stored and displayed. Specimens within a collection continue to transform and decay, and though their habitat alters, they participate within an ecosystem of living and non-living organisms within their subsequent environments (Swann 14; Calhoun, "Book" 460–73). What happens, then, if we conceive of the network of the collection not as a radically new environment, entirely separate from that which has come before it, but as a continuation of an ongoing, though altered, ecosystem? Extant collections would, in this case, comprise an additional stage in the long history of textual ephemera.

This altered understanding of ecosystem and life cycle allows us to account for the paradoxical period, after that of production, use, disuse, and use as waste, in which ephemeral texts might be gathered and stored and so endure. The trajectory of text moving from use to disuse is not an ending, and nowhere is this more explicit than within the continued ecosystem of the collection. William Viney's philosophical analysis of the life cycle of waste is useful for our understanding of this stage in the biography of ephemeral texts: discarded objects, Viney argues, undergo "a rich series of comings and goings," constituting "a more complex, continuous and fluid process of cycling in and out of the times of use and waste, attended by and expressed through assembly and disassembly, preservation and dispersal, retrospective legibility and dust" (60, 179). This disjointed period of "comings and goings" in the life cycle of a text, in the case of extant collections, continues into the present day and provides a direct line of connection between the environments of kitchen, privy, and seventeenth-century study, and the climate-controlled rooms and acid-free archival boxes of our modern-day archives and libraries. By paying closer attention to the period *after* which an ephemeral text has been gathered and preserved by a seventeenth-century antiquarian, we are able to dispel the myth of fixity and gain insight into the ongoing ecosystems of collected entities.

Far from permanent, the status of a collected item might radically alter. In the seventeenth century, as today, items might be discarded or sent to fellow collectors, particularly when a similar or duplicate item has been acquired. More radically, a collector's death often heralds a change in the status or make-up of a collection: often, another collector or an institution purchases the collection as a whole, and so its environment and its arrangement alters. In many instances, the collection is dispersed at auction and so enters into a new network of objects. Anthony Wood's diaries suggest the likelihood of a fate that typically went unrecorded: perceived as valueless by its inheritors, a collection of books and manuscripts might be "converted" into waste paper and put to "infimous uses" (*Life* 150, 429, 476; see also Yale 205–48). The mobility and transformative potential of a collection extend to the material make-up of individual items as well as the collection as a whole: Jeffrey Todd Knight has demonstrated that bindings were temporary structures in the early modern period (3–4), and this is certainly the case for the contents of Anthony Wood's library (see Knight, esp. 3–4). Nicolas Kiessling has revealed the striking mutability of Wood's library: much material collected by Wood, most likely as part of bulk purchases, was not deemed worthy of preservation, and so was torn up and used as slips and scraps of waste paper to repair other sheets (xxii–vi). Wood did, though, seek to preserve the ephemeral items he considered valuable: in 1681, Wood made a 112-page shelf-list of his library of printed texts, including those stored in unbound gatherings and "bundles" and "heaps." Between this date and his death, Wood worked to have these bundles of loose sheets bound in sturdy but economical bindings, providing the binder with strict instructions regarding the materials to be bound together in each volume. Although he had 295 bundles of loose sheets bound before his death in 1695, the collection was far from fixed at any stage in its history. Bequeathed to the Ashmolean Museum, Wood's collection did not undergo the waste fate he so often lamented, and instead travelled, almost whole, from his house opposite Merton College Oxford to Elias Ashmole's cabinet of curiosities in the Ashmolean. In 1860, the collection made another journey across the city to the Bodleian Library, where it remains today. A number of volumes were, though, sold to the Bodleian and to Jesus College prior to Wood's death, and almost 500 items were missing by the date of the 1860 transfer. Other bibliophiles and ephemerologists such as John Bagford, Richard Rawlinson, and Humfrey Wanley, Kiessling hypothesises, may have been culprits in the early disappearance of items from Wood's library (Kiessling xlviii). This loss and decay have continued into the present day, with valuable items cut out and stolen from Wood's volumes in the twentieth century, as well as the more mundane losses caused by rebinding and the misadventures of transporting and reclassifying large quantities of books (Kiessling x).

The waste and fragments collected by the "wicked old biblioclast" John Bagford make the temporally and materially changeable fate of textual ephemera even more apparent (Blades 118). Gathered on behalf of wealthy collectors such as Hans Sloane, Samuel Pepys, and Humfrey Wanley, much "Bagfordiana" was spread across late seventeenth- and early eighteenth-century society (for an overview of Bagford's collection, see: Nickson 51–55; Gatch; Griffiths). Bagford did, however, accumulate his own collection of printed and manuscript material, largely in fragmentary form, as part of his numerous projects including those on the histories of printmaking, papermaking, and bibliography. Purchased by Edward Harley after Bagford's death in 1716, these items can now be found in the British Library. Their material form and habitat has transformed, however, multiple times since Bagford, in many instances, first salvaged them from the piles of waste in booksellers' shops. The 1759 catalogue of the Harleian library describes much of the collection as being made up of multiple "Porte-folios," including "Several Paste-Board Covers with loose Papers" (*Catalogue* entry 5910). By 1808, these albums were bound into volumes. We might expect Bagford's fragments to remain, after this point, fixed and static in their bound volumes. These items, however, conform closely to the "rich series of comings and goings" Viney describes as characterising the status of waste within a collection (60). After 1808, the Department of Prints and Drawings was established, and the engravings and prints in Bagford's collection – previously loose, now pasted onto bound pages – were cut out from the volumes, likely at the expense of other, lesser-valued fragments.[8] Many volumes were again dismembered and rearranged in 1890–1891 when the collection was divided between the Department of Manuscripts and the Department of Printed Books, and again in 1900 between Printed Books and Prints and Drawings. It is clear, therefore, that the life cycle of the texts collected by Bagford ended neither when they were discarded as waste, nor when they were collected and entered as specimens into a library. Instead, they remain highly mobile. Initially gathered loosely between pasteboard covers and later pasted to sheets and bound in volumes, the habitats, and networks within which the items dwell continue to transform across the centuries.

Through her work to create a digital, and so explicitly palimpsestic, edition of Bagford's fragmentary albums, Whitney Trettien has characterised the enduring ecosystem within which these ephemeral specimens endure. "Each reconstellation," Trettien writes of Bagford's metamorphosing albums, "destroys some of what came before … yet it also creates something new, enabling new futures to come into being, including, in the case we are examining, our own" (55). The sheets and fragments in Bagford's collection have fluctuated between the status of text, waste, and curio multiple times in their histories, and the violent acts of discarding, wasting, and cutting that have determined their current material form and arrangement have stretched across the centuries from the seventeenth century to the present day. The "new future" that Trettien refers to is the disciplinary future of book history, one that she argues should be modelled on Bagford's own methods, methods akin to those Russell has described as a "wild bibliography" pre-dating our own (Trettien 55; Russell 96–97). Rather than conceiving of texts as fixed objects within stable bindings or neat classificatory systems, then, we should understand them as nodes – or even metamorphic, insect-like forms – within an ever-shifting network or ecosystem.

The modern-day perception of ephemeral sheets as radically distinct from stable codices, housed in different curatorial departments and demanding differing fields of curatorial and scholarly expertise, is, therefore, complicated by an attention to the imaginative overlap between text and insect in the seventeenth century. In the century prior to the development of the bibliographical category of "ephemera," the distinction between "difficult" loose sheets and bound codices was not one of type and classification, but one of time:[9] a bound book might become a loose sheet at a later point in its life cycle, and a waste sheet or fragment might find itself bound, once again, within a codex volume, and so the distinctions that have since been drawn between bibliographical categories cannot be sustained. Ephemerality before ephemera, in other words, constituted a wide-reaching sense of a text's capacity to metamorphose, to change shape, and to endure in an altered form. While adopting a similar sensibility will do little to simplify the archivist's or librarian's tasks of classifying, storing, and conserving difficult texts, or ephemera, it can play an important role in the future of book history. Attention to the long histories and the entomological nature of texts helps to remedy the distinction, outlined by Terry Cook, between archivists who tend to consider the "subsequent history of documents over time, including the many interventions by archivists," and scholars who often perceive of archives as "unproblematic storehouses of records awaiting the historian" (Cook 600–01). Scholars, like archivists and librarians, are participants within the ongoing ecosystems of early modern texts. Our source materials, whether we conceive of them as literature or as waste, remain as insect-like as their early modern users understood them to be: they have been removed, like Peacham's butterflies, from one habitat and are "preserve[d]" in another, in "close boxes," stuck with pins, or pasted "severally upon small papers," or stitched within tightly-bound volumes. Like an insect, they will continue to move, change shape, and decay, just as they have already metamorphosed at earlier points in their histories. In considering the nature of textual ephemerality before ephemera, then, we do not find the prehistory of a category of text; instead, we uncover the ephemerality, or metamorphic potential, of *all* early modern texts, as well as a distinct way of thinking about their ongoing histories and habitats and our own place within this ecosystem.

Notes

1 On the connection between metamorphosis and ephemerality, see Katherine Hunt's chapter in this volume.
2 Bookworms are not an actual category of insect but a catch-all for any insect that damages papers. Moths are included in this expansive bracket, and so texts are regularly described as being moth-eaten. See Solberg.
3 On the only gradual supersession of the theory of spontaneous generation in the seventeenth century, see Eric Jorink.
4 For an example of the book still life sub-genre, see the c. 1628 *Still Life with Books* by an unknown Dutch master, housed at Alte Pinakothek, Munich.
5 On seventeenth-century cabinets of curiosities and the broader culture of collection, see Bleichmar and Mancall, Swann, and Wiles-Portier.
6 Wood writes: 'This I found in Dr Lowers privy house 24. May 1675 in Bow Street, Lond.' and "Tobacco wrapt up in this paper in the beginning of May 1693" (quot. in Kiessling, xix). See William Claesz Heda's 1637 *Tobacco Still Life* (oil on wood; Los Angeles County Museum of Art) for a still life containing waste tobacco wrappers.
7 Gil Harris excludes in this essay still life paintings and *wunderkammern* from the multitemporal and palimpsestic model of matter he outlines in *Untimely Matter*.
8 See Bob Bearman's chapter in this collection for a comparable biography of the collections housed in Shakespeare's Birthplace Trust.
9 On the centrality of difficulty in definitions of ephemera, see McDowell (49).

Works Cited

Alpers, Svetlana. *The Art of Describing: Dutch Art in the Seventeenth Century.* Penguin, 1989.

Bearman, Robert. "What is an 'Ephemeral Archive'? Stratford-upon-Avon, 1550–1650: A Case Study." *Practices of Ephemera in Early Modern England.* Eds Callan Davies, Hannah Lilley, and Catherine Richardson. Routledge, 2023. 65–82.

Blades, *The Enemies of Books.* London, 1888.

Boehrer, Bruce. "Time's Flies: Ephemerality in the Early Modern Insect World." *Practices of Ephemera in Early Modern England.* Eds Callan Davies, Hannah Lilley, and Catherine Richardson. Routledge, 2023. 44–64.

Bleichmar, Daniela and Peter C. Mancall. "Introduction." *Collecting Across Cultures*. Eds Daniela Bleichmar and Peter C. Mancall. U of Pennsylvania P, 2011. 1–13.

Bradshaw's ghost. London, 1659.

Bramhall, John. *The Serpent Salve*. N.p., 1643.

Browne, Thomas. *Hydriotaphia, urn-burial [...] Together with the Garden of Cyrus*. London, 1668.

Bryson, Norman. *Looking at the Overlooked: Four Essays on Still Life Painting*. Reaktion, 1990.

Calhoun, Joshua. "Book Microbiomes." *The Unfinished Book*. Eds Alexandra Gillespie and Deirdre Lynch. Oxford UP, 2020.

———. *The Nature of the Page: Poetry, Papermaking, and the Ecology of Texts in Renaissance England*. U of Pennsylvania P, 2020.

A Catalogue of the Harleian Collection of Manuscripts, Vol. 2. London, 1759.

Chaucer, Geoffrey. *Troilus and* Criseyde. Ed. B. A. Windeatt. Clarendon, 1992.

Cook, Terry. "The Archive(s) Is a Foreign Country: Historians, Archivists, and the Changing Archival Landscape." *The American Archivist* 74:2 (2011): 600–01.

Dawes, Lancelot. *Two Sermons Preached at the Assises Holden at Carlile*. Oxford, 1614.

Dobson, Mary J. *Contours of Death and Disease in Early Modern England*. Cambridge UP, 2003.

Fisher, Samuel. *Christianismus redivivus Christndom* [sic]. London, 1655.

Garner, Anne. "State of the Discipline: Throwaway History: Towards a Historiography of Ephemera." *Book History* 24:1 (2021): 244–63.

Gatch, Milton McC. "John Bagford, bookseller and antiquary." *British Library Journal* 12:2 (1986): 150–71.

Griffiths, "The Bagford Collection." *Picturing Places. The British Library*. Online. Accessed 29 Nov. 2021.

Grootenboer, Hanneke. *The Rhetoric of Perspective: Realism and Illusionism in Seventeenth-Century Dutch Still-Life Painting*. Chicago UP, 2005.

Harris, Jonathan Gil. "The New New Historicism's Wunderkammer of Objects." *European Journal of English Studies* 4:2 (2000): 111–23.

———. *Untimely Matter in the Time of Shakespeare*. U of Pennsylvania P, 2009.

Higginson, Francis. *A Brief Relation of the Irreligion of the Northern Quakers*. London, 1653.

Hochstrasser, Julie Berger. *Still Life and Trade in the Dutch Golden Age*. Yale UP, 2007.

Hunt, Katherine. "More Lasting than Bronze: Statues, Writing, and the Materials of Ephemera in Ben Jonson's *Sejanus His Fall*." *Practices of Ephemera in Early Modern England*. Eds Callan Davies, Hannah Lilley, and Catherine Richardson. Routledge, 2023. 111–27.

Johnson, Samuel. "Essay on the Origin and Importance of Small Tracts and Fugitive Pieces." *The Works of Samuel Johnson, LL.D.* Ed John Hawkins, Vol. 9. Cambridge UP, 2011. 350–59.

———. *Rambler* 145 (6 August 1751).

Jorink, Eric. "Between Emblematics and the 'Argument from Design': The Representation of Insects in the Dutch Republic." *Early Modern Zoology: The Construction of Animals in Science, Literature and the Visual Arts*. Eds Karl A. E. Enenkel and Paul J. Smith. Brill, 2007. 147–75.

Kiessling, Nicolas K. *The Library of Anthony Wood*. Oxford Bibliographical Society, 2002.

Knight, Jeffrey Todd. *Bound to Read: Compilations, Collections, and the Making of Renaissance Literature*. U of Pennsylvania P, 2013.

The Life and Times of Anthony Wood. Ed. Andrew Clark, 5 vols. Vol. 1. Clarendon, 1891.

McDowell, Paula. "Of Grubs and Other Insects: Constructing the Categories of 'Ephemera' and 'Literature' in Eighteenth-Century British Writing." *Book History* 15 (2012): 48–70.

Martial. *The Epigrams of Martial*. Trans. Henry G Bohn. Bell & Daldy, 1871.

Neri, Janice. *The Insect and the Image: Visualizing Nature in Early Modern Europe, 1500–1700*. U of Minnesota P, 2011.

Nickson, Margaret. "Bagford and Sloane." *The British Library Journal* 9:1 (1983): 52–53.

Schneider, Norbert. *Still Life: Still Life Painting in the Early Modern Period*. Taschen, 2003.

Ovid. "The Poet to his Book." *Tristia*. Trans. A. L. Wheeler. Harvard UP, 1924.

Peacham, Henry. *The Art of Drawing*. London, 1606.

Peck, Robert McCracken. "Alcohol and Arsenic, Pepper and Pitch: Brief Histories of Preservation Techniques." *Stuffing Birds, Pressing Plants, Shaping Knowledge: Natural History in North America, 1730–1800*. Ed. Sue Ann Prince. American Philosophical Society, 2003. 27–54.

Pope, Alexander. *The Dunciad in Four Books*. Ed. Valerie Rumbold. Longman, 1999.

Raymond, Joad. *Pamphlets and Pamphleteering in Early Modern Britain*. Cambridge UP, 2003.

Reynolds, Anna. "'Worthy to Be Reserved': Bookbindings and the Waste Paper Trade in Early Modern England and Scotland." *The Paper Trade in Early Modern Europe: Practices, Materials, Networks*. Eds Daniel Bellingradt and Anna Reynolds. Brill, 2021.

Russell, Gillian. *The Ephemeral Eighteenth Century: Print, Sociability and the Cultures of Collecting*. Cambridge UP, 2020.

Shakespeare, William. *Hamlet*. Eds Ann Thomson and Neil Taylor. Rev. ed. Bloomsbury, 2016.

Smith, Helen. "Things That Last: Ephemerality and Endurance in Early Modern England." *Practices of Ephemera in Early Modern England*. Eds Callan Davies, Hannah Lilley, and Catherine Richardson. Routledge, 2023. 148–66.

Solberg, Emma Maggie. "Human and Insect Bookworms." *Postmedieval* 11:1 (2020): 12–22.

Stoddon, Samuel. *An Essay on a Question Relating to Divine Worship*. London, 1682.

Swann, Marjorie. *Curiosities and Texts: The Culture of Collecting in Early Modern England*. U of Pennsylvania P, 2001.

Trettien, Whitney. "Creative Destruction and the Digital Humanities." *The Routledge Research Companion to Digital Medieval Literature*. Eds Jennifer E. Boyle and Helen J. Burgess. Routledge, 2017. 47–60.

Troughton, William. *Saints in England Under a Cloud*. London, 1648.

Viney, William. *Waste: A Philosophy of Things*. Bloomsbury, 2015.

Vlieghe, *Flemish Art and Architecture, 1585–1700*. Yale UP, 1998.

Wiles-Portier, Elizabeth. *Collectors and Curiosities: Paris and Venice, 1500–1700*. Polity P, 1990.

Wither, George. *Britain's Remembrancer*. London, 1628.

Yale, Elizabeth. *Sociable Knowledge: Natural History and the Nation in Early Modern Britain*. U of Pennsylvania P, 2016.

3 Time's Flies
Ephemerality in the Early Modern Insect World[1]

Bruce Boehrer

Somewhat Like a Butterfly

From ancient times, notions of ephemerality have been bound up with the behaviour of certain insects, most particularly mayflies, day-flies, water-flies, and associated species. Carl Linnaeus included six species of these insects under the generic name *Ephemera* in the tenth edition of his *Systema Naturae* (1758) (546–57). Following his lead, modern biology, which recognizes some three thousand related species on six continents, distributes these into sub-taxa of the order *Ephemeroptera* (Kluge).

Nor was this language new to Linnaeus, although he used it in new ways. The linguistic connection to evanescence proves paradoxically durable, stretching back nearly two and a half millennia. As early as the mid-fourth century BCE, Aristotle could already refer to "a winged four-footed [sic] animal" which "lives and flies about until evening ... and dies at sunset, having lived precisely one day [sic], whence its name, the day-fly [*dio kai kaleitai ephemeron*]" (184–85). Aristotle's point is obvious enough: the name *ephemeron*, compounded of the preposition *epi* and the noun *hemera* (literally "upon the day"), registers the brevity of life as these insects' most distinctive feature.

This sense remains foremost in Sir Francis Bacon's mention of "certain *Flies* that are called *Ephemera*, that live but a day" (1627) (144) And this same sense underlies the elder Pliny's account (77 CE) of a certain "four-legged caterpillar" that "does not live beyond one day, owing to which it is called the hemerobius," for this noun also derives from the Greek *hemera* (506–07).[5] And thus when Walter Charleton refers to "*the Fly living but one day*" by the names "EPHEMERUS, Hemerobius, Diaria," he employs three synonymous Graeco–Latin derivatives, all pointing toward the limited life-span—the one-dayness, as it were—of the flies in question (951). As for the symbolic connection between mayflies and mortality, this appears as early as Cicero (c. 45 BCE):

> Aristotle says that a kind of small animal is born, which lives for a single day. ... Contrast our longest lifetime with eternity: we shall

DOI: 10.4324/9781003058588-5

be found almost in the same category of short-lived beings as those tiny creatures. (112–13)

The core associations in this case prove consistent over the long term. Yet this consistency can mislead. The ephemera identified by Linnaeus take their place in a grid of biological relations defined by anatomical similarity and encoded in binomial nomenclature. The ephemera of Aristotle, Cicero, Pliny, Bacon, and even Charleton, by contrast, exist in a more ambiguous relation to other forms of life. Early modern natural historians did not know all three-thousand-odd species of the order *Ephemeroptera*, of course, but they knew quite enough to be challenged by what they saw: a dizzying array of insect kinds associated and distinguished by countless often minute similarities and differences. Given the subject matter, elision proved inevitable.

Consider, for instance, the first entomological treatise produced in England, Thomas Moffett's *Theater of Insects*, first printed in Latin in 1634 (thirty years after Moffett's death[2]) and translated into English by John Rowland for re-publication in 1658 as an addendum to volume 2 of Edward Topsell's *History of Four-footed Beasts and Serpents*. Moffett assembled his work from the prior research of others, notably Thomas Penny, Edward Wotton, and Conrad Gesner, and his two chapters on flies contain multitudes, both of insect varieties and of human opinions. Beginning with the greater dipterans, Moffett ranges through an assortment of discordantly-related but identifiable species, from horsefly and housefly (order *Diptera*) to dragonfly and damselfly (*Odonata*) to caddis fly (*Trichoptera*) to bee-fly and crane fly (*Diptera*) to the ephemera and beyond. However, some species – Moffett's water-flies, for instance – prove hard to identify now, for various reasons. Also, Moffett often describes one species in terms of others quite different from it, with the result that differing species begin to overlap conceptually. On a typical page, thus, he writes of flies "with tails like Scorpions," of a fly "almost like the Bee in shape and color," and of another "very like the lesser Butterfly, with four silver wings full of blackish spots" (937). Nor is the confusion eased by Moffett's conventional habit of citing authority. Thus, of the difference between two kinds of biting fly, he muses unhelpfully,

> most of the Greek and Latine Authors ... make them all one. Yea even [Conrad] *Gesner* himself in this very matter could not tell what to say ... and indeed unless it were only *Pierius* [Pierio Valeriano Bolzani] and my friend *Pennius* [Thomas Penny] now deceased, no man as yet found the difference between them. (937)

When it comes to the ephemeral flies, similar confusions appear. Citing authorities from Aristotle to Hesychius, Moffett repeats the inaccurate tale of the mayfly's one-day life cycle, describes the insects as both four- and six-footed, and ponders whether they possess four or six wings (different sources say different things). Moffett then considers the possible relation between these ephemeral flies and the "*Triemerus*, or a Fly living three daies," which in turn is "somewhat like a Butterfly" (949). This done, he ends with a homiletic flourish that also erases distinctions of species, presenting the entire legion of flies, so to speak, as a collective emblem of Vanitas:

> [T]he last use of Flies ... appears to be this, that whereis [sic] none of them passe a Summer, yet some of them do not live out a short day, we should by them be put in minde of our own frailty, and of the uncertainty of this vanishing life; the which although preserved with all the dainty food that can be got, with the softest raiment, and all the best waies and means that may be for a short space, yet when it seems most to flourish, it on a sudden declines and scarce with the fly holds out an Autumn, much lesse a Winter. (951)

While this falls short as a scientific account of the order *Ephemeroptera*, it helps lay out the cluster of attributes through which early modernity processed the cultural symbology of flies: plurality, swarming, confusion of kinds, summer heat, moisture, daintiness, flimsiness, novelty, triviality, extreme brevity, and sudden putrefaction. These qualities – the key elements of what we might call early modern flyness – provide our focus of study here. Dealing largely – but not exclusively – with English literary records, we can trace the gradual adaptation of this symbology to the principal socio-ecological developments of the early modern period: population growth and incipient urbanization.

The Quick and the Dead

Moffett's *Theater*, it may be objected, represents an antiquated view of the insect world, one abandoned during the seventeenth and eighteenth centuries. In the broad sense, this is true; Moffett's book fell out of date before it ever saw print. For more cutting-edge entomological research, one need only look across the North Sea to the Low Countries. There, in the same year that finally saw the publication of Moffett's *Theater*, the Dutch scholar Augerius Clutius (Outgert Cluyt) brought forth his *De Hemerobio*, the first full-length publication to deal solely with the mayfly and "one of the first European monographs to be devoted to a specific species of insects" (Jorink 200). Some forty years later, in turn, Jan Swammerdam would produce his *Ephemeri vita* (1675), for the first time fully describing the mayfly's distinctive life-cycle while also conducting a ground-breaking microscopic inspection of the insect's anatomy.

But even for these scholars, old ways die hard. For Clutius, the mayfly's life still serves as a moral exemplum, wherein ought to be admired the power of all-knowing nature, which has blessed with life beings of varying origin and by efficient destiny condemned them to one fate. For all beings are brought to a quick end of life, although these are not all marked out with one form and character. (68, my translation)

Swammerdam, for his part, still labours to distinguish the mayfly from such creatures as "the Ear-worm, or *Forfica*," the "Dragon-flie, ... and the *Locusta* or locust" (31, 32). And Moffett's "*Triemerus*" survives into the nineteenth century in the pages of Abraham Rees's *Cyclopaedia* (1819), which describes it, almost exactly in Moffett's original words, as "somewhat like the butterfly" (n.p.).

In sum, while Swammerdam's microscope enabled him to subject the mayfly to the detailed anatomical study upon which modern taxonomy depends, earlier forms of natural history, focused less on the difference of species and more on the similarity of kind, nonetheless persisted, even within the emerging discourse of modern biology itself. As a result, the particular qualities of individual species blended together into a more general bond of association that was usually given a moral or spiritual cast. The mayfly's treatment in early scientific discourse illustrates this tendency well.

As for the contemporary visual record, this offers a similar spectacle, for similar reasons. On one hand, illustrators equipped with magnifying lenses like Swammerdam's produce ever more perfect renderings of insects like the mayfly. On the other hand, these newly precise images remain framed by a more traditional spiritual and moralistic context, thus reproducing the same tensions found in the earliest entomological writing.

For a case in point, behold Albrecht Dürer's early intaglio print of *The Holy Family with the Mayfly* (c. 1495; Figure 3.1), also known as *The Holy Family with the Dragonfly*, *The Holy Family with the Butterfly*, and *The Holy Family with the Locust*. These names have all accrued to the work belatedly, reflecting disagreement over the kind of insect located in its bottom right corner. However, the earliest catalogue of Dürer's prints (released 250 years after his death) makes no mention at all of insects in its account of the piece, to which it gives the generic title "Maria und Joseph" (B4r).[3] And in fact, Dürer's engraving provides a visual instance of the challenges faced by early natural historians as they teased out the relations between differing species. The insect's head is clearly that of a butterfly, with club-formed antennae and an extendable proboscis. However, the abdomen is just as clearly that of a dragonfly, being too elongated for a butterfly. The wings, for their part, rest vertically, like those of butterflies and mayflies but not of dragonflies. However, the scale of the wings and their relation to the abdomen better approximate the mayfly, whose signature abdominal hairtails, or cerci, nonetheless go missing.

Figure 3.1 Albrecht Dürer, *The Holy Family with the Mayfly* (c. 1495). Washington, The National Gallery of Art. This is used under a Creative
Commons Zero License (CC0).

The overdrawn back leg suggests that of a locust or grasshopper. In sum,
there is no distinguishable species here. Rather than any specific mayfly, or dragonfly, or butterfly, or locust, Dürer depicts something closer
to the collective notion of flyness, which – unlike any particular species
identification – claims central importance within the work as a whole.

For at heart, Dürer's print stages the relationship between time and
eternity. The latter dominates the image, extending vertically from

top to bottom of the picture plane, radiating downward from God the Father's appearance in a rent in the clouds, through the mediating figure of the Holy Spirit, into the foregrounded dyad of Virgin and Child. The temporal realm, in turn, surrounds and holds the holy family, framing it with a scene of exuberant complexity: land and water, ships and buildings, flora and fauna, the diversity and detail of created nature. The composition thus arranges itself around two contrapuntal secondary figures, with the diminutive Father, central and aloft, balanced against the even tinier form, marginal and below, of the unidentified insect. In its species ambiguity, the insect contributes to this arrangement in at least two complementary but distinct ways. If we read it as a mayfly, it figures forth the brevity of earthly affairs and the apparent incompatibility of the transient and the eternal. If we read it as a butterfly, however, it embodies connection, metamorphosis, contact, and becoming, the "transformation from caterpillar to winged insect" conventionally symbolizing "the resurrection and redemption of the soul" (Heard and Whitaker 79). So viewers find themselves challenged by an anamorphic representation of time. On one hand, the present moment remains walled off from the eternal, confined to the now, yet the eternal simultaneously appears in and through the ephemeral, which cradles it and gives it presence, making it perceptible to time-bound beings.

Beyond this, ephemerality informs the technical character of Dürer's print, which takes its own disposability for granted. Here, arguably for the first time, we confront the work of art in the age of mechanical reproduction, for, in Dürer, we encounter an artist who designs his work with mass production in mind. Equal parts draftsman and entrepreneur, Dürer early understood the profit potential of inexpensive reproducible art objects. *The Holy Family with the Mayfly* takes the market for such objects as a given, and in the process, it engineers a new kind of deliberately ephemeral art, one that embodies several of the core attributes of flyness: plurality, flimsiness, novelty, and confusion of kinds – as witness Dürer's problems with piracy (Koerner 208–12). Indeed, when such prints were not pasted into commonplace books, or slipped between the leaves of albums, or tacked to a wall as cheap decoration, they were "often purchased precisely to be copied as models," thus effecting a paradoxical self-effacement by self-multiplication, and vice versa (Koerner 209). In this way, the medium of Dürer's *Holy Family with the Mayfly* embodies its message: while any single copy of the print can expect a quite limited life-span, the multiplication of exemplars ensures that at least a few will survive over the long term, marshaling the resources of ephemerality to achieve, if not eternal life, at least a much-enhanced extension in time.

While comparable in size to Dürer's *Holy Family with the Mayfly*, Joris and Jacob Hoefnagel's *Allegory of Life and Death* (1598; Figure 3.2) could scarcely differ more in terms of the process and purpose of its creation.

Figure 3.2 Joris and Jacob Hoefnagel, *An Allegory of Life and Death* (1598). By permission of the British Museum, London.

The Hoefnagels work in an essentially medieval medium, the miniature, to produce a unique image for an aristocratic collector – the foremost connoisseur of his day, Emperor Rudolf II. The piece is every bit a bespoke luxury item, painted on vellum with watercolors compounded in part from pulverized semiprecious stones and highlighted with gold leaf. A product of courtly patronage relations rather than early market capitalism, it appears to have been created in part to secure future employment for the younger Hoefnagel, Joris's son Jacob, whose skill as a figure painter features prominently in the central roundel (Vignau-Wilberg 186). As in Dürer's *Holy Family*, the insects and other animals in this piece remain confined to the margins. However, Joris Hoefnagel's images conform much more closely to the emerging "specimen logic" of modern scientific illustration – this despite the fact that, like Dürer, he produced imaginary, composite insect forms in other contexts (Neri xi–xii, 3–26). Where the insect in Dürer's *Holy Family* appears within its natural setting, for which it serves as a kind of metonymy, Hoefnagel's specimens are abstracted from their surroundings, juxtaposed, and serially displayed as objects of study, all rendered in their representative particularity. Reconstituted thus as "animal things," they offer themselves as a site for the circulation of knowledge and exercise of mastery (Fudge 86–100).[23]

As a result of this presentation, Hoefnagel's animal subjects can be readily identified with particular species or species complexes: house mouse (*Mus musculus*), water frog (genus *Pelophylax*), wood scorpion

(*Euscorpius*), grove snail (*Cepaea*), centipede (class *Chilopoda*). The insects prove a bit more challenging, but not impossible. Along with a damselfly (suborder *Zygoptera*), a seven-spotted ladybug (*Coccinella septempunctata*), a deer fly (family *Tabanidae*), and a red admiral caterpillar (*Vanessa atalanta*), there appear two butterflies, the one to left clearly a pierid, perhaps some kind of checkered white, and the one to right perhaps a species of copper. Predictably, the hardest specimens to identify are the smallest: the two chrysalises (bottom left), the two mealworms, the small beetle at the bottom center, the miller moth (bottom right), and the minor dipteran just above it. Amidst all this, Hoefnagel introduces not one but two mayflies, on either side of the piece. To judge by wing conformation and abdominal tilt, these are different species. The one to the right greatly exceeds the other in length, and while elsewhere Hoefnagel plays with proportion, enlarging some figures (like the caterpillar) while diminishing others (like the frog) in a way that suggests their fungibility as specimens, in this case, I believe the size difference indicates difference of kind. If so, one may venture that the righthand image represents *Palingenia longicauda*, the largest of European mayflies, a well-known species in central Europe.

In sifting this mass of detail, we generate a catalogue, and rightly so, for the items catalogued represent a collection. If we add the reasonable likelihood that some of the figures in this collection were modelled on specimens already in Rudolf II's curiosity cabinet, then we see the miniature for what it is: a collectible designed for inclusion in the same collection it depicts. The work takes shape as a celebration of the collector's mania, simultaneously object, expression, and representation of the urge to possess, which it configures under the sign of death. For death lies everywhere in this image, even – or especially – where it is not. The central medallion, with its skull-bearing putto and monitory hourglass, makes that point plain enough. "*Non sum quod es*," says putto to skull in the old *memento mori* formula, to which the skull replies, "*Sed eris*" (see e.g. de Bry 70). It remains for the hourglass to chart the merger of *quod sum* with *quod ero*, a convergence that seems never to occur and yet always to have happened. Which grain of sand in the glass will mark our conversion from flesh to bone? The answer, of course, trades in paradox: no one alone, only all together, countless ephemeral moments sedimented into the fixity of the grave. Thus Hoefnagel *père* teases viewers with the lively deadness, and dead liveliness, of his subjects: the clearly departed frog and mouse, the seemingly robust snail and caterpillar, the butterflies – by their very insect nature challenging "the natural philosopher's capacity to distinguish between living and nonliving bodies" – clinging to cut roses (Wolfe 115). All stages of insect life save the egg appear here, with the pupae in the left-hand corner looking – as they tend to do – like inert things, while the mealworms inspire thoughts of vermiculation.

Like Dürer before him, Hoefnagel has depicted the temporal paradox that connects the ephemeral with the enduring. But, whereas Dürer's work generates a vision of lasting life, Hoefnagel's heads in a darker direction. One would not exaggerate in describing *An Allegory of Life and Death* as corpse art, down to the vellum it is drawn on and the brushes used to apply the paint: an image of corpses composed on skin to remind the prospective collector of his own ongoing encorpsement. The metamorphic entanglement of life and death here anticipates the dynamics of seventeenth-century still-life painting as discussed elsewhere in this volume by Anna Reynolds. But here the emphasis remains clearly on the downside. Joris Hoefnagel regularly paired his images with explanatory mottoes that serve up the philosophical purpose of the device, but in this case, fittingly, the provided banderole remains blank (Bass 16–39). One may be tempted to think of it as a visual portrayal of Hamlet's final words, and more generally, *An Allegory of Life and Death* seems to reach out to various literary parallels: not just Hamlet, but also Eliot's butterfly-like Prufrock, pinned and wriggling on the wall, and the self-reflexive heroine of Sylvia Plath's last poem, perfected in death.

Ut Pictura Poesis

When turning specifically to the verse and drama of the early modern period, we encounter much predictable carryover from the material just surveyed. For instance, we re-engage with the tendency to elide differing insect species into a general notion of flyness – a tendency made explicit in the archaic usage of the noun "fly" to denote "[a]ny winged insect; as the bee, gnat, locust, moth, etc." (*OED* s.v. "Fly" 1.a). The title of Thomas Moffett's didactic poem *The Silkwormes and their Flies* (1599) thus uses the word to refer to the moth of the silkworm caterpillar (*Bombyx mori*). Likewise, Michael Drayton's "Nymphidia" (1627) imagines the angry fairy king Oberon "encountering with a waspe" in similar terms: "He in his arms the Fly doth claspe, / As though his breath he forth would graspe" (287–309).

Following this general usage, early modern writers also maintain the conventional association of flyness with fragility, brevity, and vanity. Shakespeare's most notable flies – e.g., the "harmless fly" that Marcus kills in *Titus Andronicus* (c. 1592) (3.2.63) and the butterfly "mammock'd" by young Coriolanus (c. 1608) (3.2.63; 1.3.65) – participate in this frame of reference, as does Gloucester's despairing complaint, "As flies to wanton boys are we to th'gods, / They kill us for their sport" (4.1.36–37). So too do non-Shakespearian flies like Edmund Spenser's Clarion, the ill-fated lepidopteran hero of "Muiopotmos" (1590):

But what on earth can long abide in state,
Or who can him assure of happie day;

Sith morning faire may bring fowle evening late,
And least mishap the most blisse alter may? (115–22)

But these conventional formulas by no means remain static. Instead, tropes of flyness acquire shifting social affiliations that parallel the move from feudal agrarianism to market capitalism, with its attendant relocation of people and repurposing of land.

The resulting affiliations assume both residual and emergent form, with fairy-lore like Drayton's "Nymphidia" providing an instance of the former. Adapted from elements of an increasingly "debased agrarian culture," the fairytale matter of "Nymphidia" and similar works – Shakespeare's *Midsummer Night's Dream* (c. 1597), Ben Jonson's *Oberon* (1616) – celebrates conservative modes of social order, with the peculiar result that early modern aristocrats proved "unusually prone to identify themselves, and to be identified with, fairies" (Lamb 4, 31). But the ancient connection of fairy-lore to superstition and nature-worship produces another set of symbolic ties entirely, one suggesting "the commensurability of insects and fairies" (Borlik 26). Hence the conflated preciosity of an insectoid fairy chivalry, equipped with "Hornets sting" rapiers and "Bettles head" helmets (Drayton 501, 505): such fantasies hover quaintly on the edge of self-parody, at once ennobling and diminishing their subjects. Much the same holds for a poem like Spenser's "Muiopotmos," which discards the fairy-lore while retaining the core association between insect life and aristocratic culture. Here, too, the bond between flyness and the chivalric ethic enfeebles the latter, thereby complementing Spenser's "focus on the vanity of human things" (MacFaul 144). Given the increasing pressure upon elite identity in the early modern period – whether understood as a decades-long crisis of the aristocracy or as a less dramatic transition from warrior to leisure class – such matter seems over-determined. It reads like phylogeny recapitulating ontogeny: a proleptic meditation on the end of a way of life.

By extension, the flyness of aristocratic culture also displays itself relative to courtly manners, where it inspires pejorative images of flattery, favouritism, and parasitism. One sub-group of these images foregrounds the pleasant vices of palace life: delicate diet, splendid raiment, extravagant sexuality, all subject to the sudden rise and fall of courtly fortunes. Here we encounter Lear's hopeful fantasy of prison life with Cordelia:

So we'll live,
And pray, and sing, and tell old tales, and laugh
At gilded butterflies, and hear poor rogues
Talk of court news; and we'll talk with them, too –
Who loses and who wins; who's in, who's out –
...
...and we'll wear out,
In a wall'd prison, packs and sects of great ones

That ebb and flow by th' moon. (Shakespeare, *King Lear* 5.3.
11–15, 17–19)

And here too we meet Hamlet's "water-fly," the ridiculous courtier
Osric (5.2.82). In Lear's case, the phrase "gilded butterflies" evokes the
fleeting excesses of courtly fashion. Hamlet's "Dost know this water-
fly?", by contrast, refers to behaviour: Osric has just saluted the prince
with an affected curtsey that recalls the exaggerated fluttering of a mayfly in swarm. Flyness acquires upscale sexual overtones, too, as when
John Donne exhorts his mistress to let "curious traitors, sleavesilk
flies,/Bewitch poor fishes' wandering eyes," she herself needing "no
such deceit,/For thou thyself art thine own bait" (44). The conceit here
is typically tricky: seeing hungry fish drawn to the mating swarms of
water-flies, early anglers modelled their own artificial flies after species
like the mayfly, oak fly (genus *Rhagio*), and hawthorn fly (*Bibio marci*)
(Walton 112–13). The resulting admixture of passion and predation –
ardent flies pursued by hungry fish pursued by hungry people disguised
as ardent flies – provides the perfect foil for Donne's mistress, herself her
own bait, collapsing the difference between hunter and hunted, eater
and eaten.

A subtly different image of fashionable sexuality occurs in Jonson's
Epicoene (1609) as Truewit warns Morose about the dangers of taking
a wife: "If she be fair, young, and vegetous, no sweetmeats ever drew
more flies; all the yellow doublets and great roses i' the town will be
there" (2.2.57–59). While the context here remains elite – the trendy
yellow doublets and lace roses of gentlemen's attire – this language carries a distinctly unsavoury feel, imagining the female body as a high-
class comestible already subject to decay and crawling with insects.
Here, the flyness of delicacy yields to the flyness of putrefaction, which
generates another sub-group of associations with court life and court
manners. Thus, Jonson's image of flies crawling on food also appears
a couple of years earlier in Shakespeare's *Timon of Athens* (c. 1606),
where it attaches to Timon's faithless flatterers: "Feast-won, fast-lost;
one cloud of winter show'rs, / These flies are couch'd" (2.2.170–71).
Emphasizing the brevity of bought loyalties, this language also points to
a central weakness of the patronage ethic: its endless need to transform
present largesse into future security, to cobble distinct units of time into
comforting cohesion. Unhappily for Timon, his flatterers exist only in
the moment. "Fools of fortune, trencher-friends, time's flies" (3.6.96),
they embody a moral rot that mimics the decay of the food on which
they feed.

But there exists no greater literary monument to the flyness of putrefaction than the character Mosca in Ben Jonson's *Volpone* (1606). The
play's charactonyms, recalling Aesop, cast the plot as a chain of predation by patronage. The legacy hunters Voltore, Corvino, and Corbaccio

(Volpone calls them "Vulture, kite, / Raven and gor-crow, all my birds of prey") compete to feed upon Volpone when he "turn[s] carcass" (1.2. 89–90, 91); with Mosca's help, Volpone feeds on them in the meantime; and in a final reversal, Mosca turns the tables on everyone else, in effect feeding on them all. Read as animal fable, this reversal flips the food chain upside down, with megafauna falling prey to microfauna. Hence the enraged Voltore, when Mosca gets the better of him: "Well, flesh-fly, it is summer with you now; / Your winter will come on" (5.9.1–2). Voltore's predictable Vanitas imagery merges with a singular view of Mosca as flesh-fly, "the biggest of all other" biting flies, frequenter of "the flesh-market or Shambles," where it taints the meat with its "fly-blowes" – i.e. its eggs and maggots. (Moffett 934). Flyness of putrefaction indeed.

Further, Mosca's trickery embodies not only zoological but also social inversion, the ignominy of gentlemen bested by a servant. This, more than anything, infuriates Mosca's betters, who splutter with indignation over it. "I'm cozened," Corbaccio cries, "cheated, by a parasite-slave;/ Harlot, th'ast gulled me" (5.3.64–65). "Outstripped thus by a parasite? a slave?", wails Voltore, "Would run on errands? And make legs for crumbs?" (5.7. 1–2). The thought annihilates, and the word Jonson chooses to denote Mosca's inferior status – sometimes coupled with "slave," as above – is "parasite." It occurs nineteen times in *Volpone*, always in connection with Mosca, always in its prevailing early modern sense, drawn straight from the Greek, which designates a recipient of patronage: "One who eats at the table or at the expense of another" (*OED* s.v. "Parasite" 1). By contrast, the word's current biological sense – "an animal or plant which lives in or upon another organism" (*OED* s.v. "Parasite" 2) – will not enter usage for over a century; the *OED* first records it in 1727, as a metaphorical extension of the word's root meaning. Yet Mosca's flyness anticipates this later usage, in reverse: if we now speak of literal flies as figurative parasites, Jonson imagines Mosca, a literal parasite, as a figurative fly. In the process, he gives us the English language's earliest association of parasitism with non-human animal behaviour.

For Mosca, indeed, parasitism unites the food chain of animal fable with the feeding chain of patronage: "All the wise world is little else in nature / But parasites or sub-parasites" (3.1.12–13). And for Mosca, the essence of parasitism lies in illusion, dissemblance, sleight of hand:

> [Y]our fine, elegant rascal, that can rise
> And stoop (almost together) like an arrow;
> Turn short, as doth a swallow; and be here,
> And there, and here, and yonder, all at once;
> Present to any humour, all occasion;
> And change a visor swifter than a thought!
> This is the creature had the art born with him. (3.1.23–30)

But Mosca's "art" entails a strangely fraught relationship with time. For what Stephen Greenblatt says of Volpone applies to his servant, too:

> In committing himself to a fictive existence, to a life of masks and pseudo-relationships, [he] cuts himself off from the experience of duration. He must renew himself each moment ... lest the whole performance simply cease and vanish. (100)

As con man, as actor, as parasite, Mosca consigns himself to an oxymoronic half-life of endless ephemerality. This too marks a form of flyness.

Empire of the Flies

Of the literary references cited hitherto, all function as lagging cultural indicators. They attach themselves to residual social arrangements: patronage, the chivalric ethic, notions of aristocratic hierarchy, and privilege. But flyness also functions in early modern writing as a leading indicator, connected to emergent historical trends, in particular population growth and urbanization. For the English experience of the seventeenth and eighteenth centuries, these developments prove crucial, of course. Between 1600 and 1650, the population of London roughly doubles, from 200,000 to 400,000, and by 1800, London becomes the first modern European city with over a million inhabitants (Sacks 22). This unprecedented growth generates a new environmental reality, with increasing numbers of human beings and commensal animals occupying an ever-more-crowded urban space.

Within this context, flyness acquires down-market associations through the foregrounded qualities of multiplicity, swarming, novelty, and heat. In itself, of course, a flyness of swarming is nothing new to early modernity, nor is its disparaging connection to various social groups. As one medieval poet complained, "Fleas, flies, and friars sorely afflict the people of God," the affliction in each case clearly compounded by number (Wright and Halliwell 91, my translation). But in the crowded setting of early modern London, quantity acquires a quality all its own, associated with specifically urban places and urban situations and the meaner sort of city-dwellers. We get an early glimpse of this usage in Shakespeare's *3 Henry VI* (c. 1590), as the dying Clifford laments Henry's loss of popular support: "The common people swarm like summer flies, / And whither fly the gnats but to the sun?/ And who shines now but Henry's enemies?" (2.6.8–10). While these fly-like commoners as yet lack a clear urban affiliation, their fickleness anticipates Shakespeare's disparaging treatment of city mobs in *Richard II* (c. 1595), *Julius Caesar* (1599), and *Coriolanus* (c. 1608) – the first of which likens England to "a sea-wall'd garden ... / Swarming with caterpillars" (3.3.42, 46), while the last casts aspersions on the "multiplying spawn" of the Roman people (2.2.78).

A more arcane Shakespearian allusion, when unpacked, offers intriguing specifics of time and place. In *Henry V* (c. 1599), King Henry seeks aid from the Duke of Burgundy anent his courtship of Princess Katherine:

K. HEN: [G]ood my lord, teach your cousin to consent winking.
BUR: I will wink on her to consent, my lord, if you will teach her to know
    my meaning; for maids, well summer'd and warm kept, are like flies
    at Bartholomew-tide, blind, though they have their eyes, and then
    they will endure handling, which before would not abide looking on.
K. HEN: This moral ties me over to time and a hot summer; and so I shall
    catch the fly, your cousin, in the latter end, and she must be blind,
    too. (5.2.304–14)

With nudge-wink humour, Burgundy counsels Henry to get the princess in the mood; once fed and warmed up ("well summer'd and warm kept"), she'll "endure handling." As for the interloping fly-simile, with its talk of blindness, this may sound like mere nonsense to a modern ear. However, Moffett affirms the tale, assigning it specifically to large biting flies like the horsefly and deer-fly:

In the months of *July* and *August*, by reason of the extremity of heat
they are most fierce, and do miserably handle Oxen and Horses and
young cattel, ... which they follow by sent of their sweat, because
they cannot reach them with their sight, being very weak sighted.
(936)

Once the princess has been properly blinded with dinner and a little heat, Burgundy assures Henry, she may be grasped "in the latter end" just like such a fly.

The image can only be described as gross, and the more one considers it, the grosser it gets. Beginning in fashionable prurience, it descends straight to the meat-stalls of summer, in the process making all too clear Henry's view of his bride-to-be. The calendar specification of "Bartholomew-tide" makes perfect sense here, Saint Bartholomew's Day falling smack in the dog days of late August. But it makes a kind of topographical sense too, given the seasonal occurrence of Bartholomew Fair on the northwest edge of London, near "the Pens (or foldes) in Smithfield," the city's principal meat and livestock market (Stow 304, 309–11). Among other things, Henry's language transforms Katherine from one of a kind – princess of the royal blood of France – to one of a crowd: of women, flies, cattle, whatever. And the "Bartholomew-tide" crowd in question carries marked vulgar associations, as it also does for the gentlemen of quality in Jonson's *Bartholomew Fair* (1613). There, as the play's assorted ninnies and knaves sally forth to Smithfield, Quarlous and Winwife agree to keep them company, but pointedly not for the attractions on offer at the fair itself. For while "none goes thither of any quality or fashion" (1.5.116), the folly and vice of the fairgoers provide their own amusement; as Winwife puts it, "These flies cannot, this hot season, but engender us excellent creeping sport" (1.5.123–24). Here in Jonson's comedy, the flyness of urban swarms and summer heat serves as an instrument of satirical deprecation. Quarlous and Winwife consort with the other fairgoers not in solidarity, but with the paradoxical aim of enforcing difference, of marking their own superiority to the group.

In the longer term, such language proves congenial to the satirical bent of Restoration and eighteenth-century literature, with Jonathan Swift supplying a prominent case in point. As Lucinda Cole has noted, "Although his talking horses have received a great deal of critical attention, Swift's vermin are more numerous and, in some ways, more revealing" (Cole 145). They figure humankind as a swarming pestilence, as when "Verses Occasioned by the Sudden Drying Up of St. Patrick's Well" (c. 1729) describes the English colonists of Ireland:

> Emblems of insects vile, who spread their spawn
> Through all thy land, in armour, fur and lawn;
> A nauseous brood, that fills your senate walls
> And in the chamber of your Viceroy crawls. (*Jonathan* 375, ll. 55–58)

Swift applies such language to oppressor and oppressed alike, not just the interloping English but also the Irish beggars who "infest" Dublin like so many "Caterpillars" (Cole 145–49; *Proposal* 23). More than an instrument of satirical abuse, it underlies his sense of the human condition.

Following this vein, Swift's flyness achieves its most disturbing formulation in the second voyage of *Gulliver's Travels* (1726), as Gulliver makes his way in Brobdingnag. There, surrounded by beings vastly larger than he, Gulliver faces off against the local fly population:

> The Kingdom is much pestered with Flies in Summer, and these odious Insects, each of them as big as a *Dunstable* Lark, hardly gave me any rest while I sat at Dinner, with their continual humming and buzzing about my Ears. They would sometimes alight upon my Victuals, and leave their loathsome Excrement or Spawn behind, which to me was very visible, although not to the Natives of that Country, whose large Optics were not so acute as mine in viewing smaller Objects. Sometimes they would fix upon my Nose or Forehead, where they stung me to the quick, smelling very offensively, and I could easily trace that viscous Matter, which our Naturalists tell us enables those Creatures to walk with their Feet upwards upon a Ceiling. (102)

Gulliver's reaction to these insects – a mixture of revulsion and fear – anticipates his later response to the Yahoos of his fourth voyage, and a shared disgust links this earlier scene to Swift's later account of the land of the Houyhnhnms. Both cases present Gulliver with a crisis of similarity. While differing from his aspirational companions – the king of Brobdingnag, his Houyhnhnm master – in ways that can be neither remedied nor ignored, Gulliver finds himself thrust instead into the unwelcome society of flies and Yahoos. Forced to abandon his rational ideals in face of his excremental embodiment, he bears horrified witness to his kind's degradation on the Great Chain of Being. Thus the king of Brobdingnag:

> [B]y what I have gathered from your own Relations, and the Answers I have with much Pains wringed and extorted from you, I cannot but conclude the Bulk of your Natives, to be the most pernicious Race of little odious Vermin that Nature ever suffered to crawl upon the surface of the Earth. (123)

In effect, Gulliver's dilemma reverses the posture of Quarlous and Winwife in Jonson's *Bartholomew Fair*. Jonson's gallants encounter the teeming life of Smithfield in order to spurn it with gestures of mockery and contempt. Gulliver attempts similar self-distancing only to find himself consigned to life among the very beings he abhors. To be swarmed upon by others, to lose oneself in the crowd: it is a distinctly urban horror fantasy, one that also acquires specific associations in the eighteenth-century English literary market. For that market was itself an urban artifact, centered on London, shaped by the city's history, deriving its local habitation and name from the city's topography. Will Tullett's essay in the present volume notes how "The coffee-house, arguably the interior urban venue most associated with ephemeral print in the early eighteenth century, had its own distinct 'buzzing' soundscape to match" (214). Likewise, writing of London's iconic downscale literary enclave, Paula McDowell observes, "it is no accident that the derogatory label 'Grub Street' draws heavily on the word 'grub,' meaning 'the larva of an insect, esp. of a beetle; a caterpillar, maggot'" (54). In fact, the etymological connection proves less direct than this implies: the street apparently earned its name from an adjacent sewage-ditch, via the Old English verb *grybban*, to dig (Clarke 9). But by the mid-1700s, Grub Street, its denizens, and the products of their literary labour had all acquired creeping, insectoid associations. Queen Dulness, in Alexander Pope's *Dunciad* (1728–1743), sets the tone here when, surveying the "Journals, Medleys, Merc'ries, [and] Magazines" produced by the "Grub-street race," she beholds "Maggots half-formed in rhyme exactly meet,/And learn to crawl upon poetic feet" (ll. 42, 44, 61–62). Similar language recurs, minus the local geography, when Samuel Taylor Coleridge critiques "the present mode of conducting literary journals" in his *Biographia Literaria* (1817):

"Gnats, beetles, wasps, butterflies, and the whole tribe of ephemerals and insignificants, ... may hum and buzz and jar ..., unchastised and unnoticed" (381; see also McDowell 53, 59–60, 64).

But the trope of literature-as-ephemeral-insect receives its most forthright treatment in George Crabbe's *The Newspaper* (1785), which revisits Gulliver's nightmare of the mob from a specifically journalistic standpoint. Crabbe worries about the accelerating pace of the London news cycle, which he considers inimical to serious writing, especially verse. Hence his opening complaint: "A time like this, a busy bustling time, / Suits ill with writers, very ill with rhyme" (43). Crabbe figures the problem here as an excess of literature that negates literature: papers, journals, and broadsheets "flying forth" in a "daily swarm, that banish every Muse" (43), an overabundance of language that creates a collapse of meaning. An accomplished natural historian himself, Crabbe reaches instinctively for entomological metaphor when describing the news sheets:

> In shoals the hours their constant numbers bring,
> Like insects waking to th'advancing spring:
> Which take their rise from grubs obscene that lie
> In shallow pools, or thence ascend the sky;
> Such are these base ephemeras, so born
> To die before the next revolving morn. (44)

Crabbe's satire thus frames a clear set of oppositional categories: news versus art, ephemerality versus eternity, plurality versus singularity, commerce versus contemplation, insects versus humanity. Welcome to the empire of the flies.

Yet having established these contrasts, Crabbe proceeds at once to break them down, for he locates the real horror of journalism not in its alliance with the ephemeral, but in its elevation of the ephemeral to the status of the eternal. Continuing his entomological metaphor, Crabbe therefore draws a contrast between the natural evanescence of flies and its artificial journalistic counterpart:

> Yet thus they differ: insect-tribes are lost
> In the first visit of a winter's frost;
> While these remain, a base but constant breed,
> Whose swarming sons their short-lived sires succeed:
> No changing season makes their number less,
> Nor Sunday shines a sabbath on the press! (44)

In place of seasonality and cyclical recurrence, the press gives us nature denatured, a torrent of information both eternal and ephemeral and therefore neither. In this sense, London's newspapers function as a synecdoche of the world that creates them, and Crabbe deplores the contents of both: politicking, advertising, gossip, and social blather. Given the differences of scale distinguishing the Georgian era from our own, this indignation seems both prescient and somehow quaint. On one hand, Crabbe recognizes the potential for overload and redundancy inherent to increased modern media circulation; on the other hand, he has no way of knowing just how bad the problem will become.

A Tomb of One's Own

Crabbe's hostility to the newspaper business takes shape around an implied contrast between literary trifling, figured as frantic and swarming and brief, and literary attainment, figured as calm and unique and durable. The trifling finds apt embodiment in images of flyness like those examined here. As for the attainment, it has its own metaphors, with monumental and architectural comparisons prominent among them.

As Katherine Hunt notes elsewhere in this volume, Horace provides a *locus classicus* for such metaphors, exulting, "More durable than bronze, higher than Pharaoh's / pyramids is the monument I have made" (182). His boast proves popular among early modern English poets, who refashion it in various ways. Shakespeare recasts it most famously in Sonnet 55: "Not marble, nor the gilded monuments/ Of princes shall outlast this powerful rhyme" (1–2). Jonson then transfers the metaphor to Shakespeare himself: "Thou art a monument without a tomb" ("To the Memory" 264 l.22). John Milton follows suit, asking, "What needs my *Shakespear* for his honour'd Bones / The labour of an Age in piled Stones?", then concluding, "Thou in our wonder and astonishment / Hast built thyself a live-long Monument" (61 ll. 1–2, 7–8). Less sanguine, Edmund Waller complains, "Poets that lasting Marble seek / Must carve in *Latine* or in *Greek*" (237).

Can it be accidental that such monuments all assume funerary form? We might well conclude this essay by pondering the nature of a literary dispensation that imagines failure as hot and active and multiple and insectoid, while conceiving success as static and marmoreal and singular and – not to put too fine a point on it – dead. Perhaps the last word should go to Andrew Marvell, who summons the figures of the insect and tomb once more to indicate the nature of the problem here:

> Thy beauty shall no more be found;
> Nor, in thy marble vault, shall sound
> My echoing song: then worms shall try
> That long-preserved virginity. (51)

As tempting as it may be to inhabit a tomb of one's own, only the living can read and love. *Vivamus, mea Lesbia, atque amemus*! For despite all the talk of lasting marble, worms eat books and corpses alike.

Notes

1 I'm indebted to Anne Coldiron and Tom Yanosky for their very generous help with this essay.
2 Moffett readied this work for the press in 1588–89, and an original title-page was imprinted with the latter date. However, financial issues prevented final publication for nearly fifty years.
3 At least three of the print's four current titles were in circulation by the late nineteenth century; see Boston Museum of Fine Arts Print Department, *Exhibition of Albert Dürer's engravings, etchings, and dry-points, and most of the woodcuts executed from his designs.* Boston, 1888. Cat. no. 2 (1–2). The print's insect has also been identified as a praying mantis (Strauss 8).

Works Cited

Aristotle. *History of Animals: Books IV-VI*. Trans A. L. Peck. Harvard UP, 1970.

Bacon, Francis. *Sylva Sylvarum, or, A Natural History in Ten Centuries.* London, 1658.

Bass, Marisa Anne. *Insect Artifice: Nature and Art in the Dutch Revolt.* Princeton UP, 2019.

Borlik, Todd Andrew. "Shakespeare's Insect Theater: Fairy Lore as Elizabethan Folk Entomology." *Performing Animals: History, Agency, Theater.* Eds Karen Raber and Monica Mattfeld. U of Pennsylvania P, 2017. 123–40.

de Bry, Theodor. *Emblemata Nobilitatis.* Frankfurt, 1592.

Charleton, Walter. *Onomasticon zoicon.* London, 1668.

Cicero. *Tusculan Disputations.* Trans J. E. King. Harvard UP, 1989

Clarke, Bob. *From Grub Street to Fleet Street: An Illustrated History of English Newspapers to 1899.* Ashgate, 2004.

Clutius, Augerius. *De Hemerobio*, in *Opuscula duo singularia.* Amsterdam, 1634.

Cole, Lucinda. "Swift Among the Locusts: Vermin, Infestation, and Natural Philosophy in the Eighteenth Century." *Animals, Animality, and Literature.* Eds Bruce Boehrer, Molly Hand, and Brian Massumi. Cambridge UP, 2018. 136–55.

Coleridge, Samuel Taylor. *Biographia Literaria. Samuel Taylor Coleridge: The Major Works.* Oxford UP, 2009.

Crabbe, George. "The Newspaper." *The Poetical Works of George Crabbe.* Eds R. M. and A. J. Carlyle. Oxford UP, 1914. 42–49.

Donne, John. "The Bait." *John Donne: The Complete English Poems.* Ed A. J. Smith. Penguin, 1971. 44.

Drayton, Michael. "Nymphidia." *The English Spenserians.* Ed. William B. Hunter, Jr. U of Utah P, 1977. 287–309.

Fudge, Erica. "Renaissance Animal Things." *New Formations* 76 (2012): 86–100.

Greenblatt, Stephen. "The False Ending in *Volpone.*" *Journal of English and Germanic Philology* 75.1/2 (January–April, 1976): 90–104.

Heard, Kate and Lucy Whitaker. *The Northern Renaissance: Dürer to Holbein.* Royal Collection Publications, 2011.

Horace. *The Odes and The Centennial Hymns.* Trans James Michie. Bobbs-Merrill, 1963.

Hunt, Katherine. "More Lasting than Bronze: Statues, Writing, and the Materials of Ephemera in Ben Jonson's *Sejanus His Fall.*" *Practices of Ephemera in Early Modern England.* Eds Callan Davies, Hannah Lilley, and Catherine Richardson. Routledge, 2023. 111–27.

Jonson, Ben. *Bartholomew Fair. The Alchemist and Other Plays.* Ed. Gordon Campbell. Oxford UP, 2008. 327–433.

———. *Epicoene. The Alchemist and Other Plays.* Ed. Gordon Campbell. Oxford UP, 2008. 119–210.

———. "To the Memory of My Beloved, the Author Mr. William Shakespeare." *The Complete Poems.* Ed. George Parfitt. Penguin, 1976. 263–65.

———. *Volpone. The Alchemist and Other Plays.* Ed. Gordon Campbell. Oxford UP, 2008. 1–118.

Jorink, Eric. *Reading the Book of Nature in the Dutch Golden Age, 1575–1715.* Brill, 2010.

Kluge, Nikita. J. *Ephemeroptera of the World.* Saint Petersburg State University, 2020. *insecta.bio.spbu.ru/z/Eph-spp/index.htm.* Web. Accessed 17 Nov. 2021.

Koerner, Joseph Leo. *The Moment of Self-Portraiture in German Renaissance Art.* U of Chicago P, 1993.

Lamb, Mary Ellen. *The Popular Culture of Shakespeare, Spenser, and Jonson.* Routledge, 2006.

Linnaeus, Carl. *Systema Naturae.* Stockholm, 1758.

MacFaul, Tom. "The Butterfly, the Fart, and the Dwarf: The Origins of the English Laureate Micro-Epic." *Connotations* 17.2–3 (2008): 144–64.

Marvell, Andrew. "To Hs Coy Mistress." *Andrew Marvell: The Complete Poems.* Ed. Elizabeth Story Donno. Penguin, 1986. 50–51.

McDowell, Paula. "Of Grubs and Other Insects: Constructing the Categories of 'Ephemera' and 'Literature' in Eighteenth-Century British Writing." *Book History* 15 (2012): 48–70.

Milton, John. "On *Shakspear.* 1630." *The Riverside Milton.* Ed. Roy Flannagan. Houghton Mifflin, 1979. 60–82.

Moffett, Thomas. *Insectorum sive Minimorum Animalium Theatrum.* London, 1634.

———. *The Silkwormes and their Flies.* Ed Victor Houliston. Medieval and Renaissance Texts and Studies, 1989.

———. *The Theater of Insects.* Trans. John Rowland. *The History of Four-footed Beasts and Serpents.* Edward Topsell. Vol. 2. London, 1658.

Neri, Janice. *The Insect and the Image: Visualizing Nature in Early Modern Europe, 1500–1700.* U of Minnesota P, 2011.

Pliny the Elder. *Natural History 3: Books VIII-XI.* Trans. H. Rackham. Harvard UP, 1983.

Pope, Alexander. *The Dunciad.* Ed Valerie Rumbold. Pearson, 2009.

Rees, Abraham, ed. *The Cyclopaedia; or, Universal Dictionary of Arts, Sciences, and Literature*, 39 vols. London, 1819.

Reynolds, Anna. "What do Texts and Insects have in Common?; or, Ephemerality before Ephemera." *Practices of Ephemera in Early Modern England*. Eds Callan Davies, Hannah Lilley, and Catherine Richardson. Routledge, 2023. 25–43.

Sacks, David Harris. "London's Dominion: The Metropolis, the Market Economy, and the State." *Material London, ca. 1600*. U of Pennsylvania P, 2000. 20–54.

Shakespeare, William. *Coriolanus. The Riverside Shakespeare*. Eds G. Blakemore Evans et al. Houghton Mifflin, 1997. 1440–88.

———. *Henry V. The Riverside Shakespeare*. Eds G. Blakemore Evans et al. Houghton Mifflin, 1997. 974–1021.

———. *3 Henry VI. The Riverside Shakespeare*. Eds G. Blakemore Evans et al. Houghton Mifflin, 1997. 711–47.

———. *King Lear. The Riverside Shakespeare*. Eds G. Blakemore Evans et al. Houghton Mifflin, 1997. 1297–354.

———. "Sonnet 55." *Sonnets. The Riverside Shakespeare*. Eds G. Blakemore Evans et al. Houghton Mifflin, 1997. 1853.

———. *Timon of Athens. The Riverside Shakespeare*. Eds G. Blakemore Evans et al. Houghton Mifflin, 1997. 1489–525.

———. *Titus Andronicus. The Riverside Shakespeare*. Eds G. Blakemore Evans et al. Houghton Mifflin, 1997. 1065–100.

Spenser, Edmund ."Muiopotmos." *The Complete Poetical Works of Edmund Spenser*. Ed. R. E. Neil Dodge. Cambridge UP, 1908. 115–22.

Stow, John. *A suruay of London*. London, 1598.

Strauss, Walter. L., *The Complete Engravings, Etchings, and Drypoints of Albrecht Dürer*. New York, 1973.

Swammerdam, Jan. *Ephemeri vita*. London, 1681.

Swift, Jonathan. *A Proposal for Giving Badges to the Beggars in All the Parishes of Dublin*. Dublin, 1737.

———. *Gulliver's Travels*. Ed. Robert Demaria, Jr. Penguin, 2010.

———. *Jonathan Swift: The Complete Poems*. Ed. Pat Rogers. Penguin, 1983.

Tullett, William. "Extensive Ephemera: Perfumer's Trade Cards in Eighteenth-Century England." *Practices of Ephemera in Early Modern England*. Eds Callan Davies, Hannah Lilley, and Catherine Richardson. Routledge, 2022. 210–28.

Vignau-Wilberg, Thea. *Joris and Jacob Hoefnagel: Art and Science around 1600*. Hatje Cantz, 2017.

Waller, Edmund "Of English Verse." *Poems, &c. Written Upon Several Occasions*. London, 1686. 236–38.

Walton, Izaak. *The Complete Angler*. London, 1668.

Wolfe, Jessica. "Circus Minimus: The Early Modern Theater of Insects." *Performing Animals: History, Agency, Theater*. Eds Karen Raber and Monica Mattfeld. U of Pennsylvania P, 2017. 111–22.

Wright, Thomas and James Orchard Halliwell, eds. *Reliquiae Antiquae. Scraps from Ancient Manuscripts*. 2 vols. London, 1843.

4 What Is an 'Ephemeral Archive'? Stratford-upon-Avon, 1550–1650

A Case Study

Robert Bearman

It is a common experience, especially when sorting through one's own papers, "academic" or otherwise, to come across items that were never intended to be kept – rough working notes, shopping lists, reminders of things that needed doing – which in effect had become redundant as soon as they had (or had not) been acted on or worked up. Had they, within a day or two, been destroyed, then they would, by the original definition of the word, as given in the *Oxford English Dictionary*, have been ephemeral – that is, they would only have been in existence for a very short time (A.1.b.). When unearthed some years later, we might still regard them as ephemera *manqué* and destroy them anyway. On the other hand, the passage of time may have added to their interest, in some cases providing a fuller or alternative record of what had occurred, especially helpful in cases where a more formal written record of what had taken place may never have existed, or has itself since disappeared. And at a distance of 400 or 500 years, it can be persuasively argued that *any* fragment of archival material will, due to its chance survival, yield useful additional information about the event that led to its production.

The *OED* does allow for a less rigid definition of the ephemeral, namely something that is "in existence, power, favour, popularity, etc. for a short time only; short-lived; transitory" (A.2.a). This opens up a wider field and also serves as a reminder that ephemerality applies not only to physical objects but also to abstract thoughts and memories. Before increased popular literacy allowed "facts" to be set down in writing, this was the basis on which many aspects of life were conducted. Any discussion of archival ephemera, therefore, needs a working definition. Here, I have applied it to material that, at the point of creation, was thought of as transitory only and certainly not created with a view to its becoming a "deliberate" part of the historical record – and, for the purposes of this chapter, that it refers to material in handwritten or hand- drawn form. I will then move on to assess to what extent such material, preserved against the odds in the administrative archive of the Stratford-upon-Avon Corporation, can still be of assistance in the writing of history.

DOI: 10.4324/9781003058588-6

In today's world, distinguishing between records worth keeping for a while (in case one needs to refer to them) and records that should be regarded as of historical importance (and so worth permanent preservation) falls to records management (at least until the "born digital" age) – a skill designed to restrict an excessive accumulation of hard copy from finding its way into the permanent historical record. Destruction schedules are therefore commonplace, broadly based on a pyramid view that some of the records at the bottom can be dispensed with if a more refined digest exists at a higher level. Indeed, ephemera, if defined by its original meaning, is not even part of this process, having been more or less immediately consigned to the waste-paper basket.

In early modern England, however, an orderly process of this kind did not exist. Although the preservation of the formal record was by then accepted as important, what happened to the mass of informal documentation – the "working papers," in modern parlance – was nobody's responsibility beyond those who had created them. But paper, being valuable in its own right, was not routinely destroyed, especially if any spaces left blank allowed for some unconnected reuse. Neither was there any official guidance either on the desirability, or not, of preserving a draft once a final version had been agreed on or a need to keep detailed records of expenditure after formal accounts had been drawn up and audited. Moreover, though such guidance can be professionally applied today to the long-term preservation of business or administrative records, it cannot be so easily imposed on personal papers, whether these survive in huge unsorted accumulations or occupy only a single folder.

Many of the documents relating to events that happened 400 years ago have, "ephemeral" or not, come down to us simply by chance. Those who initially drew them up and then filed what they thought were worth keeping were in general terms not doing so because they might one day prove of historic interest but rather in the belief that such records might prove helpful in the transaction of future business or as evidence that they had discharged their duties in an honourable manner. Over time this could become less and less a reason for their retention and huge tranches of records, once thought worth filing, were repurposed to new functions or, by accident or design, lost or deliberately destroyed. As likely as not, many of those that endured owed their survival to the fact that storage facilities were sufficiently capacious that they did not have to be thrown away, languishing instead in hidden corners until "discovered" hundreds of years later. This is not to say that, especially in more recent times, accumulations of records, in terms of sheer bulk, have not come to serve as evidence of a family's or institution's long and glorious history, regardless of the value of individual items. Nevertheless, by and large, what has survived, and in decreasing quantities the further back we go, is inevitably a motley collection of material.

How relevant is it, then, to identify historical administrative records as "ephemeral"? Though a distinction can be drawn between those that were formally preserved and those that survived almost by accident, is this more than an academic exercise? After all, what has survived of the written record, whether intentional or not, is a large part of what we have in order to write history. On the other hand, material identified now as "ephemeral" can be of great assistance in reading between the lines of the formal record. More significantly, without this ephemera, some events would now be completely unknown to posterity. It might also be a matter of regret that, in cases where only the formal record survives, there are no ephemera to fall back on to fill out the picture of what had really happened. In what follows, I seek to determine to what extent the importance of one collection – the records of the Stratford-upon-Avon Corporation – depends on the survival of material that at the point of production was never considered as of more than passing significance.

The Stratford-upon-Avon Corporation: its Archives, Both "Deliberate" and "Ephemeral"

Stratford upon-Avon at the turn of the sixteenth century was a medium-sized market town of some 2,000–2,500 inhabitants, its governance and economy typical of what is to be expected of a settlement of that size and with no obvious distinguishing feature to set it apart from others – at least at that time (for background, see Dyer). However, from a modern standpoint, there is a very real difference: the survival of its records, particularly those of its governing body, the Stratford-upon-Avon Corporation. Stratford's is no unique case, but for a town of its size to have retained such a rich archive is somewhat unusual. Edited texts of the Corporation archives, documenting its activities from its creation under a charter of 1553 to the year 1610, currently fill 1,215 pages in a series of six volumes, with a further printed volume to be added shortly, of another 500 pages or so, covering events to 1620 (*Minutes*).[1] Even this is not the whole story. For reasons of space, it was decided not to include every surviving document of an official, or semi-official, nature on the grounds, it was thought, that its content was not deemed worthy of inclusion.[2]

Of this accumulation, it is not difficult to identify what can be called the Stratford Corporation's "deliberate" archive, namely those items that were held to be of such fundamental importance that permanent storage was required. These are best represented by a series of so-called minute books (better described as order books), the first three covering the period 1553 to 1657 (BRU 2/1–3).[3] By and large, these record the principal orders made at official meetings of the Council, without which little would be known about how the Corporation managed its affairs. However, their content is generally limited to decisions that could be consulted if disputes arose over the terms of a lease or the use of its buildings, or for the recording of orders against which the behaviour of its elected members, officers, and townsfolk could be measured. As a result, the recorded proceedings of a single meeting rarely exceed a page: of the 124 meetings held between 1599 and 1608, only 115 pages were used up, even more extraordinary in that, more often than not, half a page was taken up with a table of Council members, marked up to note whether they were present or not.

It is clear, though, that much more business must have been discussed. Some Council meetings were divided into morning and afternoon sessions with no indication, in the amount of recorded business, as to why this was necessary. In other words, there is little record of discussions leading up to the issue of an order, nor a record of any other business which did not need more than routine attention. Very occasionally a note was made that insufficient members were present to allow for any decisions to be taken; on the other hand, of the 124 meetings held between 1599 and 1608, around half were attended by between 19 and 21 members (out of a possible 28), with another 40 higher than that (*Minutes* 6: 7).

Another "deliberate" archival sequence to survive in an almost unbroken series, at least from 1563, comprises the annual accounts submitted by a succession of chamberlains. The charter of 1553 had imposed on the Corporation the task of maintaining a school and almshouses, and for paying the vicar's salary and finding him a house. To provide the necessary income, the Corporation received a significant block of property, both in terms of real estate and a portion of the tithes, formerly belonging to religious institutions recently suppressed. This required the keeping of accounts, mainly rental income set against payments. A summary for the year 1558 establishes that these were routinely submitted (*Minutes* 1: 79; see also rent roll for 1561 at 108–15), and from 1563 annual accounts survive in an almost unbroken series until the end of our period.[4] These order books and accounts were clearly produced as a permanent record, to be referred back to as required.

However, even in this deliberate archive, there are examples of a change of use or function, offering an insight into the impermanence of texts despite their preservation within a formal archive. A good example is a volume acquired in March 1641 used to record "A note specifying howe all ye money contributed to our late losse by fire is disposed of" with, at the end of the volume, and in reverse: "A perticuler account of all such summes of money as were contributed towards our late losse by fire" (BRU 16/1). Despite the obvious implication that considerable business was anticipated, only 11 of its 88 leaves were used for its original purpose and in the 1720s it was adapted to record poor law matters instead. Something similar happened with a volume of accounts begun in 1524 by the Guild of the Holy Cross concerning the maintenance of

Clopton Bridge (BRT 2/1). This responsibility was taken over by the Corporation in 1553 and the volume was used for the same purpose until 1562. But a few years later, it was decided to devote it instead to more general real estate matters, with the greater part subsequently taken up by a series of surveys, from 1614 to 1675, of the Corporation's property, detailing the leases by which each property was held. Other important records were preserved as separate documents: successive borough charters, a fine set of leases of Corporation property, "books" of orders, and regulations observed by various trading companies, all destined in the minds of those who created them, to become part of a "deliberate" archive of the Corporation's business and administrative activities.

However, these formal "top-level" records more often than not are deficient in terms of human involvement in their creation, and to fill this gap an accumulation of supporting material can often be fallen back on. Under the wider definition of ephemera already discussed, the survival of such material may at the time of its creation have never been thought of as more than transitory. On the other hand, the contribution they can now make is invaluable. Moreover, and ironically, it is often the case that, though the Corporation may have had the best of intentions, archive material to which they attached great importance has since been destroyed, leaving for posterity only fragmentary pieces of "transitory" evidence, which at the time nobody would have thought worth keeping, to work out what had happened.

Institutional Processes and the Ephemeral Archive

The routine reporting of decisions as recorded in the order books occasionally includes glimpses of personal interaction. On 9 May 1565, for instance, one of the aldermen, William Bott, who had allegedly "spoken evell wordes … that ther was never a honest man of the Councell or the body of the Corporacion," was sent for to explain himself but, after failing to appear, was "expulsed of the Company" (*Minutes* 1: 144–45). In 1588, a similar fate befell William Smith, after his obstinate refusal both to serve as bailiff or "to come to the halles when he hathe byn sent for"; and in 1601 John Smith, serving that year as Capital Alderman was accused of multiple "abuses" including his refusal to hand over the Corporation's mace which he had illegally taken home together with the key to a cupboard or chest which housed the Corporation's archives (*Minutes* 4: 29; 6: 143). He too was expelled. But can ephemera help to provide a more rounded picture of what happened in the lead-up to this formal decision-making?

One example is what appears to be Richard Quiney's rough agenda for a meeting of the Corporation late in December 1601, over which he was due to preside as bailiff. After heading it, "In the name of God Amen," he then jotted down a list of eighteen issues he thought worth discussing, prefacing three of them "Remember" (BRU 15/1/142, in *Minutes* 6: 169–70). These occupy one side of a sheet of paper and at the meeting which followed, the Council, it may be assumed, began to work through them. However, when they got to Item 4 – "to see what leases be expired & howe we maie speedielyest make some fines to bringe ourselves out of debett" – Quiney evidently turned the page over and jotted down six-teen (unnumbered) tenancies to which this might be applied, probably as suggested at the meeting. He later crossed out two but added against one of the others: "Mr Gybbes [an alderman present] will speak to hym [the lessee]." However, the order book's account of the three meetings held in December record no business for those held on either 2 December or 18 December (although both were attended by nineteen members, with the second one extending into the afternoon); and during the third, held on 30 December, the only order issued was to survey the Council's property and its state of repair (item 5 in Quiney's list) (*Minutes* 6: 164–65, 167–68, 171–72). The chance survival of Quiney's "agenda" thus provides a much fuller picture of what a Corporation meeting was like: the active part, for instance, that the bailiff was expected to play beforehand; the true volume of business that came up for discussion; and the delegation of business to fellow aldermen. Still lacking, of course, is an account of these discussions and whether the order book's silence reflects the fact that no firm decisions were reached. But if Quiney had disposed of this note once it had become redundant, there would not even be this rare insight into the conduct of meetings. Instead, he apparently just decided to use it as a wrapper for a packet of papers which he endorsed: "Matters concerning our town cawsses."

Quiney is the source for other incidental memoranda that he jotted down in the summer of 1602 whilst compiling a list of legal arguments for and against matters in dispute between the lord of the manor and the Corporation. In some respects, these notes themselves can be regarded as ephemeral, ending as they do with some disjointed afterthoughts about actions that still required attention (*Minutes* 6: 131–35). But what makes this list of particular interest is Quiney's use of the same piece of paper to jot down a few personal items under the head: "Remember myne owne Buysenes" dealing mainly with leases of his own property but ending: "Speiek with Bess Quiney [his wife] concerning a meyde." An earlier fragment is similarly revealing (ER 3/677). Around 1598, Quiney had in his possession a formal letter from Simon Stone recommending to the recipient that he offer the bearer (probably Quiney) "your best helpe & furtherance in a matter where with he will acquaint yow." How-ever, once it had served this purpose, Quiney used the blank space to begin a draft petition to the government concerning its promise "to have our [Stratford's] Subsedies & Tenthes of Taxe remitted." This in itself could be thought of as ephemeral, as it was then abandoned, but even better Quiney later picked it up to add in an empty space: "Remember to write to Mr Warborton, to Mr Parsons & to my cosen *William* Walford. Item to my father concerning Thomas Jones." In a similar vein, he jotted down, on the back of another letter sent to him the cost of seafood in London: "Smeltes, 8^d; Shrimptes, 2^d; Flownders, 4^d; Soales, 6^d; Lampernes, 3^d; Barbelles, v^d Lobsters, 16^d" (BRU 15/5/149). Such examples serve as a reminder, then, that in this process of repurposing, information of an entirely personal nature could find its way into the archives of an official body: despite its lack of an organised system of record-keeping, it was able to provide a more secure home than if the material of this sort had remained in private hands.

Returning to the order books, voting is rarely recorded except in the vaguest terms, as, for instance, in 1614 when Francis Smith was elected bailiff, "by full consent, noe man gaynseyinge" (BRU 2/2 p.269). In 1609 the order book had been slightly more helpful in its formal record that eleven capital burgesses, albeit unnamed (out of thirteen present) and nine aldermen (out of fourteen) voted for Henry Wilson to succeed to the post of chief alderman (180). But in 1619 something more ephemeral allows further insight: whereas the order book records only that William Wyatt was chosen "by the most of voycis," the town clerk's rough working notes record that he received fifteen votes, and the two other candidates seven and three votes respectively (376; BRU 15/16/74). The form in which he made these calculations is also of interest, with a series of symbols against the names of the candidates, indicating that votes were cast in succession verbally, enabling the clerk, at the end of the process, to declare the result "by the voices" of those present. The piece of paper recording this process, being still blank on one side, became valuable scrap paper, and the following year was used to record the votes cast for a new inmate of the almshouses, with the names of the voters this time recorded. An example of voting by rote is even better demonstrated during a succession of votes at a meeting in September 1620 when they are numbered almost certainly by seniority of those present (BRU 15/13/2).

Another example of the re-use of blank space is an autograph letter dating from the summer of 1619 from John Strayne, a tenant of Corporation property, to the borough chamberlain, requesting help in the repair of his house following damage caused by a fire breaking out in a neighbouring property (BRU 15/5/23). Some action may have been taken, as Strayne was excused his rent that year, but more relevant in the context of this discussion is the use of the blank space on the back of the letter for a couple of notes, one recording votes cast in the election of Thomas Ainge as a sergeant-at-mace on 12 January 1621. The order book merely records his election: the loose note records that five candidates stood – good evidence of the popularity of a remunerated appointment in the Corporation's service – with the aldermen's or capital burgess's names recorded against their chosen preference.

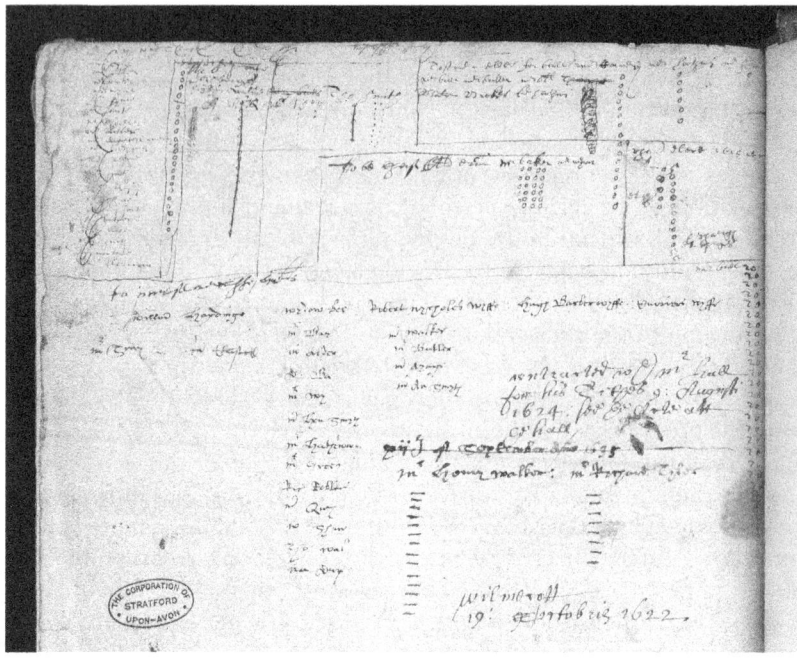

Figure 4.1 The final leaf of the Stratford Corporation's second order book (BRU 2/2 531) with miscellaneous jottings by the clerk not included in the formal record. In the top right corner are the votes cast on 7 September 1625 for the election of a new bailiff, namely, sixteen for Arthur Cawdrey, six for Robert Hathaway, and none for William Shawe. Below is a record of the unanimous choice, at the same meeting, of Daniel Baker to serve as chief alderman. Below that again, in June 1628, is set out the names of four local people seeking admission to the almshouses, and the measure of support each received from named aldermen and burgesses. Only the outcome of this voting was formally recorded. © Shakespeare Birthplace Trust.

These scrappy notes are not the only examples of jottings never regarded as of more than transitory significance. The final leaf of the second order book, 1593–1628, was used, in its later years at least, to jot down things that cropped up during the meetings even though these details never found their way into the official record (BRU 2/2 531, Figure 4.1). On 7 September 1625, when a new bailiff was elected, these notes are the only indication that the successful candidate, Arthur Cawdrey, received sixteen votes, whereas other candidates, Robert Hathaway and William Shawe, received six votes and none at all, respectively. Even more revealing, on 6 June 1628, the names of the aldermen and burgesses are recorded against votes cast for a suitable person to be admitted to one of the almshouses, with their choice overwhelmingly in favour of Francis Bee. Other notes jotted down relate to the election of a chief alderman in September 1625, following the death of the alderman who would have succeeded to the office, showing very strong support for Daniel Baker (twenty-three votes as opposed to none cast for, one suspects, a straw candidate), following which Baker reluctantly agreed to serve. Even the voting for the bailiff in September 1635 occurs on this leaf of jottings, seven years after a new order book had been opened: perhaps this was thought too new for the recording of such notes.

Another category that might be considered ephemeral consists of items that were quickly overtaken by events but that have nevertheless survived. Evidence for petitions, for instance, had to be collected and then worked into a draft, and then a re-draft, before formal submission. This process might run for just two or three days, perhaps even a few weeks, but generally speaking, given the essentially transitory nature of such material, it is unlikely that they would ever have been formally filed away for use at a later date. From a historical perspective, however, their accidental survival can preserve important information, most often in a slimming down or rewording designed to improve the chances of success; and, although later events turned on how the official version was received, earlier drafts still reveal the original extent of the petitioners' ambitions. In Stratford's case, one example is the approach to the crown in 1610 for the grant of a new charter. The final version of its petition was restricted to seven additional privileges, all but one of which (the right to pontage for those using the bridge) was granted. The drafts, however, show a gradual whittling down of the Corporation's ambition. At the start of the process, there survives an outline of the claims with a note in the hand of Thomas Greene, the town clerk, that the lord of the manor, "Sir Edward Grevill be spoken withall," and naming seven aldermen who could be called on to back up the claims. This led to an early draft to serve as the basis for discussions with the government (BRU 15/10/20). As a result, some of the rights petitioned for were dropped: for example, the extension of the medieval borough boundary to include the whole parish, and the right to nominate the vicar and schoolmaster.[5]

A collection of material arising out of the Corporation's opposition to a proposed enclosure of open fields to the north-east of the town is a further example of institutional deliberations generating ephemeral notes and paperwork, the survival of which gives insight into the way local political bodies functioned. The dispute ground on for five years involving the preparation of four petitions, some of which were drafted more than once. Their final form is not always clear and this is not helped by the fact that, having been cast aside, what were consecutive pages were separated and have since been bound up haphazardly in a series of sixteen volumes of "Miscellaneous Documents," further discussed below.

The petition drawn up in March 1616 is of particular interest. It begins with a rough draft in Thomas Greene's hand with multiple crossings out and interlineations, supplemented by a series of sixteen numbered incidents, with marginal notes naming the witnesses who could vouch for their having taken place.[6] The next draft, of the petition only, is in a more careful hand, presumably that of Greene's clerk. No fair copy of the "incidents" is extant but they must have been signed off, as Greene records on the draft, "except that which are Crossed as thinges superfluous." Amongst these was the accusation that one of the workmen engaged on the enclosure work had exclaimed: "shyte on his Lordshipps order [against enclosure work], he cared not for yt or wordes to such effect." Against this Greene had instructed his clerk: "Spare this."

Another illuminating example is a draft of a petition prepared towards the end of the dispute, indicating the work that went into such an exercise. Here phrases such as "Heere let the article come in concerning the yll usage of Mr Wall[ford] & Mr Chaundler" and "Joine this with the 9th artickle" bear witness to the work involved, but only known to posterity because of the survival of this draft (BRU 15/7/23). Also revealed here, of course, are the informal social relationships between those responsible for important drafting work. Whereas the final, carefully preserved official copy was often the work of a professional scrivener, the hard work that had gone on in its preparation is only to be found in these drafts.

From Henry Smith's year as bailiff (1616/17) there survives what was clearly once a packet of papers containing a number of items that might today be described as ephemeral. At some point in 1616, Smith had picked up a draft of an earlier letter from the Corporation to John Marston, the dramatist, seeking help over any "evidences" that might survive relating to a matter on which the Corporation had sought the advice of Marston's father, a Coventry attorney (BRU 15/13/23). Given its imperfect state, this draft in itself might be classed as ephemeral, but Smith then used the blank space on the back to draft another letter to an unnamed justice of peace, reporting the successful outcome of a case he had been instructed to deal with arising out of certain "misdemeanours of some persons in our burrough agaynst goodw[ife] Knight, a widow in the same Towne." Without this casual repurposing, there would be no record of either of these events.

In October of the same year, Smith received a letter from a local gentleman, Clement Throckmorton. He was writing on behalf of a Stratford attorney, Thomas Lucas, urging the settlement of a dispute between Lucas and two other Stratford lawyers (ER 1/1/79). To this, Smith drafted a reply to the effect that as two of the parties were in London nothing could be done straight away (ER 1/1/80). However, immediately below this first draft is another longer and more confused reply seeking to excuse the Corporation of any discrimination it had shown against Lucas. Something similar happened the following year on the resignation of Thomas Greene as town clerk. The High Steward, George Baron Clopton, in a letter to the Corporation, expressed his desire that

Greene's successor should be his brother John (BRU 15/17/1). In a draft reply, it was explained that, before the request had been received, the place had been offered to someone else, whose reply was awaited, but in any case expressing some doubt as to whether John Greene was sufficiently well qualified. However, on realising that this might be taken as disrespectful, this was slimmed down to a far simpler draft statement: "We before Easter terme last made choice of one Mr Frauncys Collyns an Attorney and one of whom we thought very well to Succed … but hadd your Lordships Letteres come before such eleccion mad, We should have bene reddy in all duety to have observed your Lordship as had bene meet" (BRU 15/16/27a, BRU 15/17/1v). In both cases the outcome is not entirely clear (final copies no longer exist) but it can still be argued that the "working papers" provide more by way of background than any final copy would.

The "Creation" of an Ephemeral Archive

Many more similar examples could be cited of scraps of papers retained mainly because, having served their immediate purpose, they still retained enough blank space for the addition of further notes. To assess how meaningful a contribution these "scraps of paper" make to the overall collection, I now turn to look more closely at the "Miscellaneous documents" section mentioned earlier. They are preserved now in a series of volumes created by J.O. Halliwell-Phillips in the 1850s. There is little evidence on how they were stored prior to that, but, in 1862, Halliwell had published a *Brief Handlist of the Records Belonging to the Borough of Stratford-on-Avon* describing the collection as housed, in a seemingly orderly manner, in a set of eight drawers, a single chest trunk, eight iron boxes and a series of thirty volumes. However, whereas the contents of the drawers and chests are then listed, sixteen of the volumes turn out to be a series of "Miscellaneous Documents." On closer examination these prove to be what, prior to Halliwell's "re-organisation," must have been a mass of papers ("several thousand" by his calculation) that until that point had been stored with little interest as to their content. Some of the material is grouped well enough to suggest that Halliwell might have found them together. For example, three papers concerning a dispute over the tithes of Luddington are bound up together in one volume and, given other similarities in their appearance, were probably once attached to one another in some way (BRU 15/10/12, 13, 15). However, other papers in the same case are scattered across three further volumes, only one of many examples where the generally unsorted accumulation of papers led to a displacement of related material (BRU 15/3/12, 15/12/113, 15/16/82). In another instance, for example, five separate papers relating to the holding of the borough sessions in January 1604 are now scattered through four volumes of "Miscellaneous Documents" (BRU

15/3, 7, 12, 16 and brought together in *Minutes* 6: 283–91). In some cases, even pages of the same document have become separated: for the 1613 draft petition against the enclosure of common land, with articles attached, the full picture only appears after consulting three separated documents in two different volumes (BRU 15/7/25, 15/8/2, 182). Nevertheless, the binding up of this miscellanea reflects Halliwell's passion to ensure that anything that might reflect in some way on the history of the town during the town's Shakespearean age – extended at both ends by considerable margins – should be kept; and whereas much of similar accumulations – if they had survived that long – might well have been treated as waste paper, in Stratford's case they were preserved and catalogued in a 475-page calendar that Halliwell published the following year (*Descriptive*). These collections had already been looked at by earlier antiquarians – Edmond Malone, James Saunders, and R.B. Wheler, for example – but they had been looking for, and copying out, material that piqued their, mainly Shakespearean, interest. They even took some home and then failed to return them (Bearman, *Shakespeare* 60–75). Halliwell too was aware of their importance from a Shakespearean angle, but his underlying aim was different, to arrange and preserve the collection, warts and all, not only as a memorial but as a source for future research, and inspired by the belief that almost anything that had survived for a century or more was worth preserving.

One only has to look at some of the material preserved to appreciate that very little, if anything, was thrown away. One volume in particular, the sixteenth in the "Miscellaneous Documents" series that Halliwell created, has many scraps of paper, the date and purpose of which defeated him when compiling his calendar but which he still made sure were preserved for later researchers to puzzle over. There are around a hundred items in this volume, very few of which had ever been regarded as administratively important, hence their survival in this mass of unsorted miscellanea. There are some which were not strictly "ephemeral": an autograph letter of 1614 from the vicar, John Rogers, to the Corporation petitioning for the use of a piece of land to keep a couple of pigs, or the official record of proceedings at the borough sessions of January 1606, signed or bearing the marks of the jurymen (BRU 15/16/21; *Minutes* 6: 350). Of the same date is a final list of known recusants dwelling within the borough, and an early seventeenth-century apprenticeship indenture binding John Finch to the glover Clement Burman (BRU 15/16/29, *Minutes* 6: 350, 73). But these are outnumbered by a miscellaneous collection of items that had only a very brief administrative function. Around a dozen are draft petitions or notes for drawing them up. From a historical point of view, as already discussed, these are of some importance, especially when completed versions have been lost, but in their compilers' eyes an almost pointless survival once the redrafting was complete. Six pieces of paper record voting on multiple

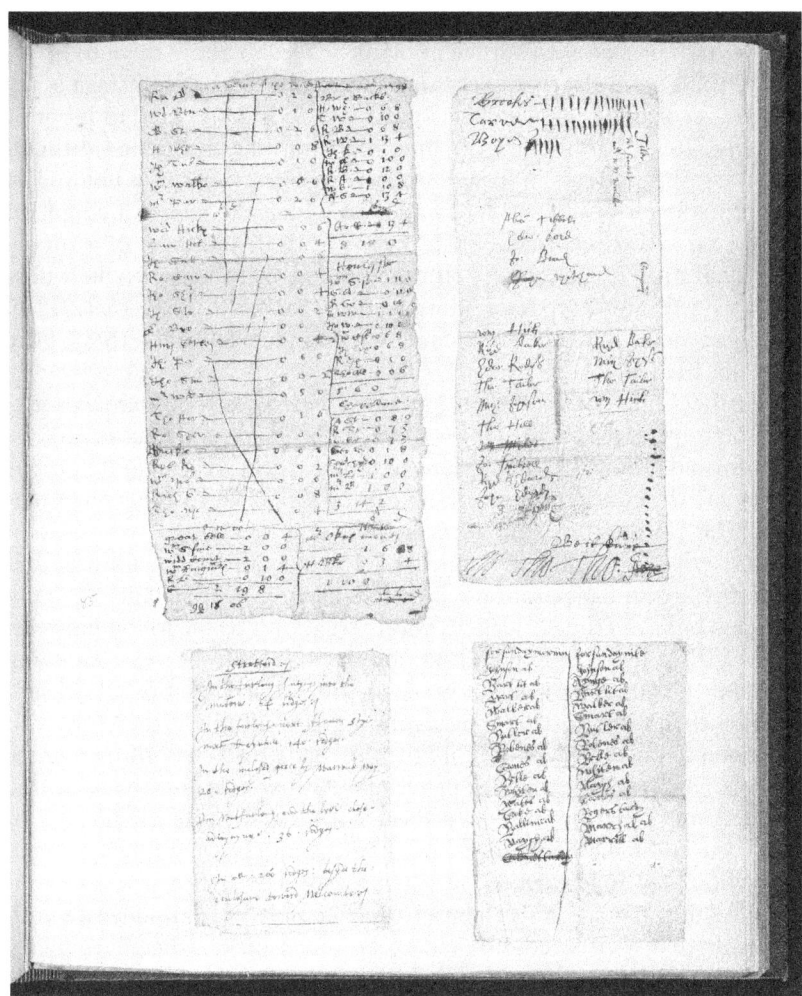

Figure 4.2 A page from 'Miscellaneous Documents', Vol 16 (BRU 15/16/85). Much of this volume is taken up with scraps of paper pasted into it, part of J.O. Halliwell's effort to ensure the survival of everything that had survived even though its original purpose was far from clear. Holes were cut on the page so that notes written on the other side were also preserved. The top left is part of a draft of a rental of Corporation property of c. 1600; below is a note relating to the Welcombe enclosure, c. 1615. The purpose of the item top right has not been identified but below it, in a late seventeenth-century hand, are two columns of names apparently concerning church attendance. © Shakespeare Birthplace Trust.

occasions, not retained for official purposes once the order books had been written up but with sufficient blank spaces to allow them to be re-used. Others were clearly of very short-term use: draft jury lists, a scrap of paper recording the "watchers" and "warders" appointed to monitor one of the town fairs, scraps of paper reporting the constables' difficulties in arresting offenders, rough notes assembled prior to a holding of the borough sessions, a scrap of paper on which the fate of a couple of migrant poor was recorded, and a corrected draft of a part of a survey of Council property, at some point torn in two with the other half now found pasted into a separate volume (BRU 15/16/28, BRU 15/12/119). Other fragments dutifully pasted in are incomplete (BRU 15/16/87, 90b, 91a, 91b, 91c).

A further clutch of papers in the same volume concern financial matters. Some are in the form of bills, some are brief accounts but others are just informal notes and calculations of money spent. It is a moot point as to how far the concept of ephemera can be stretched to cover such material. The Corporation's main record, the annual account, was written up in a series of booklets, balancing receipts against expenditure, and submitted at the Corporation's January meeting. The balance, usually an excess but sometimes a deficit, was carried over to the following year. Some of these items of expenditure are dated late in the year, implying both that the fair copy was not made up until shortly before submission and also that some sort of rough running account must therefore also have been kept. However, of this there is little evidence. Moreover, in this early period, a neat series of receipts and vouchers to back up the final account is hardly to be expected, not least because the literacy of large sections of the population could not be taken for granted. Indeed, for the first fifty or so years of the Corporation's existence, it was not unusual for the chamberlains themselves to be only partially literate with the result that their accounts had to be made up for them. Ancillary documentation, for Stratford at least, is thus unusual if not rare, reflecting the fact that all accounting processes at this date, whether private or public, were, in any case, carried out without the "paper trail" that one would expect later.

A crude survey may not initially appear to bear this out, with perhaps up to a thousand individual receipts extant for the years 1553 to 1687 (BRU 5, most of the sixteenth and seventeenth centuries at BRU 5/1).[7] However, for the first eighty years of our period – until around 1630 – it was not uncommon for only three or four invoices to survive for any one year. Indeed, it is not until the post-Restoration period that there are significant numbers, and even then there are gaps.[8] And were it not for a rare clutch of ten bills for the early 1630s – once wrapped in a bundle endorsed "to be provided to Hen: Normans Accompte" presented in January 1633 – there would be little to suggest that it was normal practice to have kept what receipts there were, even if most of them were later ditched. Nevertheless, their rarity – whether the result of routine destruction once they had ceased to have any administrative value or because most transactions in these early years were not neatly documented anyway – tempts an "ephemeral" classification.

A closer examination of those that have survived is often an improvement of what can be deduced from the summary accounts. For instance, late in 1601, a bill was submitted to the Corporation by the brother of the vintner, John Smith, unsettled on the latter's death earlier in the year, for food and wine supplied for a number of otherwise undocumented civic events. Before payment, however, the bailiff Richard Quiney struck out three items which "we allowe not" (BRU 5/1/20 40). Later, between 1624 and 1626, Thomas Wilson, the vicar spent over £5 on building work done on his house, eventually submitting an elaborate bill, under twenty-one heads, for materials and labour charges in far more detail than the chamberlain's account records (BRU 5/1/73). Another bill from the end of 1626 gives a detailed account of work done by "Goodman Greene" on the council house and the chapel (BRU 5/1/79). In 1626, one of the constables sent in a claim for payments he had made "for keeping a criple from Satirday night to Monday morning" and then paying to take him to Clifford Chambers. Later he gave support "to a poore sick woman & a child to carry her to Shottery & for maintenance for her" (BRU 5/1/82). In 1630, Ann Phillips neatly signed a receipt for £1 2s 0d for claret and sack, which she had supplied to the Corporation at Easter (BRU 5/1/86).

Richard Quiney's notes and papers discussed above are paralleled by those of Thomas Greene. He was not an elected member of the Council but served as the borough's steward, or town clerk, from 1603 to 1617, drawing an annual salary of £5, then £7, for his services. But he combined this with other income derived from his professional status as a Middle Temple barrister. He kept chambers there for life and spent considerable blocks of time in London during the four legal terms. In 1609, he decided to invest in property in Stratford, buying a large house adjoining Holy Trinity Church and investing in a half share of a lease of the tithes due from a large part of the parish. These investments seem to have proved his undoing, and in 1617 he sold up and left Stratford, using the money he raised largely to pay off debts. The result, as fortunate for the historian as was Quiney's death in office, is that he failed to clear his desk properly before departure. As a result, some of his papers, either left at the Guild Hall or even at his own house, were swept up into the Corporation archive with no real attempt to sort them out (for more on Greene, see Bearman, "Thomas"; "Shakespeare"; for his wife Lettice, see Lilley).

Some of this material has already been discussed, particularly the numerous draft petitions against the planned enclosure to which the Corporation was opposed for fear that it might adversely affect the value of its tithes. Greene was thus placed in a difficult position. On the one hand, he was expected to defend the Corporation's position but on the other hand, as a lessee of part of the tithes, he had to protect himself from any threats to his income. His reaction was to keep some notes of the main events, now preserved on four paper leaves. These partly served as an aid to drafting the successive petitions he submitted on the Corporation's behalf but he was also concerned to cover himself against accusations of double-dealing. The record that has survived, accidentally or not, is very revealing, not least because of the personal angle it provides on what was going on but also for those insights into his domestic life rarely documented in other sources.[9] But can it be regarded as ephemeral?

Looking at the record, it was evidently not intended as a formal record. Greene's official handwriting is challenging enough but these notes were clearly kept for his own use only and are sometimes so cryptic or hastily written as to become indecipherable. They are also peppered with crossings out and interlineations, with marginal notes to help him refer back to significant events or to add information he had forgotten about or had discovered later. His frequent references to meetings with members of the enclosure party, and his discussions with them to ensure that he was not going to suffer personally as the result of the enclosure, also make it clear that these notes were for his own use, including details it would have been imprudent to have divulged to others, especially his employers. Moreover, as the dispute dragged on, but with the enclosure party in retreat, entries become increasingly desultory to the extent that when Greene sold up and moved to Somerset (having surrendered his lease of the tithes) he left these notes behind as being of no longer any interest to him. In other words, it was an informal and personal record, made finally redundant when he left town, to become instead part of a bundle of working papers which, to be on the safe side, the Corporation did not destroy but that were not looked at again – or at least not for over 150 years when antiquarians working their way through these various accumulations happened upon them and found to their delight that Greene had included in his notes four entries concerning the lessee of the other half of the tithes – William Shakespeare. So delighted, in fact, that one of them took a sheet home and never returned it, leaving it to his sister, after his death, to do the decent thing.

* * *

This essay set out to determine to what extent the archive of the Stratford-upon-Avon Corporation is composed of material that, though not ephemeral by the original definition of the word, can be regarded as records that those who created them had never regarded as more than of a very transitory, or "ephemeral," nature. In fact, their chance of survival often depended on the fact that the paper they were written on was regarded at the time as of more value than what was written on it but allowing in retrospect a greatly enriched understanding of their lives. With only the formal record to guide us, it would still be possible to track the Corporation's reactions to the challenges it faced. However, with the aid of what, taking a generous view of what can be defined as ephemera, insights are afforded into those "behind-the-scenes" activities and personal interactions of which the formal record leaves very little trace. In other words, the informal or ephemeral archive material to be found today amongst the records of the Stratford Corporation enhances the perception of how this body went about its work. What they wished to record for posterity was formally written down and, in comparative terms, carefully preserved, often in volume form. Other material likely to involve the accumulation of loose papers – court cases both civil and criminal – might also have been filed for legal purposes. However, though significant tranches of these official records have since disappeared, this is more than made up for by the survival of material that, conversely and by a strange irony, was never seen as worth keeping but now enriches the understanding not only of how the Corporation functioned but also, and sometimes accidentally, how the activities and behaviour of its members and employees impacted the local community.

Notes

1 "Governing body" is here used somewhat loosely, especially for the early period, as the activities of the manorial court leet (though curtailed over time) and the parish also need to be taken into account.
2 A rough estimate would put this at least 80,000 words.
3 In 1862, these and two other order books were securely located in "the iron safe" (James Orchard Halliwell-Phillipps (23–24).
4 At first they were incorporated into the first order book (BRU 2/1) but from 1590 they survive as individual booklets bound up into volumes in the nineteenth century. The years to 1647 are now found in BRU 4/1–3.
5 For these modified petitions, see BRU 15/7/112; ER 1/1/60. The charter as granted is at BRU 1/2.
6 The first draft of the petition is at BRU 15/5/155–56 and a tidier version at BRU 15/7/25. The "articles" survive in a rough draft only, at BRU 15/8/2 continued as BRU 15/8/182.
7 Most of these were bound up, roughly chronologically, in a separate series, now BRU 5 (with sixteenth- and seventeenth-century examples at BRU 5/1).
8 None survive, for example, for 1676 but there are twenty-seven for 1675.
9 The pages survive at BRU 15/13, 26a, 27, 28, 29 and were edited and translated (though not without mishap) by C. M. Ingleby, *Shakespeare and the Enclosure of Common Fields at Welcombe*, 1885.

Works Cited

Bearman, Robert. "Shakespeare and the Replingham agreement." *Shakespeare on the Record*. Ed. Hannah Leah Crummé. Bloomsbury, 2019. 165–78.
———. *Shakespeare in the Stratford Records*. Sutton, 1994.

————. "Thomas Greene: Stratford-upon-Avon's town clerk and Shakespeare's Lodger." *Shakespeare Survey* (2012): 290–305.

BRU 2/1–3. MS. Shakespeare Centre Library and Archive. Stratford Upon Avon, UK.

BRU 4/1–3. MS. Shakespeare Centre Library and Archive. Stratford Upon Avon, UK.

BRU 5 (series). MS. Shakespeare Centre Library and Archive. Stratford Upon Avon, UK.

BRU 15 (series). MS. Shakespeare Centre Library and Archive. Stratford Upon Avon, UK.

BRU 16/1. MS. Shakespeare Centre Library and Archive. Stratford Upon Avon, UK.

Dyer, Alan. "Crisis and Resolution: Government and Society in Stratford, 1540–1640." *The History of an English Borough: Stratford-upon-Avon 1196–1996*. Ed. Robert Bearman. Sutton, 1997. 62–96.

ER 1/1. MS. Shakespeare Centre Library and Archive. Stratford Upon Avon, UK.

ER 3/677. MS. Shakespeare Centre Library and Archive. Stratford Upon Avon, UK.

Ingleby, Clement. M. *Shakespeare and the Enclosure of Common Fields at Welcombe*. Birmingham, 1885.

Halliwell-Phillips, James Orchard. *A Brief Handlist of the Records Belonging to the Borough of Stratford-on-Avon*. London, 1862.

————. *A Descriptive Calendar of the Ancient Manuscripts and Records in the Possession of the Corporation of Stratford-upon-Avon*. London, 1863.

Lilley, Hannah. "Lettice Greene of Stratford-upon-Avon and her World." *Middling Culture*. Online. Accessed 29 Nov. 2011.

Minutes and Accounts of the Corporation of Stratford-upon-Avon. Eds Edgar I. Fripp, Richard Savage, Levi Fox, and Robert Bearman. 6 vols. Dugdale Society, 1921, 1924, 1926, 1929, 1990, 2011.

5 Paper and Elite Ephemerality

Alison Wiggins

Paper has long been used in metaphors for what is abstract, unreal, or hypothetical, or to mean flimsy, impermanent, and insubstantial. Delicately cut table-decorations "pared out of papure purely" evoke the chimerical qualities of the castle depicted by the *Gawain*-poet (l. 802).[1] Tearing a paper bill and crowning with a paper crown signal delusional and fragile beliefs with paper-based props and stage directions in Shakespeare's plays (3 *Henry VI* 1.4.505.1; *Two Gentlemen* 4.4.1967). Yet alongside these associations with the frail and fleeting was paper's rapidly expanding role in early modern archives to ensure longevity, where paperwork was gaining status as evidentiary proof that would stand the test of time (Hindle; Shapiro). Both senses are encapsulated by the rhetorical instruction in early modern epistolary discourse to "burn after reading," which relies on the capacity of a letter written on a sheet of paper to be as easily destroyed as preserved and dramatises the moment of receipt as a precariously balanced decision point between keeping and throwing away (Hunt). Likewise, the everyday metaphor "on paper" may mean a plan that is abstract and unpromising or, conversely, one that is concrete and realistic (Gitelman; Hunt). These are the paradoxes of paper. Paper has the potential to be preserved for posterity alongside its capacity to be instantly destroyed or slowly to deteriorate, to be recycled, or gradually to biodegrade. Its twin affordances of disposability and durability gave it a unique place in early modern social interactions. To conceptualise the materiality of early modern paper is to scrutinise the culturally contingent motives, attitudes, and intentions that existed at the boundary between durability and ephemerality.

This chapter considers the materiality of early modern paper in the 1597–1607 financial accounts of William Cavendish of Hardwick Hall.[2] It asks what early modern financial accounts from an elite household can tell us about paper—not only through quantitative data about forms and costs but also qualitative assessment of the vignettes and personalisations indicative of paper's functions and performances (Prescott). During the decade covered by these financial records, William Cavendish's household was located at Hardwick Old and New Halls in Derbyshire, the palatial residence he shared with his mother the dowager

DOI: 10.4324/9781003058588-7

countess of Shrewsbury and would soon inherit. Mother and son each kept their own servants and sets of financial records for their distinct yet connected and overlapping households. While mostly located at Hardwick, William Cavendish was often himself in London during the law terms, in addition to which he and members of his own and the dowager countess's households visited other family properties that included nearby Chatsworth House. Their households were the operation centre for running the Cavendish family estates, businesses, and overseas ventures, as well as being the base for the maintenance of social networks, the location for the education of William's children, and the home to his niece, the courtier Arbella Stuart. The financial records, far more than lists of extractable raw costs, sharpen our sense of paper's contemporary uses, its actual and perceived value, its availability to these individuals and groups, and its social and cultural place in Shakespeare's time. Another reason to select William Cavendish's financial records is that they are especially meticulous and detailed, not least for recording textual cultures. Whereas the Signet Office or the Dutch East India Company have given us examples of paper used at enormous scale and quantity, what we gain from William Cavendish's accounts is granular detail about the daily routines of a wealthy investor that show us how he and his mother prospered thanks to a meticulous grasp of finance (Birkenholz; Williams; and Andreani). He gives us an extraordinary record of paper's ephemeral and durable role in the remarkable rising fortunes of the Cavendishes, as they progressed on their way to becoming one of England's most rich and powerful families.

The financial accounts that are the focus of this chapter are held today in the Devonshire Collection at Chatsworth House Archives and are mostly in one codex: a vellum-bound volume with three leather straps and a buckle fastening, of 203 folios on paper that is grape watermarked and larger in size at 32 x 44cms (Figure 5.1).[3] Here we find the stream of daily disbursements that flowed through William Cavendish's household, among which were around 20 purchases of blank paper per year as sheets, quires, reams, or blank books, alongside other paper-based items coming in and out of the household.[4] These records were written up by the London and Derbyshire receivers from receipts and bills, then audited by William. Very few of these original loose receipts and bills themselves survive, except accidentally. Turning the pages we come across sweet-wrapper-sized squares written with sums being worked out; a postcard-shaped receipt for loads of coal and ditching dated 28 December 1606; and a torn-out scrap that was perhaps a draft letter turned bookmark with contemporary writing on the back about a dawn duel at sword point.[5] These are still there as rare treasures, either pasted in by a conservator or tucked into the gutter, that we must be careful to leave in place for the future. They are chance survivals, neither intended to be kept nor collected later. Neither ephemeral nor ephemera,

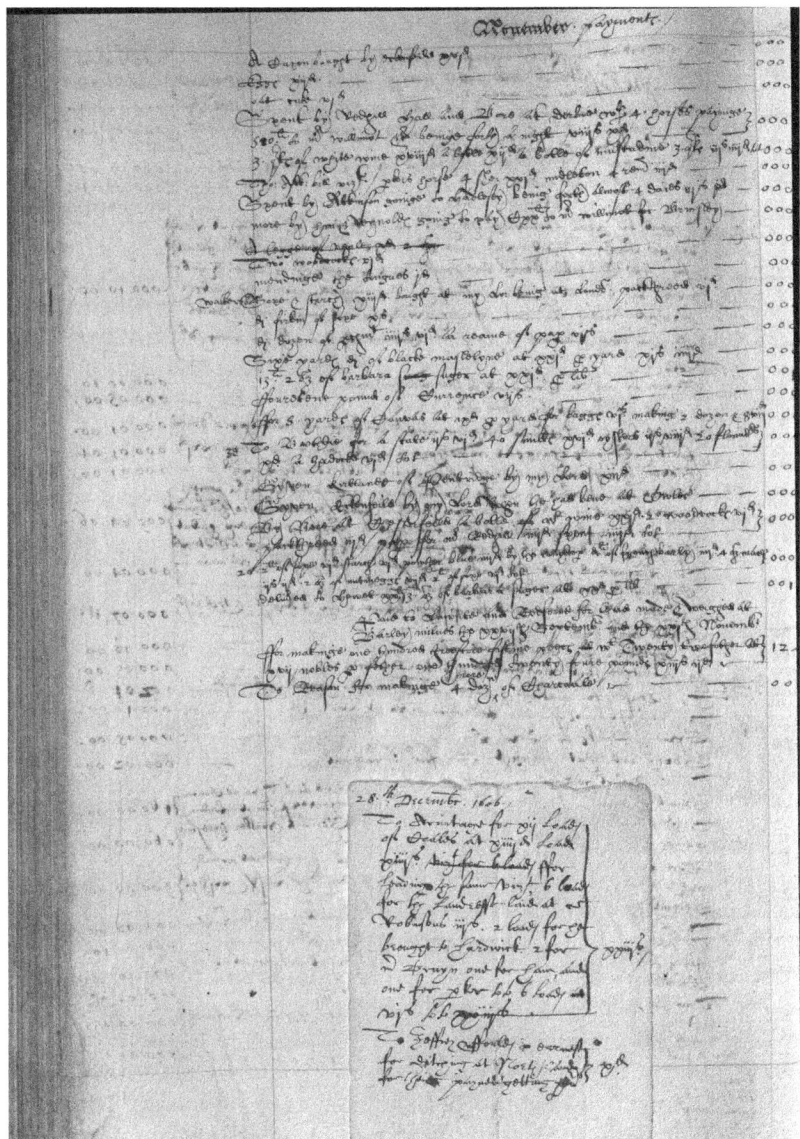

Figure 5.1 Financial account book of William Cavendish 1599–1607, Devon-
shire Collection Archives, Chatsworth, HMS/1/5 (formerly HM/23).
The image shows entries from November 1606, fol. 195v, and the
loose receipt for coal and ditching from 28 December 1606. © The
Devonshire Collections, Chatsworth. Reproduced by permission of
Chatsworth Settlement Trustees.

but archival materials that resist either category. We might call them accidental ephemera.[6] They are the last remaining material fragments of the sea of paper notes that were copied in condensed form into this large book. It was an accounting system different from that used by William Cavendish's mother, who tended to keep more of the material papers themselves. Each set of accounts was, as Jemima Matthews in this volume puts it, "a negotiated 'thing' on paper" that also captures "the life of other paper things," being a dynamic object in use as well as the surface to record transactions. More than an inert list of prices, the financial records were part of the papery fabric of the household depicted by Elaine Leong and give us a spectacularly detailed picture of paper's ephemeral and durable performances. They tell us about uses of paper in the moment and at specified times and places, by the co-head of the household, his family, children, secretaries, and servants in a gendered hierarchy, depicting paper in its mobile, animate social world. Poets and playwrights have given us paper castles and paper crowns as metaphors for insubstantiality; for the Cavendishes, paper became the material basis on which they built palaces, a business empire, and a family dynasty.

Buying and Using Blank Paper

William Cavendish's 1597–1607 household disbursements record 219 purchases of blank paper, which cost in total over £20 13s 5d and bought more than 21,199 sheets of loose blank paper and 31 blank paper books. We cannot be sure how incomplete or selective this is as a record, but we can say that this recorded amount spent over the course of a decade was eminently affordable to William Cavendish, whose rental income was around £5,000 per year, to which can be added his profits from lead smelting and overseas trade.[7] There is no doubt his household could source, transport, and easily pay for many thousands of sheets of paper, which was one of its lesser expenses. It is important to emphasise this point because the practice of fastidiously recording small sums of money could potentially, to anyone unfamiliar with early modern financial accounts, give the impression of concerns over pennies. This recording of costs to the penny was not to do with a shortage of money, but was a feature of the broader culture of accounting, described by Jacob Soll among others as a recordkeeping impulse: it reflected a desire to keep a close track of the running of the household, something that itself was a factor driving purchases of paper. Heather Wolfe and Orietta Da Rold have done much to revise some of the persistent over-generalisations about paper, in particular the flawed and over-simplified presumptions that medieval paper was used because it was cheap and convenient and, conversely, that early modern paper was expensive and scarce (Da Rold 13, 21, 58–59; see also Leong 34). This analysis of William Cavendish's accounts offers a constructive response to their calls to describe early modern paper more accurately, from its forms and functions to its cost relative to wealth and income and its social interactions. We know that "paper is not just one thing" but an object and a technology with multiple "affordances and connotations," varying in price, availability, and function (Da Rold 185, 214). The multiple valences of paper are immediately recognisable when we read William Cavendish's accounts.

As we would expect and as is vividly apparent here, William Cavendish and his receivers were alert to distinctions between different types of paper. The terms used were conventional and distinguish paper type by its watermark (Crossbow, Grape, Pot), size (Demy, Imperial), origins (Dutch, Frankfurt, Venice), and intended use or material features (Brown, Cap, Coarse, Fine, Gilt, White, Writing) (for these and other terms, see Wolfe, "Letter-Writing" 25; for size and shape of paper, see Da Rold 170). While the forms and terms are known from other sources, William Cavendish's accounts give us a vantage point from which to observe an impressive range of paper types active for one household over a defined period at specific points in time. For present purposes, these paper types can be considered in four groups: (i) unsized paper, (ii) ordinary 4-pence-per-quire paper, (iii) more expensive paper, (iv) blank paper books. The following discussion considers how each of these paper types had a different relationship with ephemerality.

Unsized Paper

A total of 39 of the 219 payments were for Brown paper, which usually cost a penny a quire. Brown paper cost only 2.8% of the total recorded outlay spent on loose sheets but amounted to 10.2% of the number of loose sheets purchased. That is, calculated per-quire, this was the cheapest sort of paper and was purchased regularly, in both Derbyshire and London. Brown paper was unsized (as, it is likely, were the Cap and Coarse paper), so was not suitable for writing; being porous, it would soak up liquid such as ink, making it more like blotting paper or tissue than a surface for carrying text. Brown paper's pliability, softness, and relative strength made it ideal for wrapping. Purchases sometimes directly state that it was bought to "lap" or "carry" an item. It was often bundled with purchases of thread, packthread, tape, cord, baskets, trunks, or a combination of these, such as for "brown paper and cord for a basket 2d" (Riden 2: 267). Brown paper had the capacity to deal with sticky or powdered materials so was used to wrap 18lbs of white lead, probably in powder form for paint pigment or cosmetics (Riden 2: 233).[10] In other entries, while it was not directly stated to be a wrapper, its grouping together with items suggests that function, such as the entry for "½ ell of cloth for socks 12d, 2lb soap 8d, brown paper 2d, total 1s 10d," where the Brown paper was to wrap the soap and perhaps also the cloth (Riden 2: 371, 397). As we see here, Brown paper could function

Summary overview of purchases of paper in the 1597–1607 Financial Accounts of William Cavendish[8]

Type of paper	Cost per quire	Number of payments	Quantity purchased	Quantity purchased as sheets	Total spend	Total spend as pence
Brown	1d (rarely 2d or 3d)[9]	39	87 quires (estimated)	2,175 sheets (estimated)	8s (estimated)	96
Cap	3d or 4d	2	3 quires (at 4d per quire + 1 unspecified quantity costing 3d)	More than 75 sheets	1s (estimated)	12
Coarse	unspecified	1	1 unspecified quantity (2d for a candle and coarse paper)	-	Less than 2d	1
Crossbow	6d	4	4 quires	100 sheets	2s	24
Demy	7d	1	1 quire	25 sheets	7d	7
Dutch	6 – 6.5d	5	34 quires	850 sheets	17s	204
Fine	4.6 – 6.6d	2	4.5 quires	112 sheets	2s	24
Fine Venice	6.9 – 7.2d	2	2 reams (i.e. 40 quires)	1,000 sheets	£1 3s 6d	282
Frankfurt	15d	1	2 quires	50 sheets	2s 6d	30
Gilt	10d	1	19 quires	475 sheets	15s 10d	190
Grape	4d	1	3 quires	75 sheets	1s	12
Imperial	30d	1	5 quires	125 sheets	12s 6d	150
Paper	4d (rarely 3d or 6d)	139	618.5 quires (estimated)	15,462 sheets (estimated)	£9 12s 2d (estimated)	2,306
paper books	various costs	12	31 blank or ruled paper books of various kinds	-	£6 5s 11d	1,511
Pot	4d	5	26 quires	650 sheets	8s 8d	104
White	unspecified	1	unspecified	-	3d	3
Writing	4d	2	1 quire (plus one unspecified amount costing a penny)	More than 25 sheets	5d	5

as a barrier against contaminators, and elsewhere we find it paired with payments for clean laundry, bedding, and wool for a quilt (3: 39).

In other cases, Brown paper appears in the context of William Cavendish's personal spending as he walked around London, such as the December day when he took the ferry to Westminster to visit Parliament, bought himself some rosewater, "a little wine glass 6d," and "a book 4d," and spent another 4d on a link to light his way home (2: 338). He also spent a penny on Brown paper that day. Perhaps the Brown paper was to hold the link or to wrap the wine glass or book. We do not know the quantity of Brown paper that he received for a penny, but the impression here (and in similar cases) is that this was a purchase made on-the-fly, as he walked about, so we might wonder if it were just a few sheets. The context is suggestive of an ephemeral and elite function for Brown paper where, costed per sheet, it may also have become a relatively expensive paper type. Buying Brown paper in transit, such as a sheet or two whilst shopping, to keep hands or purchases clean and dry, was an elite function rarely visible in the historical record. It reminds us that cost is not necessarily fixed or intrinsic to an object but could depend on its use in context.

Brown paper was regularly purchased by William and his agents in small quantities at the point of sale with other items, which was often the case when shopping in London, but also in Derbyshire. It accompanied specialist purchases, such as the penny spent on Brown paper grouped in the same entry with "a pen and inkhorn 8d, a box for civet 8d" (3: 345). Or, where 2 pence were spent on Brown paper bought with "a clyster pipe 8d" (a sort of syringe) (3: 6). Its ability to offer padding meant it was used for hard durable items like these, to avoid damage during transit. We know that wastepaper and parchment were in demand among soap-sellers and chandlers for wrapping up their goods (Reynolds). Although, here, it seems, it was new paper that was available at the point of purchase and for a range of types of items. We might wonder if there were a choice provided between new paper and wastepaper, or if the distinction mattered, and if it were on offer in every shop. Another notable feature in the disbursements are the references to small amounts of Brown paper to accompany donations or payments of money, sometimes with pins or thread: "To the poor and for brown paper 3d"; "given by my Lord to his godchild at Leicester 12d, brown paper 2d"; "Barbing my Lord 12d, pins 6d, brown paper 2d" (2: 388, 3: 285, 3: 217).[11] Repeatedly, we find these kinds of records of small quantities of Brown paper along with gratuities and gifted coins, all of which involved William Cavendish himself in the transaction whilst he was out and about visiting or shopping. Again, on 10 May 1601, after visiting St Paul's Churchyard to hear a sermon, William gave 3d given to prisoners at Ludgate Gaol at the same time paying a penny for "brown paper" (2: 310). The regular pairing of donations and brown paper means we should ask if the coins were handed over in sachets or wraps, either twisted, pinned, or tied shut; and, if so, whether this was a widespread practical use of Brown paper, or, as seems more likely, more of an elite refinement to the culture of deference.[12]

By contrast with these ad hoc point-of-sale purchases in small quantities, there were bulkier buys of between four and six quires of Brown paper with other groceries for the house at Hardwick alongside quantities of mutton, starch, barley, and mace (3: 283, 269, 383). The many applications of Brown paper in the spheres of medicine, horticulture, and cooking has been well documented, and its affordances gave it the capacity to strain, filter, wipe, ignite, make poultices and plasters, to be mashed as an ingredient, provide a work surface, or to clean and dry a range of items (Leong). While these functions are nowhere directly stated in William Cavendish's accounts, the purchase of multiple quires with groceries may indicate such uses at Hardwick. A caveat should be made here about the nature of household accounts. Large households tended to run several single-entry account books in parallel. So, we can expect that there was once another set of financial accounts focused on the kitchens at Hardwick, whereas the record under consideration here is mostly preoccupied with William Cavendish's personal disbursements. Furthermore, while the fine-ground style of many of these entries gives an impressive sense of completeness, there are nonetheless elisions: some give copious precise detail, but others gloss over the specifics and are for "things" and "other stuff" (2: 157, 171, 283). Certainly, Brown paper for the kitchens and gardens is the least well documented in the written record that comes down to us here.

Ordinary 4-Pence-Per-Quire Paper

A total of 148 of the 219 payments were for 4-pence-per-quire paper, which was usually referred to in the accounts simply as Paper or, a number of times, is specified as being Grape or Pot watermarked paper, or as Writing or White paper.[13] The total quantity purchased was around 16,000 sheets, which was most (76.5%) of the loose blank sheets purchased, costing around £10 2s 6d, almost half the total spending on blank paper. It was purchased at a variety of locations in the English Midlands around Derbyshire: in Rotherham, Nottingham, Mansfield, Uttoxeter, and Chesterfield. But on around half of the occasions it was purchased in London, either to be used there or to be sent back to Hardwick. Individual purchases ranged in specified quantity from half a quire up to two reams. It was purchased solo ("for a quire of paper 4d") or with other items. This 4-pence-per-quire paper, as well as being more expensive than Brown paper when costed quire-for-quire, also differed because it was suitable for writing, being sized to carry ink.

As we might expect, the main function of 4-pence-per-quire paper was for handwriting, confirmed by its regular grouping exclusively with stationery: hard wax, soft wax, tape, quills, bottles of ink, "stuff to make ink," inkle, boxes, mouth glue, parchment, and "a penknife." It was used every day and is the paper type found extensively throughout the handwritten books and documents that come down to us from the Cavendish family and their network. Pot paper and Grape paper were the usual substrates for the routine correspondence of William Cavendish, his mother the dowager countess, their servants, stewards, solicitors, and a wider network of correspondents.[14] This was the paper made in Normandy, imported, and used throughout England for most early modern letters, accounts, receipts, and handwritten documents. At Hardwick Hall, we find quires distributed to William Cavendish himself, to his son Master William Cavendish, and to members of the household who included "the nurse"; Barbara, who kept the still room; Walker; and agents and upper servants who included Mr Butler, Sir Ralph (given a quire "for Calton's reckoning"), Mr Kinnersley, Mr Lowe, Mr Gay, and Mr Redhill.[15] We have texts in the handwriting of some of these individuals, plus their letters or references to them. They were provided with writing paper from the household stocks, either for their work in the household or for their own accounts, letters, bills, shopping lists, or educational purposes.

While often used for writing, there were other uses for 4-pence-per-quire paper. Most frequent are the references to its use for wrapping, where it was an alternative to Brown paper for a range of items being transported. So we find "paper to pack the plate [i.e. silver plate] in 3d" purchased along with a new trunk, "paper and packthread to lap the sugar in 6d," and "paper" for transporting "three Barbary sugar loaves" (3: 347, 364; 2: 42). There are other groupings of small quantities of paper along with items being delivered, where the paper may have been for wrapping for transportation, which included the quire of paper purchased along with "400 pippins" and another quire purchased together with a curry comb.[16] Direct references to use for covering or lining included paper to cover "rose pots" and "to cover roses," with thread "for the footcloth," with a searing candle, paired with in-person gratuitous donations, and simply for "paper and packthread" (2: 334, 336).[17] It is possible that these purchases recorded for "paper" were, in reality, for Brown paper, i.e. where scribe had written "paper" rather than specifying Brown paper. However, there is no reason to doubt the precision of the receiver's use of terms here, as these could equally indicate quantities of 4-pence-per-quire paper.

We should not too strictly try to separate the use of 4-pence-per-quire paper for writing and for wrapping, given that we know these functions were closely connected and that sized paper provided writeable wrapping and wrappable writing. In a fictional example, Shakespeare gives us a ring thrown from a casement "wrapped in a paper" written with the name of the noblewoman who threw it, which aptly captures paper's ubiquity, mobility, and flexibility *(All's Well* 5.3.110–11). In a real-world example, when "bundeles" of seeds were sent by William Cavendish's mother, these packets were "all wreten with wellem marchyngtons hande," the gardener, with exact instructions for planting to follow (x.d.428 83).[18] When, years later, the gardener Timson purchased 96 apple trees "of diverse sorts" plus 24 warden and pear trees, he also bought parchment "to set upon them," evidently as labels around the trunks (2: 262). The intention, in each case, was to select a substrate both that could be written on and had the tensile strength to be shaped into a packet or label. These were ephemeral uses that nevertheless required the writability and all-round robustness of parchment or sized paper. The twin function for 4-pence-per-quire paper—as a packet to be written on or a text to be wrapped—helps to explain the extensive use of this type of everyday paper. For this elite household, the affordances of a substrate mattered above and beyond cost. Sometimes parchment or sized paper were the most suitable choice for a temporary wrapper, sachet, or packet, and we cannot correlate cheapness and ephemerality.

More Expensive Paper

A total of 15 of the 219 payments were spread across seven other types of paper, all of which cost more than 4-and-a-half pence per quire: Crossbow, Demy, Dutch, Fine, and Fine Venice paper each at around 6 or 7 pence per quire; Gilt paper (that is, gilt-edged) at 10 pence a quire; and Frankfurt paper at 15 pence a quire. The total combined spend on these types of paper was £3 3s 5d (22% of the total spending on loose blank sheets) which amounted to 104.5 quires (2,612 sheets; 12.3% of the number of loose sheets of paper purchased). Most of this spending went on the Dutch, Gilt, and Fine Venice paper, together costing £2 16s 4d, which purchased 93 quires (2,325 sheets). The others were purchased in smaller quantities: in total 7s 1d for 11.5 quires of Crossbow, Demy, Fine, and Frankfurt paper. All of these higher-priced types of paper were purchased only in London; we never see them purchased in Chesterfield, Nottingham, or other places closer to Hardwick, unlike Brown paper and 4-pence-per-quire paper. They tended to be purchased in one large batch, or in smaller batches but clustered in a fairly concentrated period of time, viz: in April 1599 a dozen quires of Dutch paper as three purchases; in 1601 all of the four quires of crossbow paper, mostly in October; in 1603 a ream of Fine Venice paper as one purchase; in 1604 all 19 quires of gilt-edged paper as one purchase; in January 1605 another ream of Fine Venice paper as one purchase; and in 1606 a ream plus two more quires of Dutch paper. That is, there was a pattern of larger purchases made annually based on the paper type available.

These shopping patterns suggest that William Cavendish's agents sought out supplies of fine imported paper in London each year, and not all types were always on the market. It is a pattern that correlates with what we know from other sources. Angela Andreani tracks Italian Crossbow Paper at the Signet Office and observes it emerged on the scene from 1595, after which point we know that it was used by individuals in William Cavendish's network (99, 131). That at least some of the Crossbow paper William Cavendish bought was for his own personal use is indicated by the note "for my master" against one purchase, as well as his letter of 1605 written on Crossbow paper (x.d.428, letter from William to his mother).[19] We might wonder about the gap in time between the record of William Cavendish buying Crossbow paper in 1601 and sending his letter written on Crossbow paper on 23 April 1605. Either he had not used up the 100 sheets of Crossbow paper by 1605, or he had made further purchases of Crossbow paper in the intervening years not recorded in the accounts, or he was using a source other than his own paper stocks. Given he had purchased Venice and Gilt paper in 1603–1604, it is possible that, like his letter, he had a choice between types of fine paper among his own stocks, or kept stocks at different locations.[20] Unpacking the financial accounts reminds us of the effort and logistics involved in securing paper supplies. Choosing fine paper was an elite privilege and a social marker, although limited by pragmatic issues that included timing and availability.[21]

As has been so compellingly argued by Wolfe, elite letter-writers were "paper connoisseurs" who liked to communicate "power and prestige" through their choice of fine paper to high-status correspondents ("Letter-Writing" 27). The choice of more expensive paper was very deliberate and was a feature of epistolary etiquette, where the moment of reception was a fleeting opportunity to make an impression on your recipient. William Cavendish's financial accounts offer one further observation to add to those of Wolfe, which is that the etiquettes around paper choice may also apply to wrapping other deliveries. Among the payments by Cavendish's London agent Henry Travis in November 1602 were those for "200 orange 6s" along with "a basket to put oranges in 6d" and "a quire of paper 6d" grouped with "a hamper for oranges 4d" (2: 390). The basket, hamper, and paper were to protect the oranges during transit from London and, even though Brown paper or Paper would have done the same job, it was 6-pence-per-quire paper that Travis purchased. We know from other sources of fruit arriving wrapped in paper and here we might wonder if the choice of more expensive paper—equivalent to the cost of Crossbow, Dutch, and Fine paper types—was a deliberate one. That is, we might ask if the paper connoisseurship associated with letters could be extended to valued sent items or gifted consumables such as citrus fruit.

Opening a letter was an ephemeral moment that mattered to the Elizabethan elite and where higher-quality paper was expected and perceived to be worth the extra expense. We must remember that often the largest portion of the cost of sending a letter was its delivery—which, although perhaps the most overlooked part of their materiality, becomes more visible in these records. In William Cavendish's 1597–1607 finances we find £35 spent on sending and receiving letters, much more (c. £15 / 75% more) than the total recorded spend on blank paper and amounting to over 500 records of deliveries, often of multiple letters. Individual gratuities to letter-bearers were typically between 6d and 12d, but there are numerous instances of several shillings being paid and of extra expenses incurred. There is more to say about these records of delivery but, for now, we can observe again that cost was not fixed to the material object. Fine paper was purchased to be sent to a network of elite correspondents and there were expectations around how, when, and by whom a letter was delivered. As part of a web of elite social interactions, fine paper had, as it were, running costs.

Blank Paper Books

A total of 12 of the 219 payments were for purchases of 31 blank paper books, plus the one purchase of Imperial paper, stated to be for making a book, giving a total spend of £6 18s 5d (33.4% of the total outlay on blank paper). That is, over a third of the blank paper purchased was for pre-stitched books or booklets or for loose sheets to be immediately bound. Most of these blank paper books cost only a few pence or shillings each: 20 small paper books cost 9d or less each and another 5 cost 2–4 shillings each, almost all of which were for the children's education.[22] They included 10 copy-books for Master William in 1601 when he was around 10 years old and being tutored in Latin, and the books purchased by Ham the music tutor pricked and ruled for musical notation, for singing, or in 1605–1606 for teaching Master William the viol (2: 312, 336; 3: 117, 262, 308, 320, 348, 393). More substantial were the four "large paper" books costing 15s–23s 4d, all purchased by Travis in London (2: 26, 50, 317, 320). The first of these was purchased in 1598 as "5 quire of imperial paper for a book 12s 6d" plus 2s 6d for "binding the same in vellum and pasteboard" (the most expensive paper type purchased in the records). It would have made a book of over 200 sheets likely measuring slightly under 50x27cms after the sheets were folded, trimmed, and bound, making it very close in size and shape to HM/1/15 that recorded William's financial accounts from 1 January 1599.[23] If it were not this book itself, it must have been a very similar one and is indicative of intended use.

An unusual purchase was of £2 3s 6d for three blank paper books, which William bought for his niece Arbella Stuart, who lived at Hardwick and, a known booklover, letter-writer, and talented linguist, was the best educated member of the household (2: 267). The cost of these books for Arbella indicates they may have been large bound volumes for recordkeeping similar to HM/1/15. Alternatively, they may have been smaller but of fine quality, perhaps for personal or literary use.[24] We might observe the context of the timing of the purchase in December 1604, as William was preparing to leave London and return to Hardwick, making final payments due "at Christmas," spending 10d on "a dozen almanacs" for the coming year, exchanging £100 into 20s gold pieces for his mother to distribute as charity donations or New Year's gifts, and buying "toys for [his infant son] Mr James and a box to put them in 2s 4d" (2: 268). Perhaps, then, these three blank paper books were Christmas gifts for Arbella, fine quality notebooks comparable to William's purchases of expensive personal items like the "fan for my Lady 42s" bought earlier that year (3: 132). We do not know how Arbella used them, but we know that William's purchases of blank books spanned both more ephemeral and more durable uses and are characterised by elite interests and refinements that reflect both recordkeeping practices and literary and artistic cultures at Hardwick.

Defining Elite Ephemerality

The 1597–1607 financial disbursements of William Cavendish give us a remarkable overview of the blank paper purchased and its immediate contexts of use. It is a picture of an "ephemeral household" wrapped and fluttering with paper, which complements the vivid depictions of ephemeral cityscapes depicted elsewhere and in this volume (Salzberg). Paper's overlapping functions had a role in defining the meanings, value, connotations, and use of the writing it carried and the material objects it transported. For the elite, many social and interpersonal transactions were accompanied by paper, whether as letters, labels, receipts, notes, wrappers, liners, padding, lids, covers, packets, twists, or sachets. These examples are suggestive of the roles the paper played in articulating status and cultures of deference and in defining interpersonal relations and social exchanges. Paper became a wrapper around many social transactions as well as a physical barrier against damage, dirt, and wear. The financial accounts themselves provide a linguistic matrix for the household's social and interpersonal relations, one that shaped and inscribed its power dynamics and hierarchies.[25] It was a linguistic matrix carried on paper—the financial accounts themselves being paper books, keeping records carried on paper slips/bills/receipts, and capturing transactions for purchases or deliveries of paper-based or paper-wrapped goods. The impulse to record these transactions was part of the culture of account keeping, which transformed transitory interactions into durable records.

Paper gives us an ephemeral household but, at the same time, it gives us an enduring one, as it was being used to shore up the family's wealth and dynastic future. Between 1601 and 1604, William Cavendish oversaw

Figure 5.2 William Cavendish's Evidence Room at Hardwick Hall. The Muniment Room at Hardwick Hall, Derbyshire.1096567. NTPL Commissioned (NTPL). ©National Trust Images/Andreas von Einsiedel.

the building of a new Evidence Room (See Figure 5.2) on the ground floor of the south turret of Hardwick New Hall (Rowell; Purcell and Thwaite). The Evidence Room was designed for the security and preservation of documents, with iron window bars, a heavily bolted door, sheets of "white plate" as fire-proofing, and other precautions against theft, fire, damp, temperature changes, and pests (2: 327, 347, 349, 379, 405; 3: 4, 17, 76, 109). Through his financial accounts, we can track the construction of the Evidence Room piece by piece. Many large houses had such a room, but here we have a rare example of one that survives today in close to its original form and where we also have records of its creation and use, as well as some of the original collections it housed. In building the Evidence Room, William was looking to the future at the time when his mother was handing him the reins of power. This space was also another way that William Cavendish fashioned his elite identity. His choices of fittings include "coarse sleeve silk" for lining the storage boxes, drawer-pull tassels of green, blue, and yellow silk, and, he furnished his adjoining closet with "an Indian writing table and a silver pen" (2: 339, 320; Rowell 333). These tastes were contiguous with his own and his mother's long-standing interests in owning precious items and rarities imported from around the world, some purchased directly off East India Company ships, *de luxe* objects only available to the richest Europeans at this time. It was among these objects and cushioned in silk that William Cavendish's paper documents and parchment deeds were sited.

The Evidence Room saw William Cavendish drawing a boundary line between the disposable and the durable—a physical barrier against ephemerality. At least £16 was spent on over 900 new skins of parchment to make conveyances, bonds, deeds, indentures, bills, and patents. Some of this new parchment was also used for covering paper books, including the financial disbursements and records of industrial enterprises, such as the lead works. More parchment was used for covering many of the printed paper books and pamphlets that William purchased from Thomas Norton in London—he spent around £75 stocking his library in this period. William was adapting to a world where paper was an essential and increasingly voluminous dimension of documentary and textual cultures. The way to deal with this paradigm shift was a physical space large and secure enough to accommodate not only parchment property deeds but also paper-based legal, financial, and printed texts. While keeping records safe was important, the priority was access and findability and although the older system used by his mother the countess (of iron trunks for storage) may have been safer, the aim now was to optimise the documents' usability for actively managing the family estates, businesses, investments, and colonial prospecting. The Evidence Room was fitted with 492 drawers, accessible by ladder, neatly ordered, painted with numbers, and keyed to an index system in the muniment register. This was not intended to be a place of static deposit; it was an archive with a purpose—more database than deep freeze.

Within this space, the dowager countess and her second son William laid down the documentary basis that provided legal proof of ownership of their property and entitlements to lands and that ensured his inheritance of the family fortune and his purchased titles. They had worked together for many years to close every possible legal loophole and to cover all bases to secure his inheritance rights (Durant). The Evidence Room and adjoining Library show William Cavendish gearing up to expand the family interests and investments internationally. He was curating his own collection of the latest travel books to Europe, Asia, Persia, Virginia, and the East Indies, along with maps and globes. He was one of the first investors in Virginia and Bermuda, and from 1605, he invested very substantially in the East India Company (Levin; Riden 1: xxxiv-xxxvi). By the time he died in 1626, he left 100,000 acres and a portfolio of overseas ventures. Paper was vital to the extraordinary rise of the Cavendish family as they went from indebted minor local gentry to a family achieving enormous levels of economic wealth and positions of power and influence. This success did not happen by chance; it was achieved, by mother and son, through management of their interests, understanding of finance, an awareness that control over paper-based textual cultures gave them a competitive advantage, and an appreciation of the benefits (to them) of a fastidiously run archive. Paper defined how they managed their legal and business affairs, negotiated their social networks, cultivated their identities, and ultimately developed an administrative powerbase. It was the stuff by which the elite padded, lined, sanitised, inscribed, labelled, communicated, decontaminated, recorded, networked, and extended colonial ventures. Control over how to store, select, and use paper defined their webs of power and social interactions and amounted to a distinctively elite form of ephemerality.

Acknowledgements

The research for this chapter was supported by an AHRC Leadership Fellowship 2017–2019 (Project Reference AH/P009735/1). Initial findings were presented at *Paper Stuff: Materiality, Technology and Invention*, British Academy and University of Cambridge, 10 September 2018. I am grateful to the Devonshire Trust and Chatsworth House Archives for permission to access original manuscripts.

Notes

1 The simile has most recently been discussed by Da Rold (191–98). The metaphor PAPER IS WEAKNESS can be tracked through the *HTOED*.
2 William was Lord Cavendish from 1605 and 1st Earl of Devonshire from 1618. The accounts are accessible thanks to the three-volume edition prepared by Philip Riden. All the references given to the accounts are from Riden's edition and refer to the relevant volume and page number.
3 HMS/1/15 (formerly Hardwick MS 23) for the period 1 January 1599 – 4 April 1607; supplementary entries from 1597–1601 are provided in Riden's edition from William's digests (HMS/1/13 and HMS/1/14, formerly Hardwick MSS 10A and 10B; Riden 1: ix–xi).
4 In preparing this chapter, his disbursements have been compared to nine further sets of contemporary household financial accounts from 1548 until 1620, which highlight differences in the style of recording as well as some variations in prices and users. Comparison shows the very detailed style of account in HM/1/15 that makes it of special interest and importance (as highlighted by Riden 1: ix–xi). As expected for this period, all are single-entry and feature their own idiosyncrasies: from The Devonshire Collection Archives, Chatsworth, Hardwick Manuscripts (HM/1, HM/3, HM/5, HM/7, HM/8, HM/ADD catalogue details at https://archiveshub. jisc.ac.uk/ under Hardwick Manuscripts; MS X.d.486, Folger Shakespeare Library, Washington DC; Simon Adams, ed., *Household Accounts and Disbursement Books of Robert Dudley, Earl of Leicester, 1558–1561, 1584–1586*, Royal Historical Society Camden Fifth Series, 6, Cambridge UP, 1995; Mark Merry and Catherine Richardson, eds, *The Household Account Book of Sir Thomas Puckering, 1620*, Dugdale Society 45, Dugdale Society, 2012.
5 The small loose square slips with sums are in HMS/1/16 (formerly HM/29) that continues the accounts until 1623.
6 Further discussion on categories of archival materials can be found in the chapter by Robert Bearman in this volume. A conceptualisation of archival ephemerality is provided by Akkerman and Langman.

7 Riden, 1: xxii. The combined gross income of the family was over £20k per year, largely income from his mother the dowager countess's lands.

8 A quire was usually 25 sheets and is the basis for the calculations here (although it could vary between 24 and 25 sheets; Riden 2: 396). A quire was usually a twentieth of a ream, so 20 quires is calculated here as 500 sheets. Money was in coins: a shilling equals 12 pence (appearing the accounts as either "1s" or "12d"), and one pound equals 240 pence (usually referred to in the accounts as 20 shillings, written as either "i li" or "xx s"). These figures that are "estimated" in the table are where exact figures are not give in William Cavendish's records, such as where items are bundled together or a quantity can only be estimated from cost. The data was processed as an Excel spreadsheet prepared for this research.

9 The one occasion when the cost is 3 pence per quire is specified as being for "brown paper four large quire 12d" and, as Riden points out, given that a quire is a fixed quantity "large" presumably here refers to a larger sheet size, which explains the higher cost (3: 383).

10 Perhaps comparably, Da Rold suggests paper was used "to prepare sachet to store spices" from at least the fourteenth century (61).

11 Further entries consisting of a payment or gratuity plus Brown paper are: II 364, 374, 390, 395; III 217, 266.

12 Larger quantities of coins were kept in "money bags" made out of canvas (2: 328), but this refers to cash stored in the house rather than money carried around and spent in small quantities, which is where the paper may have come in. A relevant discussion of cultures of deference is by Merry and Richardson (57–59).

13 Wolfe confirms that the typical cost, that can be established from a range of sources, or "ordinary pot paper" or "ordinary writing paper" was 4d per quire ("Letter-Writing" 27). The variation in terms and the greater specification at these points likely reflects that these purchases were made in London at the same time as other types of paper and there was therefore a perceived to be a need to find a way to distinguish between them.

14 Examples can be found The Thomas Gravell Watermark Archive (www.gravell.org), among the Folger Cavendish-Talbot papers.

15 "For a quire of paper 4d., most of this Barbara had" (2: 146). "For a quire of paper delivered to my master," (2: 239) (4d). "A quire of paper for Mr William 4d" (2: 352). Paper to make a lead book a quire (2: 355). "For a quire of paper for Mr Butler" (2: 385). "A quire of paper for Sir Ralph Calton reckoning 4d..." (3: 150). "...paper for Mr Redhill 4d ..." (3: 374). "... two quire of paper for Mr William 8d..." (2: 354). "For three quire of paper, whereof nurse had half a quire" (2: 230) "...for paper for him" (2: 341). "To a groom of the stable at [the] mews 6d, paper 2d, total 8d (II 387). Paper bought for my Lady 1d" (3: 208).

16 "For a quire of paper 4d, 400 pippins at 4s 6d per 100" (3: 45). "For a curry comb 6d, a quire of paper 4d" (3: 69). We also find it paired with purchases of books (2: 382; 3: 217).

17 "For a quire of paper to 'Civer' rose pots and for [transporting/wrapping] three Barbary sugar loaves 4d" (2: 42). "Paper to cover roses 1d" (2: 299). "Paper for the footcloth 3d, thread 2d, total 5d" (3: 226). "1 oz of silk 2s 8d, searing candle and paper 4d, total 3s" (3: 266). "Paper 4d, to the poor 3d, needles 4d, total 11d" (3: 130). "Given to the waits of Westminster 12d, paper 3d, a ruler 3d, total 1s 6d" (3: 273).

18 Lady Elizabeth St Loe (known as Bess of Hardwick, later dowager countess of Shrewsbury) to her servant James Crompe, 8 March [1560?], Papers of the Cavendish-Talbot family.

19 Visible online at Gravell Watermark Archive at CRSBW.002.1.

20 We know that in 1592 his mother had purchased multiple 1,600 sheets of different kinds of writing paper, including both Frankfurt and Venice paper, which Wolfe describes as the "most striking example of an elite person acquiring multiple quires of paper," thus giving us a family precedent ("Letter-Writing" 27).

21 The link between paper stocks and time in the Signet Office is discussed by Andreani (99). While paper moved more slowly through the Cavendish household by comparison to the Signet Office, time and availability were likewise factors.

22 At 4, 6, or 9 pence each, they were most likely made from a single quire of ordinary 4-pence-per-quire paper each. Wee are told elsewhere that the intended use of one such quire was "to make a lead book," presumably to keep the financial accounts of William's lead mill at Barlow (Riden 2: 355 and editorial note 10).

23 The size of Imperial paper is discussed by Riden (2: 26, citing the *OED*) and Da Rold.

24 The cost indicates these were not heirloom treasures decorated with gold and jewels such as we find elsewhere purchased by the Cavendishes. On 10 May 1550, William's father Sir William Cavendish has bought his wife a gold and bejewelled book that cost him £14 6s (Folger Shakespeare Library MS X.d.486, fol. 24r); William himself had spent over £250 on bejewelled buttons (3: 330–31).

25 Further critiques of uncritical uses of financial accounts are offered by Scott-Warren and by Wiggins.

Works Cited

Akkerman, Nadine and Pete Langman. "Accidentally on Purpose: Denying Any Responsibility for the Accidental Archive." *Archives: Power, Truth, & Fiction*. Eds Andrew Prescott and Alison Wiggins. Oxford UP, 2023.

Andreani, Angela. *The Elizabethan Secretariat and the Signet Office: The Production of State Papers, 1590–1596*. Routledge, 2017.

Bearman, Robert. "What is an 'Ephemeral Archive'? Stratford-upon-Avon, 1550–1650: A Case Study." *Practices of Ephemera in Early Modern England*. Eds Callan Davies, Hannah Lilley, and Catherine Richardson. Routledge, 2023. 65–82.

Birkenholz, Frank. "Paper, Pepper and Merchant-princes: The Dutch East India Company's Paper Policies." Presentation. *The Politics of Paper in the Early Modern World*. 9–10 June 2016.

———. "A Paper Company: Exploring the Materiality of the Dutch East India Company's Information Management and Paper-Based Governance." Presentation. *Paper Stuff*. University of Cambridge. 10 Sep. 2018.

Da Rold, Orietta. *Paper in Medieval England: From Pulp to Fictions*. Cambridge UP, 2020.

Durant, David N. *Bess of Hardwick: Portrait of an Elizabethan Dynast*. Peter Owen, 1977.

Gitelman, Lisa. *Paper Knowledge: Towards a Media History of Documents*. Duke UP, 2014.

Hindle, Steve. *The State and Social Change in Early Modern England 1550–1640*. Palgrave Macmillan, 2000.

HMS 1 (series). MS. Devonshire Collection Archives, Chatsworth House, Derbyshire, UK.

Hunt, Arnold. "'Burn This Letter': Preservation and Destruction in the Early Modern Archive." *Cultures of Correspondence in Early Modern Britain*. Eds James Daybell and Andrew Gordon. U of Pennsylvania P, 2016. 189–209.

Leong, Elaine. "Papering the Household: Paper, Recipes, and Everyday Technologies in Early Modern England." *Working with Paper: Gendered Practices in the History of Knowledge*. Eds Carla Bittel, Elaine Leong, and Christine von Oertzen. U of Pittsburgh P, 2019. 32–45.

Levin, C. "William Cavendish, first earl of Devonshire (1551–1626). *Oxford Dictionary of National Biography*. Online. Accessed 1 Nov. 2021.

Matthews, Jemima. "Maritime Ephemera in Walter Mountfort's *The Launching of the Mary*." *Practices of Ephemera in Early Modern England*. Eds Callan Davies, Hannah Lilley, and Catherine Richardson. Routledge, 2023. 173–90.

Merry, Mark and Catherine Richardson. *The Household Account Book of Sir Thomas Puckering, 1620*. Dugdale Society, 2012.

Prescott, Andrew. "Tall Tales from the Archive." *Medieval Historical Writing: Britain and Ireland, 500–1500*. Cambrdige UP, 2019. 356–69.

Purcell, Mark and Nichola Thwaite. "Libraries at Hardwick, 1597–1957." *Hardwick Hall: A Great Old Castle of Romance*. Eds David Adshead and David A. H. B. Taylor. Yale UP, 2016. 177–91.

Reynolds, Anna. "'Such Dispersive Scatteredness': Early Modern Encounters with Binding Waste." *Journal of the Northern Renaissance* 8 (2017): n.p.

Riden, Philip, ed. *The Household Accounts of William Cavendish, Lord Cavendish of Hardwick, 1597–1607*, 3 vols. Derbyshire Record Society 40–42. Dinefwr Press, 2016.

Rowell, Christopher. "Appendix 2 The Hardwick Evidence House." *Hardwick Hall: A Great Old Castle of Romance*. Eds David Adshead and David A. H. B. Taylor. Yale UP, 2016. 333–36.

Salzberg, Rosa. *Ephemeral City: Cheap Print and Urban Culture in Renaissance Venice*. Manchester UP, 2014.

Scott-Warren, Jason. "Early Modern Bookkeeping and Life-Writing Revisited: Accounting for Richard Stonley." *Past and Present* supplement 11 (2016): 151–70.

Shakespeare, William. *All's Well that Ends Well. Shakespeare's Works*. Eds Barbara A. Mowat and Paul Werstine. Folger, 2016. Online. Accessed 1 Nov. 2021.

———. *3 Henry VI. The New Oxford Shakespeare: Modern Critical Edition*. Eds Gary Taylor, John Jowett, Terri Bourus, Gabriel Egan. Oxford UP, 2016. 331–406.

———. *Two Gentlemen of Verona. The New Oxford Shakespeare: Modern Critical Edition*. Eds Gary Taylor, John Jowett, Terri Bourus, and Gabriel Egan. Oxford UP, 2016. 59–116.

Shapiro, Barbara J. *A Culture of Fact: England, 1550–1720*. Cornell UP, 2000.

Sir Gawain and the Green Knight. Eds J. R. R. Tolkien and E. V. Gordon. 1925. 2nd ed. Ed. Norman Davis. Clarendon, 1967.

Soll, Jacob. *The Reckoning: Financial Accountability and the Making and Breaking of Nations*. Penguin, 2014.

Wiggins, Alison. "Money, Marriage, and Remembrance: Telling Stories from the Cavendish Financial Accounts." *Bess of Hardwick: New Perspectives*. Ed. Lisa Hopkins. Manchester UP, 2019. 36–77.

Williams, Megan K. *Paper Princes* (paperprinces.org). Website. Accessed 29. Nov. 2021.

Wolfe, Heather. "Letter Writing and Paper Connoisseurship in Elite Households in Early Modern England." *Working with Paper: Gendered Practices in the History of Knowledge*. Eds Carla Bittel, Elaine Leong, and Christine von Oertzen. U of Pittsburgh P, 2019. 17–31.

———. "Was Early Modern Writing Paper Expensive?" *The Collation*. Online. Accessed 29 Nov. 2021.

X.d.428. MS. Cavendish-Talbot MSS. Folger Shakespeare Library, Washington DC.

Part II
Matter/Metamorphosing

6 Recipes and Paper Knowledge

Elaine Leong

Amongst the vast archive of estate and personal papers deposited by the Fortescue family of Castle Hill in the Devon Heritage Centre is a folder filled with loose paper slips.[1] Varied in size and shape, they document a lively exchange of recipe knowledge between Margaret Boscawen, her daughter Bridget Fortescue and their extensive circle of family, kin and friends at the turn of the eighteenth century, and reflect recurring health concerns affecting the family and their attempts to reach out for cures and therapies.[2] Together with the family's numerous bound recipe books, these circa 150 loose slips formed a complex paper archive of recipe knowledge (1262M/0/FC/6–8). As historians have noted, collections of culinary, medical and craft recipes can reveal sickness experiences, everyday knowledge practices, social alliances, global trade networks and much more.[3] While bound notebooks of recipes have received considerable attention, less has been paid to recipes written on loose slips of paper. As such, the slips in the Fortescue papers offer an opportunity for exploration and invite complex readings about ideas of ephemerality and durability.

Some of the loose slips in the Fortescue family papers are folio-sized and had clearly been folded, sealed and sent as letters with the recipe (and perhaps some accompanying text) written on one side and the recipient's name and address and remnants of a wax seal on the other side. Other slips are long and thin, clearly torn from a larger piece of paper, perhaps a letter. Most common though, are small slips of paper with a recipe written on one side and the title of the recipe on the other with no additional identifying or contextualising information. At first sight, it is tempting to view these slips as ephemeral objects. After all, small bits of paper can be easily lost and there is some evidence that recipes written on paper slips, particularly trustworthy and/or valued ones, were often copied into recipe books.[4] However, on examination, it is clear that the status of such paper slips, as material and epistemic objects, is fluid and changing.

A case in point is the series of four paper slips recording remedies for rickets. One of the slips is part of a letter dated 26 February 26 1695 from Fortescue's aunt offering recipes and a plea for help in recovering

DOI: 10.4324/9781003058588-9

a loan of 35 pounds from "cousin Thomas Clinton." As in so many
other cases, the offer of recipe knowledge was in response to specific, often fleeting circumstances and entangled with other social interactions.
These are the stuff of the everyday and evoke the ephemeral nature of
recipe exchange. Another slip offers a set of three recipes titled "The
Broth," "The Diet Drink" and "The oyntment," with "for ye riketes L
norcort" written on the top right-hand corner. The inscription and wax
seal on the reverse side of the paper indicate that the recipe was sent via
post to Bridget Fortescue (Figures 6.1 and 6.2) Aside from the address,
a later hand (likely Fortescue's) wrote 'my Lady Norcotts Receipt for ye
Ricketts' on the top right hand corner. In fact, almost all the slips have
the recipe title and name of the donor written on the reverse side of
the paper. For example, the next slip has "the Lady Bamphylds general
course for the Ricketts" inscribed on one side and three recipes on the
other. This kind of careful endorsement and information categorisation
suggests that the survival of these slips was not by chance, rather they
were part of a complex system of paper tools designed to sort and store
recipe knowledge, much like those used by early modern scholars such
as Ulisse Aldrovandi or Conrad Gessner.[5] As with other similar paper-
based information management systems, the loose slip format enabled

Figure 6.1 Paper slip with address, recipe title and wax seal. Devon Heritage
    Centre, 1262M/0/FC/8. Image reproduced with kind permission
    from the Countess of Arran.

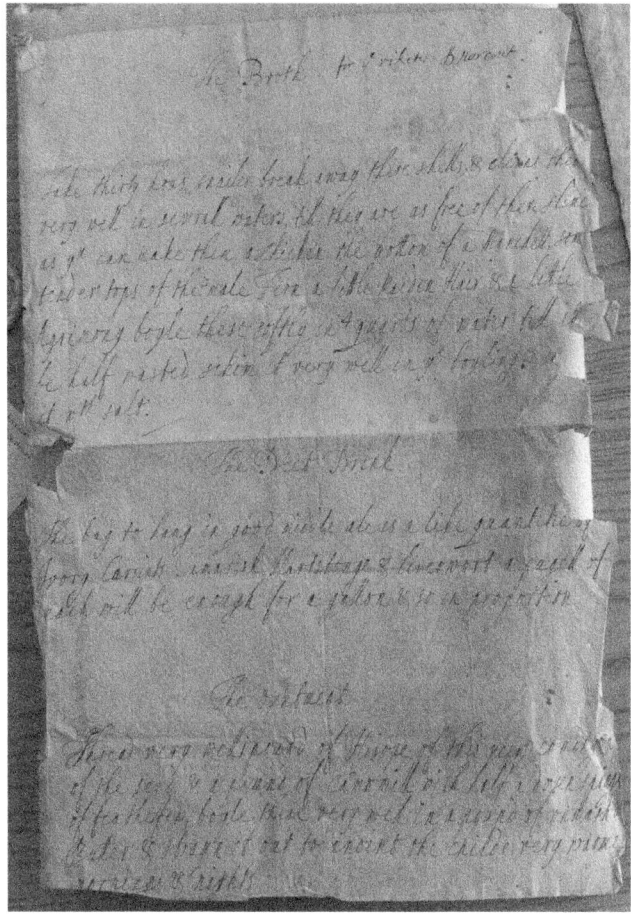

Figure 6.2 Paper slip with recipe for tickets from Lady Norcott. Devon Heritage Centre, 1262M/0/FC/8. Image reproduced with kind permission from the Countess of Arran.

the family to build a flexible archive that was at once ephemeral and durable.

The final tiny paper slip in the series reinforces this idea. It has only an untitled recipe written on one side of the paper with the endorsement "Diet Drinke for the children yt hath the Ricketts this reset I find in my mothers large boke" inscribed on the reverse (Figures 6.3 and 6.4). The same recipe can be found in the family's bound notebook where it is part of a series of cures comprising a plaister, a drink, an ointment and a syrup, all gathered under the title "A present Remedy for the Ricketts a Recaite which is very Exceelent Cozen Barretts Recaite". The presence of the same recipe across the loose paper archive and the bound notebook suggests a dynamic and changing connection between

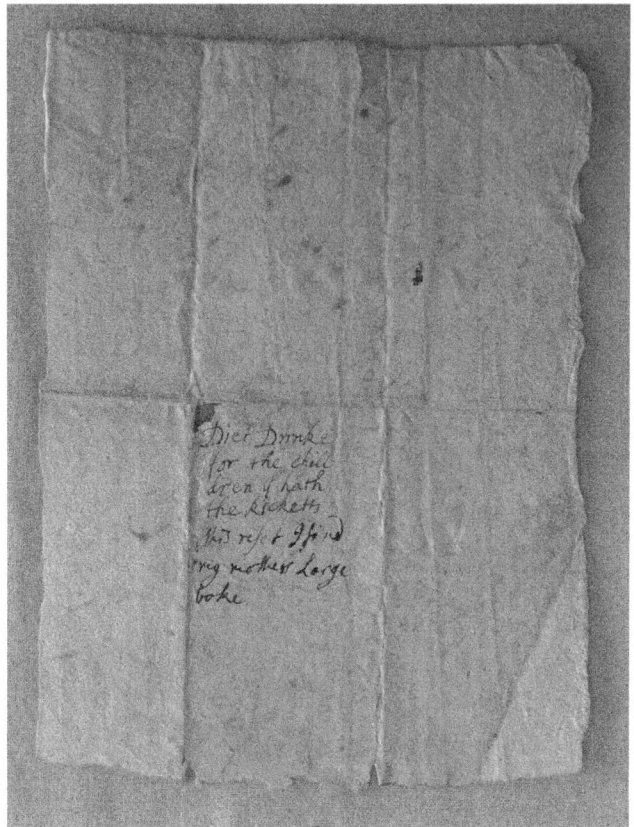

Figure 6.3 Paper slip with note from Bridget Fortescue. Devon Heritage Centre, 1262M/0/FC/8. Image reproduced with kind permission from the Countess of Arran.

the two parts of Fortescue family's collection. Other similar examples can be found within the archive, indicating that recipe knowledge was compared, tested, and transferred across the notebooks and loose slips, and the epistemic status of each recipe was continually negotiated as the family sifted through, assessed and reassessed the know-how. In recent years scholars have shed light on similar knowledge management practices used by learned men; archival examples such as the Boscawen/Fortescue papers extend existing studies to include new actors and knowledge fields (Blair; Blair et al.; Cevolini). Alongside paper evidence such as the salvaged documents in book bindings described by Megan Heffernan in this volume, they push us to reimagine past worlds of paper and reconsider notions of ephemerality and durability in knowledge practices.

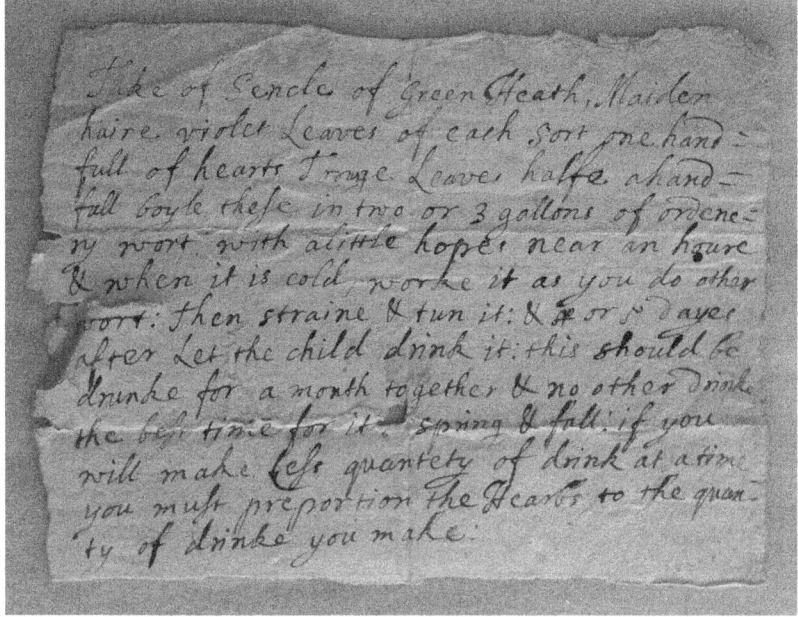

Figure 6.4 Paper slip with recipe for rickets. Devon Heritage Centre, 1262M/
0/FC/8. Image reproduced with kind permission from the Countess
of Arran.

Acknowledgements

It was a pleasure to participate in this project and I thank the editors, Catherine, Callan and Hannah, for bringing the group together and for their leadership. I also extend huge thanks to other contributors in the volume for their comments and feedback. Finally, I am grateful to the Countess of Arran for permission to reproduce images of the Fortescue family papers.

Notes

1 The Fortescue Family of Castle Hill made multiple deposits to the Devon Heritage Centre. The loose slips discussed in this article were part of the first deposit which included other correspondence, recipe books and estate papers: Devon Heritage Centre, 1262M/0/FC/8.

2 For an overview of the Boscawen/Fortescue family's household medical activities, see Stobart. I am grateful to Anne Stobart for introducing me to the Fortescue archive.

3 There is a rich literature on historical recipe studies. See, as a selection focused on the English context, DiMeo and Pennell; Leong; and Wall.

4 While we have little information about how and where these particular slips were kept at Castle Hill, there is evidence that other families kept similar items in wooden chests: Leong, Chapter 5.

5 On paper slips, see, for example, Charmantier and Müller-Wille; Considine; Kraemer and Zedelmaier. On the idea of paper technologies, see te Heesen. For a general overview of gender and paper practices, see Bittel, Leong, and von Oertzen.

Works Cited

1262M/0/FC/6–8. MS. Devon Heritage Centre, Exeter, UK.

Bittel, Carla, Elaine Leong, and Christine von Oertzen, eds. *Working with Paper: Gendered Practices in the History of Knowledge.* U of Pittsburgh P, 2019.

Blair, Ann. *Too Much to Know. Managing Scholarly Information before the Modern Age.* Yale UP, 2010.

Blair, Ann, et al. *Information: A Historical Companion.* Princeton UP, 2021.

Cevolini, Alberto, ed. *Forgetting Machines: Knowledge Management Evolution in Early Modern Europe.* Brill, 2016.

Charmantier, Isabelle and Stefan Müller-Wille. "Carl Linnaeus's Botanical Paper Slips (1767–1773)." *Intellectual History Review* 24.2 (2014): 215–38.

Considine, John. "Cutting and Pasting Slips: Early Modern Compilation and Information Management." *Journal of Medieval and Early Modern Studies* 45.3 (2015): 487–504.

DiMeo, Michelle and Sara Pennell, eds. *Reading and Writing Recipe Books, 1550–1800.* U of Manchester P, 2013.

te Heesen, Anke, "The Notebook: A Paper-Technology," *in Making Things Public: Atmospheres of Democracy*, ed. Bruno Latour and Peter Weibel (Cambridge, MA and London: The MIT Press, 2005), 582–89.

Heffernan, Megan. "Expired Time: Archiving Waste Manuscripts." *Practices of Ephemera in Early Modern England.* Eds Callan Davies, Hannah Lilley, and Catherine Richardson. Routledge, 2023. 21–24.

Kraemer, Fabian and Helmut Zedelmaier, "Instruments of Invention in Renaissance Europe: The Cases of Conrad Gesner and Ulisse Aldrovandi," *Intellectual History Review* 24, no. 3 (2014): 321–41.

Leong, Elaine. *Recipes and Everyday Knowledge: Medicine, Science and the Household in Early Modern England.* U of Chicago P, 2018.

Stobart, Anne. *Household Medicine in Seventeenth-Century England.* Bloomsbury, 2016.

Wall, Wendy. *Recipes for Thought: Knowledge and Taste in the Early Modern English Kitchen.* Material Texts. U of Pennsylvania P, 2016.

7 More Lasting than Bronze

Statues, Writing, and the Materials of Ephemera in Ben Jonson's *Sejanus His Fall*

Katherine Hunt

What are the opposites of ephemera? Things that are durable, reliable, permanent; famous, valued, and remembered? Many of the essays in this collection consider not only ephemera but also the forms of attention that these ephemera demand from us: the way they force us to dwell on the interaction between the fleeting and the lasting. In this essay, I explore the relay between durability and ephemerality and how this relationship is expressed in writing, objects, and writing about objects. I focus on Ben Jonson's play *Sejanus His Fall* (1603; published 1605). This play stages the rise and fall of the Roman soldier and prefect Sejanus, paired with the rise and fall of the bronze statues made to honour him. The humanist practices of *imitatio* that Jonson employed when writing the play, as well as what we know of its performance and textual history, repeatedly question what it is possible to salvage from the past, or send into the future. These dynamics make *Sejanus* a meditation on what lasts and what does not.[1]

As I was thinking about Jonson's description of statue destruction in this play, similar scenes were played out, over and over again, on my computer screen. Statues were torn or taken down in North Carolina, Brussels, Bristol, Cape Town, and many more places across the world: their removal is a powerful symbol of resistance to the endurance of racism and colonialism in our present. The Black Lives Matter protests of summer 2020 were about police brutality and endemic racism: more important things than public sculpture. But the statue protests, and the debates about them which are ongoing, form a related current that focuses on how we want to counter and remember injustice, and the ways in which the past persists in the present.

The statues themselves provide a kind of telescoping of time. Take the bronze statue of the slave trader Edward Colston, for example, which was torn down on 8 June 2020 and thrown into Bristol harbour, the site from which Colston's own slave ships left. He died in 1721 but it was only in 1895 that the statue was erected, the limping conclusion of a motion (not, in fact, ever particularly popular) to put up a figurative monument to him. What is being remembered in this nineteenth-century statue? The bronze figure of Colston already represented an imagined

DOI: 10.4324/9781003058588-10

past. When the statue splashed into the harbour the years 2020, 1895, and 1636–1721 (the dates of Colston's life) collided for a moment. And all this was happening in pandemic time, which stretches and snaps, endlessly rebounds on itself so that we keep on feeling as though we're back at the beginning of the whole thing once again. Our senses of time themselves keep shifting; at the same time, my own mention of these events will date this essay to a particular point in our earlyish twenty-first century.

Sejanus His Fall echoes powerfully in this moment in which I'm writing. It is concerned with how structures of power exert their influence on our lives, and how our built and adorned environment mirrors these power structures. This essay analyses Jonson's use of the materials of duration—the stone and bronze of which statues and buildings were made. Through his engagement with these materials, and the ways in which they can be reflected or contested in writing, *Sejanus His Fall* forces us to question how and what we are able to remember and forget.

Writing and Permanence

Statues operate in *Sejanus* as signs and synecdoches of the rise and fall of the play's main character. The play begins with a vacuum of authority in Rome: the emperor Tiberius is self-absorbed and selfish, and he is losing interest in the running of the empire. Sejanus takes advantage of the emperor's weaknesses and makes a bid for power; he comes so far as to share the consulship with Tiberius, now retired to Capri. More and more bronze statues are raised to Sejanus as the play progresses, mirroring the increasing power he holds over the empire. But he has many enemies in the Senate, and his control over Rome starts to crumble. After a scene in which a statue of Fortune herself turns her back on him, the citizens revolt against Sejanus and both he and his avatars in bronze are pulled down, fragmented, and, in the case of the statues, remade into new objects.

Sejanus His Fall was, famously, a flop when first performed in 1603 (see Cain 199–201 for a summary of what we know about the play's first performance). In his dedicatory epistle to Lord Aubigny in the 1616 Folio, Jonson even compared the audience's reaction to *Sejanus* the play to the Romans' rejection of Sejanus the man: the play, he writes, "suffered no less violence from our people here than the subject of it did from the rage of the people of Rome" (Jonson, "To the No Less Noble" 212).[2] But Jonson was determined that the play would avoid obscurity. In its first published form, the quarto of 1605, Jonson purposefully turned his back on *Sejanus*'s failed performance. By adding and privileging specifically textual, rather than performance, elements (including special printed characters, and extensive marginalia) Jonson signalled, Tom Cain suggests, the quarto's "radical originality as a primarily literary artefact" (209).

Sejanus His Fall was composed of fragments from classical texts, and in the quarto Jonson (and his printer George Eld and bookseller Thomas Thorpe) shows off the commonplacing humanism that has forged the play.[3] Printed marginal notes give a scholarly gloss to the text, directing the reader not only to the classical authors but often to the specific editions and pages of their works in print: to the relevant nugget of source material from which Jonson has drawn for that moment.

In the margins, we see proof of Jonson's debt to Dio Cassius, Suetonius, and, in particular, Tacitus as the leading sources for the play. Tacitus also operates as the model of authorship presented to us here, as Darryl Chalk explains: Jonson uses Tacitus both as "the source of his story and as a means of defending his right to retell it" (389). Chalk's important work on *Sejanus* illuminates these twinned ways in which Jonson makes use of Tacitus in the play, and my discussion here draws directly on his arguments. For Tacitus, the historian was responsible for representing people of the past in ways that correctly reflect their virtues (or vices). These people may not have received their proper reward (or punishment) in life, but the writing of their history can rectify this and praise or damn them, as appropriate. In his adoption of a Tacitean model, Jonson "conflates the role of the poet with the duties Tacitus assigns to the historian," and makes the writing of this play the means of commemoration or condemnation of the figures about whom he writes (Chalk 394).[4]

The quarto calls attention to its own processes of creation as a literary artefact, then, but also as a specifically, and rigorously, humanist artefact. Humanist scholarship was concerned with what could be made of the fragments that had survived from the antique; a sense of loss pervades this work, because so much had not lasted (Greene; Hui). But humanist imitation was also, always, concerned with remaking new knowledge from these fragments. In the margins, we see this commonplacing humanism at work—we are placed in the middle of Jonson's process, of making something new from the old. In the quarto, print operates as the medium of monumentalisation—of classical writing, of the play, and of Jonson himself (Chalk 387–405).

Jonson's interest in writing was not only concerned with print on paper, though, and his humanism extended beyond text to material culture, too. A notable (and much-noted) feature of the quarto is its inclusion, in particular moments, of typography that imitates Roman epigraphy: writing on stone that would have covered the city (Cain "*Sejanus:* Textual Essay"). And there are further hints at Jonson's interest in the material environment. John Kuhn has uncovered how, in his research for the Fortuna scene in Act 5, Jonson drew on ancient texts, contemporary antiquarian scholarship, and archaeological evidence to develop a realistic and scholarly dramatic depiction of Roman ritual.[5] Kuhn joins with other scholars to persuade us that, despite Jonson's own disavowing of the theatre in the quarto of *Sejanus*, his work was nonetheless deeply invested in performance, and his pointed antitheatricality was not necessarily to be taken at face value (see also Syme; Bourne). The quarto is, then, deliberately intended to call attention to its own status as a learned, written object. But *Sejanus* was also deeply invested in questions of drama, performance, and the material, and in the interactions between them, and Jonson was fascinated by the question of what might persist, and what decay.

Writing and Materiality

The questions of writing and materiality signal one of the play's important sources: Horace. In Ode 3.30, Horace contends with the materials of monumentality, but ultimately urges that writing itself could be an agent of duration:

> I have finished a monument more lasting than bronze, more lofty than the regal structure of the pyramids, one which neither corroding rain nor the ungovernable North Wind can ever destroy, nor the countless series of the years, nor the flight of time. I shall not wholly die, and a large part of me will elude the Goddess of Death.

> Exegi monumentum aere perennius
> regalique situ pyramidum altius,
> quod non imber edax, non Aquilo impotens
> possit diruere aut innumerabilis
> annorum series et fuga temporum. 5
> non omnis moriar. (Horace, Ode 3.30, ll. 1–6.)

Horace's attention to matter and its deterioration in 3.30 is sensitive. The bronze and the pyramids that he calls upon, both of which seem to be so enduring, are in fact subject to the decay caused by violent wind or "corroding" (*edax*) rain. The very environment will, bit by bit and with time, destroy these monuments. Horace is really talking about his own poetry here, and the opposition he sets out—writing versus bronze—uses bronze as a foil: this metal that seems to be so solid and durable is nothing compared to the lastingness of literary production and literary fame. By making the durable ephemeral, Horace's famous ode reframes our senses of time (see Kunin). Like timelines in natural history museums that show us how minuscule the human era is compared to the life of the earth, we are thrust into a new understanding of time and, further, what ephemera might mean, or be.

Horace's ideas echo in many other places in classical writing, including in his near-contemporary Ovid's many references to similar processes (*tempus edax rerum* "time, devourer of all things," from Ovid, *Met.* 15.234–36, for example). And Renaissance writers returned again and again to Horace's lines—and to the comparison of bronze and writing.

Think, for example, of the book in a bronze tomb with which Rabelais opens *Gargantua*, or the decaying stone and metal that Shakespeare repeatedly compares to his sonnets. Horace's lines refract in these texts and even serve to prove his claims: Horace's writing does indeed live on in these later works, even when (as in the sonnets) the authors who quote him are themselves questioning the permanence of writing.

Jonson's own indebtedness to the Ode is made explicit in the first act of *Sejanus*, in a moment that shows the play's mixture of Horatian and Tacitean influences. Brian Chalk argues that the transition from *Poetaster* to *Sejanus* shows "a transition from a Horatian mode of authorial self-representation to a Tacitean one" (394). Tacitus is crucial to *Sejanus* as source and model, as we have seen. But Horace was Jonson's "chief literary model" through the whole of his writing career, and Jonson continues to be inspired by him here (Moul 2). The Ode influences the play's engagement with materiality, and with questions of ephemerality and durability, and it works as a kind of animating spirit of the whole.

In Act 1, the Emperor Tiberius (perhaps played by Shakespeare in the play's first performances) invokes Ode 3.30 when paraphrasing part of Tacitus's *Annals*.[6] In the section from Tacitus (to which Jonson points the reader in his marginal gloss) Tiberius declares that, following Augustus's example, he has agreed to have a single temple dedicated to him and his mother. He claims to be reluctant to have more temples raised in his name. In the *Annals*, Tacitus reports of this moment that the emperor wants his actions, and his respect towards his ancestors, to be "my temples in your hearts, these are my fairest and most lasting monuments. For those which are raised of stone, if the judgement of posterity turns to hatred, are scorned as sepulchres" (Tacitus, *Annales* 4.38).[7] The use of the phrase 'lasting monuments' indicates that Tacitus is pointedly referencing Horace here. But when Jonson comes to write this speech for his version of Tiberius, he brings the Ode to the fore even more. Virtues 'shall be to us', the Tiberius of the play declares,

> Temples and statues, reared in your minds,
> The fairest and most during imagery;
> For those of stone or brass, if they become
> Odious in judgement of posterity,
> Are more contemned as dying sepulchres
> Than ta'en for living monuments. (6.1.484–90)

These lines are a clear and close paraphrase of Tacitus, but one of Jonson's few changes is to amplify the reference to Horace's Ode that Tacitus had made in the *Annals* by adding brass to the list of materials from which the futile monuments might be made. By adding brass here, Jonson not only reminds us of the bronze statues that will play a big part in this story but also offers a more emphatic nod to Horace's fallible materials of commemoration.[8]

Bronze and the Techniques of Reuse

In fact, bronze is imperishable in a way that Horace's claim doesn't recognise. Because this metal can be endlessly recycled, it never "wholly dies." To make a statue in bronze, the metal (a mixture of copper and tin) is heated until molten; it is then poured into a carefully-constructed mould.[9] When the metal has cooled, it is removed from the mould, having assumed (barring a few finishing touches) the form of the statue. The copper and tin which make bronze are available only in limited quantities from place to place; when melted, bronze can easily be reformed into a new shape—or separated back into its various elements (this is why church bells and even Henry Moore sculptures are sometimes stolen when the price of copper goes up). The story of bronze manufacture in the Renaissance, and earlier too, is one of reuse—a kind of recycling that annihilates the older objects now dissolved and subsumed within the new. In the *Natural History*, Pliny the Elder even contends that pre-used bronze might be better matter than new, and easier to work.[10] Form might be ephemeral, but matter is very much not—bronze can be remade, again and again.

In his study of the medieval bronze object, Ittai Weinryb explains that

> The ability to extract material from older sculpture and to recast it resulted in an ever-changing map of bronzes. We can assume that many medieval bronzes were cast from ancient sculptures that had been melted down to be made anew, while much of the bronze sculpture of the Renaissance was similarly made from medieval bronzes melted down and reused in turn. The biography of the bronze object is therefore embedded in the material rather than in the form. (3)[11]

Weinryb suggests an intriguing possibility: that matter can carry memory (in its "biography") even when form is lost. This creates for bronze a complicated relationship to time. Form is never conserved but matter always is, although its shape can change over and over again. A bronze object does not presume permanence. This is Weinryb's point: bronze itself, as matter, is always multitemporal.[12] Bronze objects were almost always made out of other bronze objects—and, even if they were made from freshly-mined copper and tin, their future iterations of casting and recasting were presumed, and immanent, within their matter. Bronze has a different relationship to time than other materials discussed in this collection. The form of the manuscript fragment that Megan Heffernan describes, for example, has changed through a process of attrition and reuse, rather than through the more wholesale annihilation and reformation that bronze anticipates.

The radical temporalities of bronze come even more sharply into focus when we compare this material with the stone ruin. The European Renaissance was obsessed with ruins—so much so that one recent critic thinks we should rename it the "ruin-naissance" (Hui 1). Ruins (particularly of Rome) show the fallibility of stone, once monumental but now crumbling, ramshackle, and overrun with weeds. The Renaissance's self-conscious "rediscovery" of the antique, including the unearthing of statues and buildings from the ground, brought these ruins into literal and metaphorical focus (Barkan). For late-medieval and Renaissance writers from Petrarch to Du Bellay, Spenser, and beyond, ruins operated as "the material sign that marked the rupture between themselves and classical antiquity" (Hui 2; see also Greene 220–41). Unlike bronze, endlessly remakeable, the stone ruin stood as an object to be apprehended, one which showed the markings of time—perhaps even one by which time might be measured.[13]

Anne Lake Prescott, Kent Hieatt, and Charles Hieatt began a study of the fad for ruins in early modern England, focusing on the adoption of a kind of self-conscious linguistic archaism that they called "Ruinish":

> a lexical force-field made of walls, *tempus edax*, bloody foundations, civil broils, 'ruinate', 'injurious', 'of yore', prideful self-containment, giants, maps, 'wear', 'outworn', 'map', and more. (Prescott 135; see also Hiett)

Spenser, of course, is the main figure for this trend, which uses the mournful sight of ruins to hark back to a particular (and perhaps imagined) English past. But Prescott *et al.* found that Jonson almost never adopted this manner of writing (135). In fact, in *Sejanus*, he did the opposite: Hannah Crawforth has shown how Jonson repeatedly uses English words, in sometimes surprising ways, that expose their Latin roots (for example, "'pietie,' to mean 'dutifull affection', from '*pietas*'"). He does this "in order to show how deeply enmeshed Roman culture – and, implicitly, religion – is in the history of the vernacular" (85). For Crawforth, this is because *Sejanus* is a play that is, in part, reckoning with Jonson's own Roman Catholic experience. But even without that gloss, it is clear that Jonson is modelling a very different kind of etymological exercise to that of the poets who wrote in "Ruinish."

The play's title—*Sejanus His Fall*—is itself a linguistic play on the Latin translation of the noun "fall" as *ruina*. Jonson is hinting at how the destruction of physical monuments lies at the heart of the play, but even here Jonson is interested in the potential of ruin not just as an object but also as a process. The ruin Jonson is interested in is not the old bits of stone lying on the ground, but rather the event of their destruction—their fall. In one of George Chapman's dedicatory poems in the quarto of the play, he describes Jonson's treatment of Sejanus in a way that also emphasises the ongoingness of the latter's moment of disgrace: "he presents thee to all marking states/As if thou hadst been all this while in falling" (ll. 7–8).[14] The gerund here reminds us that the fall is an action which, because this play has been written (and performed) continues to be in progress. We might even think back to the typography in the 1605 quarto that recalled epigraphy—writing on stone which might, in Jonson's time, now litter Rome as ruins. In the playbook of *Sejanus*, though, these ruins are not dead objects: instead, they show writing that is alive— writing that is part of action, and that is intended to be read.

When Jonson was interested in the stone ruin, it was—as with Horace—as a foil for his own writing. In paratexts to the printed editions of the play Jonson (and the writers of other paratextual material) seems to refer back to the Ode, and in particular to the discourse of the ruin. In a presentation copy of the 1605 quarto which Jonson gave to Sir Robert Townsend, he writes a brief note in manuscript to his "noble friend": Jonson's "affection" for Townsend will, he promises, "remayne wth him, & last beyond Marble."[15] And in his printed dedicatory epistle to Esmé Stuart, Lord Aubigny, in the 1616 Folio, Jonson writes that "If ever any ruin were so great as to survive, I think this be one I send you: *The Fall of Sejanus*" (Jonson "To the No Less Noble"). Jonson is referring back to that pun on *ruina* (fall), but also making it clear that his play is durable, and will stand for ever.

Destruction and Remaking

Jonson is concerned with the poles of past and future, but he also attempts to record the moments (the fall; the process of writing) in which memory might itself be created, or destroyed. In Act 5, he calls attention to the moment of destruction of one of the statues raised to Sejanus. The equivalence of humans and statues comes to a climax in this part of the play: the life-sized bronzes of Sejanus that have stood throughout Rome are destroyed, subjected to literal falls, just like Sejanus's metaphorical one.[16] In a report to some assembled senators, the equestrian soldier (and sometime follower of Sejanus) Terentius describes how the angry crowds "tear [...] down" the statues:

> Then fastening ropes, [the multitudes] drag them along the
>   streets,
> Crying in scorn, 'This, this was that rich head
> Was crowned with garlands and with odours, this
> That was in Rome so reverenced! Now
> The furnace and the bellows shall to work,
> The great Sejanus crack, and piece by piece
> Drop i'the founder's pit. (5.752–58)

The passage is a kind of blazon: the statue is made piecemeal, first by the singling out of its "rich head," then in the description of its near future, in which the statue will drop "piece by piece." Those repeated deictics—"This, this"; "this"—force us to imagine the immediacy of the destructive action even as we encounter it at a remove, in this reported statement. The statue destroyed reflects Sejanus himself, described a few lines later, whose body is broken into so many pieces that he is "Now torn and scattered, as he needs no grave;/Each little dust covers a little part./So he lies nowhere, and yet often buried" (5.812–14). This report marks the culmination of the concordances in the play between Sejanus the man and Sejanus the statue, and the blazon is made literal in the fragmentation (and then destruction) of both bronze and real body.

The wholesale destruction of this statue reflects the Roman practice of what Harriet Flower calls "memory sanctions." The Roman culture of memory (*memoria*) was tightly policed (Chalk 390–93). Total oblivion was assumed to be the norm for most people who were deemed to be ephemeral parts of society. The culture of commemoration carefully preserved and curated the memory of those few chosen to be remembered, but the tide could turn. Memory sanctions were, Flower explains, "analogous to [...] exile": that is, just as an unwanted person could be forced to leave the territory, their memory could also be excised from the communal consciousness (Flower 5; 172–74).[17] This is what happens to Sejanus.

We return in this moment of the play to Jonson's interest not only in the fact of oblivion but also in the processes of exactly how these memory sanctions were achieved. Jonson makes much of the moment of the statue falling and the bronze melting, as well as the equipment and processes of the foundry: the furnace, the bellows, and the pit. He is concerned throughout his work with processes of manufacture, craft, and artisanship, even if he is sometimes concerned to distance himself from them. Laurie Ellinghausen teases out the "relationship between Jonson's reliance on metaphors of labor and the disdain for laborers that so frequently emerges in his writing": a contradiction personified in the complex figure of Vulcan (who is frequently referred to in Jonson's works) (65).[18] If we return to the report of statue destruction, we see that Jonson emphasises not so much the labourers but rather the apparatus of making and unmaking. The apparatus of the foundry seems to be automated, the furnace and bellows going unaided "to work." "[T]hey," the crowd, had been dragging the statue, but now everything happens without human agency—the founder is only mentioned as the owner of the pit, not as someone who actually does something here.[19] We are asked to focus on the means and machinery by which metal can lose its form.

This moment reflects a wider concern in Jonson's work with how artisanal processes might be analogues for the work of reading and writing. Jonson returned over and over to the comparison of poetry and metalworking although, as Anthony Miller argues, he didn't resolve the tension between the hard labour of the blacksmith's work and the easy *sprezzatura* of the natural poet (59). Instead Jonson focussed on being in the middle of making. *"Poesy,"* he writes in *Timber; or, Discoveries*, "is his [the poet's] skill, or Crafte of making [...] these three voices differ, as the thing done, the doing, and the doer; [...] so the *Poeme*, the *Poesy*, and the *Poet*" (579).[20] By separating out these three terms Jonson asks us to think carefully about each in turn. In the passage above from *Sejanus* Jonson asks us to focus on his middle term: not the maker, and not the thing done, or final product, but the doing. The passage from Act V draws heavily on Jonson's source, Juvenal (on whom more below), but the final line—the description of how the statue "Drop[s] i'the founder's pit"—is Jonson's innovation. His emphasis is on the moment of unmaking; the craft at work here is the fragmentation and dissolution of existing matter, ready for a new form.

In Jonson's writing of the story, the statue is destroyed—and we hear no more about it, other than as a comparison to the scattered body of Sejanus himself. But in Jonson's source, the bronze is recycled. The description of the statue's destruction is borrowed from Juvenal's Satire 10:

> Some people are toppled by their power, object of great envy, some are sunk by their long and glorious roll of honours. Down their statues come, dragged by a rope [...] Now the flames are hissing, now that head idolised by the people is glowing from the bellows and furnace: huge Sejanus is crackling. Then the face that was number two in the whole world is turned into little jugs, basins, frying pans, and chamber pots. (Satire 10, ll. 57–65)

> Quosdam praecipitat subiecta potentia magnae
> invidiae, mergit longa atque insignis honorum
> pagina. descendunt statuae restemque secuntur,
> ipsas deinde rotas bigarum inpacta securis
> caedit et inmeritis franguntur crura caballis.
> iam strident ignes, iam follibus atque caminis
> ardet adoratum populo caput et crepat ingens
> Seianus, deinde ex facie toto orbe secunda
> fiunt urceoli, pelves, sartago, matellae.

The transformation from monumental artwork to pot to piss in is of course a comment on Sejanus's disgrace. But it also makes us think about matter and about form. The bronze that made the statue is, after its dissolution, available to be reformed into this catalogue of "little" household objects; the matter is neatly reworked and recycled, with nothing going to waste. A durable monument is transformed into these quotidian objects—objects whose form indicates that they are more ephemeral than the statue, even though they are made of the very same matter.

What are we to make of Jonson's moment of unmaking in *Sejanus*, and of the omission of the source material's end of this story? Why doesn't Jonson have his statue recycled into Juvenal's pots and pans? One reason might be generic: Juvenal is writing a satire, but frying pans have no place in a tragedy. Further, the play is interested in the process of Sejanus's fall but not really in what happens next, so this gesture towards the objects' afterlife isn't appropriate. Thinking in terms of genre is important, and these ideas help us to read this moment: however, they miss out some of the aspects of the play that stray away from the language of tragedy.

There are moments of humour in this passage. When the statue is just about to fall into the pit, we hear that "The great Sejanus [shall] crack" (5.757).[21] This is, to be sure, the sound of the statue breaking up. But that "crack" speaks to other plays by Jonson, too, in which cracks signal both fireworks and farts: ephemeral, sensory, entertaining things.[22] Think of *The Alchemist* (1610), for example, which is full of farts and fireworks ("crackers in a puppet-play," for example) and in which the cracks operate as a soundtrack to the decidedly comic action of the play (Jonson, *Alchemist* 1.2.79).

In *Sejanus* the "crack," the fart, strengthens even further the association of the bronze body with the human one. And when we look a bit closer, we see that cracks run through *Sejanus*—at least in its first two acts. Arruntius declares that Romans will "Crack the world,/And bruise the name of Romans into dust" before they allow a statue of Sejanus in Pompey's theatre; Drusus, Tiberius's son, warns Sejanus that he will "crack those [his] sinews" that are swollen with pride. Sejanus uses the word, too: he proclaims to Drusus that he will "Crack" Tiberius's house "in the flame of my incensed rage," and later that the "steep fall" he plans for Caius Silius will "give the weightier crack," and terrify more thoroughly his many other potential enemies (1.545–56; 1.573; 1.147–48; 2.291–92). These examples anticipate quite precisely the final crack, of the statue in the pit; but by thinking across genres they also suggest something scatological, even funny, running along through this tragic play.

And although Terentius doesn't report what happens next to the statue, Juvenal's little jugs and pots are not absent from *Sejanus*, because Jonson scatters textual hints to them throughout. Tiberius is described as being "carried like a pitcher, by the ears," for example—this is a proverbial phrase that suggests someone being easily led, but also prepares us for the idea that people and cooking implements might be closer together than we think (1.418). Trenchers are also used to signal relations, this time of service and sex: Arruntius claims to have known Sejanus when he was a serving boy "at Caius' trencher" (1.213), that is, when he prostituted himself to Apicius. And finally, Juvenal's "chamber pots" ("*matellae*") are implied, if not actually mentioned, when Silius describes how Sejanus's flatterers are "ready to praise/His Lordship if he spit, or but piss fair,/Have an indifferent stool, or break wind well;/Nothing can 'scape their catch" (1.38–41). By being a careful and knowledgeable reader, as the marginal notes teach us to do, we are able to find hints to the source texts throughout the play.

Juvenal is also a referent for the many, many references to faces in the play (Cain counts 26, l.213, n.). Sejanus's face, *"deinde ex facie toto orbe secunda"* ('then the face that was number two in the whole world') is the last body part that Juvenal mentions in Satire 10 when the statue drops into the pit. Jonson doesn't include this line in Terentius's report of statue destruction in Act 5, though it's paraphrased in the "head [...] That was in Rome so reverenced" (5.753, 755). But this line does appear elsewhere in the play, when in Act 1 Sabinus describes how Sejanus, "the second face of the whole world" is now "reared equal with Tiberius" (1.217, 219).[23] The parts from Juvenal's satire that Jonson does not quote in Act V's report of statue destruction are present, sometimes verbatim and sometimes more obliquely, throughout the play. These textual references are scattered, so that the tissue of the playtext imitates the dissolved, fractured body parts of the statue and the man himself.

There are lots and lots of proleptic hints of the moment of melting, then, especially in Acts I and II. Jonson is alluding to the re-makeable qualities of bronze, using the processes of making with this metal as a subtle analogue for his humanist playwriting. The act of reformation on which Jonson wants us to focus is not the founder's recycling into pots, but his own patchwork play-writing of *Sejanus*, particularly in its printed form: his own play is a new form made from old material. If my references to the play here have been bitty, that's because the play itself demands this kind of reading. *Sejanus* asks us, at least in the 1605 quarto, to read across the marginalia as well as the play text, to hold ideas in mind and to knit together our references while, or after, reading. This kind of work is piecemeal—*laboured*, even—a kind of reading that mirrors the way in which the many marginal notes show the detailed, painstaking process of Jonson's own making, pointing us towards the materials and processes of the creation of the play.[24] The hyper-referential printed quarto of *Sejanus* absorbs Roman history, satire, poetry, and more into its English dramatic verse. The furnace, with its processes of dissolution and reformation—as well as the processes of melting and moulding more generally—is a model for this kind of work.[25]

More Lasting than Bronze

There was not much mention, in the statue debates of 2020, of the suggestion that we might melt down the bronze statues and remake them into new shapes.[26] Nonetheless, the statue destruction and removal in our moment has shown us several different ways to get rid of public sculpture. Colston was rolled to the harbour, then thrown in (even though he was later recovered in order to be displayed, wearing his graffiti, in a museum). In 2017, a bronze statue of a Confederate soldier in Durham, NC, was pulled down by ropes which, in a sign of its poor quality, caused it to be crumpled like a Coke can. We also saw the organised and state-sanctioned removal of statues by people in hard hats, driving machinery. The statue of Confederate General Robert E. Lee in Richmond, Virginia had to be dismantled first: workers took angle grinders to his torso and separated his body into parts before it was lifted up by mobile cranes and taken away on a procession of trucks. This moment of statue destruction was carefully planned, rather than a spontaneous outburst, but the similarities with Jonson's Sejanus are striking nonetheless.

Amongst all these removals of stone and bronze, Horace's Ode continues to resonate through our current moment. There's even a quotation from the poem in one of the spaces contested by the Black Lives Matter protests. Above a door in Cecil Rhodes House, Oxford, reads the inscription: "Non Omnis Moriar" ('I shall not wholly die'). The inscription encircles a relief of the Matopos mountains in Zimbabwe, where Cecil Rhodes himself is buried. The whole of Rhodes House, like the hated statue to Rhodes at Oriel College down the road, is a monument to this man and his racist, imperialist project. In this inscription, Horace is put to work as a threat: even if the stone statue of him in Oxford does eventually fall, as other statues of him in South Africa have already, Rhodes himself will endure.

Horace teaches us that in order to judge what is ephemeral, we need also to understand what is durable. The persistence, or fragility, of a particular material might in fact not be a good indicator of how long it will last: we need also to decide which timescales we're thinking with. The essays in this collection all suggest, in different but complementary ways, that if we want to define ephemera we must always think perspectivally. That is, we have to attend to questions of scale if we want to determine what is fleeting and what lasts. The life of a fly includes the whole of history if we can look at it from the perspective of that fly; on the other hand even solid, stable materials like stone will, if we take a long enough view, reveal themselves to be evanescent after all. Early modern ephemera forces us to consider these variable senses of time: both on contemporary terms, and from our vantage point in the future in which we are living, now. For all the period's interest in the present and the future, it always had one eye on the past (and particularly the classical past), too: this is nowhere clearer than in *Sejanus*. In this play, Jonson draws attention to the moments of a change of state or form and, in so doing, urges us to think about the processes through which memory (or oblivion) is created. Re-makeable bronze, or iterative and commonplacing humanism, might prolong or even re-create the lives of the textual and material objects on which they focus. Jonson envisions for posterity, then, a monument that is flexible: one that may not stand like a pyramid, but rather incorporates parts of the past, reforged in the present.

Notes

1 Thank you to the members of the 2019 SAA seminar on Waste, and especially Lara Dodds and Helen Hull for their feedback on an early version of this chapter; thank you too to the editors of and contributors to the present volume, for all their really generative comments and conversation. I am grateful to the librarians of The Queen's College, University of Oxford (and particularly to Tessa Shaw) for their patience; without their help, I would not have had the materials with which to write this chapter.
2 This dedication appears in the Folio only, not the 1605 Quarto.
3 Holger Schott Syme outlines the critical attention to the literary and humanist qualities of the quarto, and proposes some new avenues for its relevance to theatre historians. Cain outlines Jonson's detailed engagements with contemporary classical scholarship in ("Introduction" 207).
4 On how Jonson's Tacitean model and historical bent in this play was received in the contemporary political sphere see Worden.
5 This research shows, Kuhn argues, "Jonson's interest not just in the texts of the ancient world, but in the materiality of ancient religious practice" (80). Chalk comments on a similar topic: Jonson's interest in triumphal arches and other decorations for James's triumphal entry into London in 1604 (387–88).
6 Jonson's marginal note is to *Annales* 4.37, 38. For Shakespeare's possible involvement, see Cain ("Introduction" 197).
7 This translation is from Cain's note to I.454; the Latin is "*Haec mihi in animis vestris templa, hae pulcherrimae effigies et mansurae. Nam quae saxo struuntur, si iudicium posterorum in odium vertit, pro sepulchris spernuntur*" (Tacitus, *Annals* 66).
8 Bronze is a mixture of copper and tin; brass a mixture of copper and zinc. Early modern English did not yet have the word bronze, which was borrowed from Romance languages in the eighteenth century. The distinction between brass and bronze is somewhat misleading, however: in many cases, analysis of ancient (and later) bronzes show that sculptures were often made up of a larger mixture of metals than just these ones. This was in part due to the frequent reuse of old metal, which already contained other substances.
9 For a comprehensive discussion of the processes of making bronze sculpture see Motture and, on techniques of Roman bronze sculpture in particular, Mattusch.
10 "Sequens temperatura statuaria est eademque tabularis hoc modo: massa proflatur in primis, mox in proflatum additur tertia portio aeris collectanei, hoc est ex usu coempti. peculiare in eo condimentum attritu domiti et consuetudine nitoris veluti mansuefacti."

> The proper blend for making statues is as follows, and the same for tablets: at the outset the ore is melted, and then there is added to the melted metal a third part of scrap copper, that is copper or bronze that has been bought up after use. This contains a peculiar seasoned quality of brilliance that has been subdued by friction and so to speak tamed by habitual use.

> (Pliny, 34.97–98)

11 Weinryb, *The Bronze Object in the Middle Ages* (Cambridge: Cambridge University Press, 2016), 3.

12 On questions of polychronicity and the anachronic see Nagel and Wood; Harris.

13 This is not to say that stone ruins weren't themselves reused: stone from ruined castles and abbeys in England was used to build new walls and houses, for example.

14 Chapman wrote dedicatory poems to both the quarto and folio versions of the play, and may even have had a hand in its composition (see Cain, "Introduction" 198).

15 Manuscript notation to the titlepage of the 1605 quarto: large-paper presentation copy; four copies of this type survive. This copy is in the British Library, Ashley 3464, which is the version of the quarto that is digitised on *Early English Books Online*. See *Sejanus*'s quarto titlepage printed in Cain's edition (211).

16 Roman statuary could be bronze or marble, but it's clear that these statues are of brass, or bronze.

17 The phrase '*damnatio memoriae*' is sometimes used to describe these processes, but this term is first recorded only in 1689 (see Omissi 171).

18 Laurie Ellinghausen, *Labor and Writing in Early Modern England, 1567–1667* (Aldershot: Ashgate, 2008), 63–92, at 65.

19 It's important to note that this scene of unmaking is reported, not staged—in fact it is doubly reported, because in this speech Terentius is reporting what the "eager multitude" (l.741) have been screaming in the streets. For examples of scenes of unmaking on stage, for example in Greene's *Friar Bacon and Friar Bungay*, see Porter, and on *Sejanus* specifically, 130–31.

20 It is Jonson's adaptation of a section from Jacobus Pontanus, *Poetatum institutionem libri tres* (Ingolstadt, 1594).

21 Juvenal uses "*crepat*," perhaps better translated as "crackles," but related to one of the Latin words for fart; Juvenal uses crepitum in Satire 3.108. Jonson (perhaps picking up on the Latin *crepitus*) chooses to translate it as "crack[s]."

22 Thanks to the other contributors to this volume, and especially Bruce Boehrer, Callan Davies, and William Tullett for their ideas about these ephemeral things.

23 In the quarto (and replicated in the Cambridge edition, 248, n.39), Jonson provides a marginal reference here to Juvenal's Satire 10.63.

24 Laurie Ellinghausen teases out the kinds of labour, and labouredness, that we find in Jonson's work, and helpfully warns us against a straightforward association of Jonson with labour versus Shakespeare with "'natural' wit and 'fancy'" (63).

25 Jonson builds here on the tradition of *ut pictura poiesis* to make sculptural process an analogue to, rather than competitor of, poetic craft. On metaphors of forge vs furnace in Jonson, see Miller (62).

26 Note, however, the community project "Swords and Plowshares" (2022–26) which plans to melt down the statue of Robert E. Lee, formerly in a public park in Charlottesville, Virginia, and turn the bronze into new artworks.

Works Cited

Barkan, Leonard. *Unearthing the Past*. Yale UP, 1999.

Boehrer, Bruce. "Time's Flies: Ephemerality in the Early Modern Insect World." *Practices of Ephemera in Early Modern England*. Eds Callan Davies, Hannah Lilley, and Catherine Richardson. Routledge, 2023. 44–64.

Bourne, Claire L. M. *Typographies of Performance in Early Modern England.* Oxford UP, 2020.

Cain, Tom. "Introduction." *Sejanus.* Ed. Tom Cain. *The Cambridge Edition of the Works of Ben Jonson*, Vol. 2. Eds David Bevington, Martin Butler, and Ian Donaldson. Cambridge UP, 2012. 197–209.

———. "*Sejanus*: Textual Essay." *The Cambridge Edition of the Works of Ben Jonson.* Eds David Bevington, Martin Butler, and Ian Donaldson. Online. Accessed 22 Oct. 2021.

Chalk, Brian Patrick. "Jonson's Textual Monument." *SEL* 52.2 (2012): 387–405.

Chapman, George. ["Come forth, Sejanus"]. *The Cambridge Edition of the Works of Ben Jonson*, Vol. 2. Cambridge UP, 2012. 224.

Crawforth, Hannah. *Etymology and the Invention of English in Early Modern Literature.* Cambridge UP, 2013.

Davies, Callan. "Playing Apples and the Playhouse Archive." *Practices of Ephemera in Early Modern England.* Eds Callan Davies, Hannah Lilley, and Catherine Richardson. Routledge, 2023. 191–209.

Ellinghausen, Laurie. *Labor and Writing in Early Modern England, 1567–1667.* Ashgate, 2008. 63–92.

Flower, Harriet I. *The Art of Forgetting: Disgrace and Oblivion in Roman Political Culture.* U of North Carolina P, 2011.

Greene, Thomas. *The Light in Troy.* Yale UP, 1983.

Harris, Jonathan Gil. *Untimely Matter in the Time of Shakespeare.* U of Pennsylvania P, 2009.

Heffernan, Megan. "Expired Time: Archiving Waste Manuscripts." *Practices of Ephemera in Early Modern England.* Eds Callan Davies, Hannah Lilley, and Catherine Richardson. Routledge, 2023. 21–24.

Hieatt, A. Kent. "The Genesis of Shakespeare's Sonnets: Spenser's Ruins of Rome: by Bellay." *PMLA* 98.5 (1983): 800–14.

Horace. "Ode 3.30." *Odes and Epodes.* Ed. and trans. Niall Rudd. Harvard UP, 2004. 216–17.

Hui, Andrew. *The Poetics of Ruins in Renaissance Literature.* Fordham UP, 2017.

Kuhn, John. "*Sejanus*, The King's Men Altar Scenes, and the Theatrical Production of Paganism." *Early Theatre* 20.1 (2017): 77–98.

Kunin, Aaron. "Shakespeare's Preservation Fantasy." *PMLA* 124.1 (2009): 92–106.

Jonson, Ben. *The Alchemist. The Cambridge Edition of the Works of Ben Jonson*, Vol. 3. Eds David Bevington, Martin Butler, and Ian Donaldson. Cambridge UP, 2012.

———. *Sejanus.* Ed. Tom Cain. *The Cambridge Edition of the Works of Ben Jonson*, Vol. 2. Eds David Bevington, Martin Butler, and Ian Donaldson. Cambridge UP, 2012.

———. *Timber; or, Discoveries.* Ed. Lorna Hutson. *The Cambridge Edition of the Works of Ben Jonson.* Vol. 7. Eds David Bevington, Martin Butler, and Ian Donaldson. Cambridge UP, 2012.

———. "To the No Less Noble by Virtue than Blood Esmé, Lord Aubigny." *The Cambridge Edition of the Works of Ben Jonson*, Vol. 2. Eds David Bevington, Martin Butler, and Ian Donaldson. Cambridge UP, 2012. 212.

Juvenal. *Juvenal and Persius.* Ed and trans. Susanna Morton Braund. Loeb Classical Library 91. Harvard UP, 2004. 371.

Mattusch, Carol. "Bronzes." *The Oxford Handbook of Roman Sculpture.* Eds Elise A. Friedland and Melanie Grunow Sobocinski. Oxfordd UP, 2015. 139–54.

Miller, Anthony. "Ben Jonson and 'the Proper Passion of Mettalls.'" *Parergon* 23:2 (2006): 57–72.

Motture, Peta. *The Culture of Bronze.* V&A Publications, 2019.

Moul, Victoria. *Jonson, Horace and the Classical Tradition.* Cambridge UP, 2006.

Nagel, Alexander and Christopher Wood. *Anachronic Renaissance.* Zone, 2010.

Omissi, Adrastos. "Damnatio memoriae or creatio memoriae? Memory Sanctions as Creative Processes in the Fourth Century AD." *The Cambridge Classical Journal.* 62 (2016): 170–99.

Pliny the Elder. *Natural History*, Vol. 9: Books 33–35. Trans. H. Rackham. Loeb Classical Library 394. Harvard UP, 1952.

Porter, Chloe. *Making and Unmaking in Early Modern English Drama.* Manchester UP, 2013.

Prescott, Anne Lake. "Du Bellay and Shakespeare's Sonnets." *The Oxford Handbook of Shakespeare's Poetry.* Ed. Jonathan Post. Oxford UP, 2013. 134–50.

Syme, Holger. "Unediting the Margin: Jonson, Marston, and the Theatrical Page." *ELR* 38.1 (2008): 142–71.

Tacitus. *Annals: Books 4–6, 11–12.* Trans. John Jackson. Loeb Classical Library 312. Harvard UP, 1937.

Tullett, Will. "Extensive Ephemera: Perfumer's Trade Cards in Eighteenth-Century England." *Practices of Ephemera in Early Modern England.* Eds Callan Davies, Hannah Lilley, and Catherine Richardson. Routledge, 2023. 210–28.

Weinryb, Ittai. *The Bronze Object in the Middle Ages.* Cambridge UP, 2016.

Worden, Blair. "Jonson Among the Historians." *Culture and Politics in Early Stuart England.* Eds Kevin Sharpe and Peter Lake. Macmillan, 1994. 67–89.

8 Uncovering Ephemeral Practice

Itineraries of Black Ink and the Experiments of Thomas Davis

Hannah Lilley

Black ink is inscribed upon almost every early modern textual substrate, where it appears dry, sometimes shining, brown, holey, or shadowed by halos (Blake; Manso et al.). The substance was used for recording information to be remembered or for temporary reference, and a great deal of work went into producing well-balanced inks that lasted without corroding the surface they marked (Banik). Early modern writers used ink as a metaphor for preservation – like Shakespeare, in Sonnet 63, who imagined the "black lines" of his verse would conserve the beauty of his subject "still green" before "confounding age's cruel knife" came and "filled his brow/ With lines and wrinkles" (Sonnet 63; Mitchell M. Harris). Ink, with its memorialising textual or pictorial function, might therefore seem a strange subject for a volume on *ephemera*. Yet, when the substance is considered materially, it fits the definition of "ephemeral": it is a "transitory thing" in the sense that it does not survive as a liquid, whose natural components (commonly: gum arabic, oak galls and copperas) decayed over time, and for which the process of making was an ephemeral practice. Like many pieces in this volume, this chapter is concerned with textual objects but, rather than taking paper as the central focus, it looks beyond the substrate and into the components of ink as a writing aid.[1] This contribution therefore considers the extra-textual to expand our conception of written ephemera to encompass the material culture of ink before, and at the time of, its use on paper, to consider what its making tells us about domestic movements and material engagements. It converses with those chapters that focus on transitory materials, like Katherine Hunt's on brass, Callan Davies' on apples, and William Tullett's on smell: it concerns objects (natural and manmade) which metamorphose in form or purpose in their lifetimes.

This chapter seeks to uncover the "itineraries" of ink and its making, rooted in Pamela Smith's "material complex" – the resulting object that arises from "materials, techniques and ideas as they travel across geographic and epistemic space" (31). I consider together the passing actions, tools, and ingredients that went into making ink domestically

DOI: 10.4324/9781003058588-11

in early modern England and the wider significance of these consumption practices through the manuscript recipes of one Thomas Davis, who recorded his ink-making experiments during the first half of the seventeenth century. This method is in line with Rosemary Joyce and Susan Gillespie's argument that itineraries are "complex" object biographies which are formed out of: "the strings of places where objects come to rest or are active, the routes through which things circulate, and the means by which they are moved." These itineraries are "singular, multiple, virtual and real," and have "no real beginning other than where we enter them and no end, since things and their extensions continue to move" (3). I therefore centre the multi-dimensional mobility of things: the physical connections between makers, matter, and substances, or, in Davis' case, between his body, the equipment, the ingredients and his resulting ink. By uncovering the itineraries of early modern ink-making, Davis' subjective practices are connected to global material networks such as the trade in gum arabic and domestic utensils, and his identity as a middling, literate man emerges from a web of actions and things attached to his ink-making. This chapter therefore provides a new material perspective on a substance usually studied as text to consider how its ingredients and processes of making were connected to Davis's identity.

In order to approach these itineraries of things and actions, I first explore how the fleeting activities of making using Davis's writing can be interpreted and then move into an investigation of the interrelated matter that formed black ink. I use textual, material, and practice research evidence for the ingredients and tools Davis deployed to uncover stories of making and consumption and allow access to experiential object itineraries. Writing, materials, and making are tied together to think about what their connections suggest about Davis's identity as he constructs it in his manuscript. In this way, it is possible to explore the meanings and selves that emerge in relation to ingredients, tools, space, and making. By uncovering Davis's processes of consumption all the way from ink-making to the practice's expression of his social identity, I consider the "questions of scale, focus and perspective" that Tara Hamling and Catherine Richardson describe as "particularly important" to the study of material culture "because of the significance and complexity of the relationship between public and private activities in our period" (2016, 4). Domestic making practices drew on broader "public" activities of trade and textual engagement, and so Davis participates in a materially engaged self-situation practice, using many materials and techniques that have ephemeral lives.

Using a practice research methodology alongside an itineraries approach to Davis's recipes, tools and ingredients allows me to experiment with the possibilities for experiencing and capturing in writing ephemeral movements and things, and therefore to mirror Davis's process. Making enabled Davis's recordkeeping, and the two were inextricably linked; the material text gestured to his artisanal expertise. By deploying this approach, I draw upon the anthropological insight of Tim Ingold who describes practice as "knowing *from the inside*" where knowledge is developed "in the course of direct, practical and sensuous engagements with our surroundings" (*Making* 5). By following the processes Davis wrote down, the hope was to *know* what actions Davis completed whilst making ink, their temporal and sensual qualities, and to think through how these related to writing. In this reading, then, Davis's ink recipes are considered as entwined with domestic practices that reached out into a wider world of ephemeral things and passing actions through which he crafted a literate identity by codifying his making in writing.

Making and Writing Black Ink: Thomas Davis in Context

I take evidence for Davis's ink-making from a notebook he compiled, at intervals, over four decades which falls into a genre of manuscript known as the miscellany due to the fact that it contains texts on a variety of subjects without a clear sense of order to later readers (Vine; Eckhardt and Smith, eds). A title "liber academae" suggests the original educational purpose of the manuscript, which may have been started at grammar school, where students were recommended to keep "paper books" in which to record information (Davis 78v, p. 48).[2] The evolutionary nature of Davis' writing, however, means that although the content began with Latin Sententiae, he later compiled practical knowledge from ephemeris tables (calendars usually containing "astrological or meteorological predictions" often found in almanacs), card games, instructions for perfuming gloves, political poetry and ink recipes.[3] Like the itinerant object, which has no clear beginning or end, Davis' writing confounds a chronological reading, but his records, which have a particular mnemonic emphasis on processes, were perhaps inspired by the kind of advice touted in conduct literature that encouraged men to keep daily memoranda. Richard Brathwaite describes these as "ephemeris" or "evening accounts" and suggests that they were essential to the establishment of a gentlemanly identity, and Henry Cockeram's dictionary defines them as "day books" (Brathwaite 225; Cockeram). Ephemerides were connected to the transitory passage of time measured by days and writing's role in defying this movement by setting information into tangible memories for the future. The passing significance of the text Davis compiled, and the way it is described as containing "miscellaneous matters of very little importance" on the British Library's online catalogue, adds to the sense of this text as engaging with ephemera on multiple levels: both in its recordkeeping of fleeting processes and in its construction (Lansdowne MS 674).

One problem with interpreting Davis's ink-making practice is navigating the gap between his language and his experience. Work on early modern recipes has highlighted this difficulty, with Sara Pennell pointing out the lack of food deposits on these manuscripts and how it "make[s] one wonder whether men and women ever actually wrote [...] these books in the early modern kitchen" – demonstrating an issue with situating these texts in space as well as in relation to action (225). Looking beyond the verbal when approaching manuscripts about material processes is tricky when words function at a remove from the process they describe. Recent approaches to recipes have, however, equalised writing and other making processes. Wendy Wall has connected writing to "kitchen literacy" arguing that "manuscript recipe collections [...] reveal tactile forms of writing taking place across different media in the home," both having the status of "crafts" (Wall 387; see also Smith on vermillion). When interpreting Davis's practice, fortunately, the material evidence of his ink on the page as well as his description survives, creating a tangible result that lends itself to an "itineraries" approach by which we can explore the material traces of his stylus, his words and the broader narratives surrounding his equipment and ingredients and their functions in his making spaces. Although the ink no longer holds the lustre of fresh inscription, it is still present.

Davis's descriptions of ink-making are of varying lengths and detail throughout his manuscript, but all were made domestically. This is clear from allusions to his home, for example: "when ye sun is direct in ye chamber window it is just half an hower past 10 of ye clock" (1v [parchment]). Davis' recipes, then, although usually short, would have functioned within a dynamic domestic backdrop. One of the briefest reads:

> The 11th of March 1625
> I made inke with a pint
> of woort 2 oz of Galls
> 1 oz of Copperas (78r, p. 46)

From a short list like this, it is very difficult to get a sense of Davis's process: how did he mix these ingredients? With what equipment? What was the purpose of writing this down? The note may have acted as a memorandum of the quantities of ingredients needed or, when read alongside an observation in another recipe, it may have been a means of testing out the resulting ink. For example, on the 16 December 1630, Davis wrote that "before it was quite cold that night I put in a quarter of an oz of gum arabick & stired it togather which being dissolved it color[ed] thus" (78v, p. 48; most of this recipe is missing). This note suggests that the purpose of Davis' writing was to test the colour and quality of the ink he produced.

Unlike other early modern ink recipe writers, Davis rarely suggests heating the mixture, meaning that his usual process had to be lengthy enough to allow the substance to thicken. The standard procedure he used was to break down the galls into pieces and place them in wort or rainwater for three days, to add the copperas and let stand for another three days, stirring at intervals with a stick, and then to add the gum arabic and leave for a few more days before using. Although this might seem very explicit, there is little clear information on his different domestic movements beyond the ingredients he used. As such, there are gaps, or absences, that fall between Davis's words, which suggest that a certain degree of what has been called "tacit knowledge" went into the making of ink – "we know more than we can tell" (Polanyi 5). By recovering Davis's practices, this chapter recovers a sense of the immaterial, which Morgan Meyer has defined as "something that is made to exist through relations that give absence matter" and "performed, textured and materialised through relations and processes". Recipes are textual traces of an absent substance, or, in Davis's case, one that would have resulted in a liquid, not the words as they now appear. So by tracing Davis's practices through the materials he does mention, some substance and depth can be given to the absences that surround his listed ingredients and actions. This approach results in an understanding of the labour involved in ink production and considerations of the meanings carried by ingredients, objects, and processes and therefore illustrates Davis's writing experience beyond the moment he put quill to paper.

Davis was far from alone in writing down ink recipes, and methods of making black ink were common in early modern manuscripts and printed texts. Most of these recipes contain three core ingredients: galls ("excrescence produced on trees [...] by [...] gall wasps," "Galls," n.3 *OED*), copperas (iron II sulphate), gum arabic (binds the ink to paper), and a liquid like wine, beer, aqua vitae or water. There was occasional variation in this, with galls sometimes substituted with types of bark – even "pomegranate bark" – or lampblack used in substitution for the chemical reaction between the galls and copperas, which created the black colour (see, i.e. Sloane 1203). Printed examples often provided qualitative judgements of "good ink," but were prescriptive rather than reflective of individual practice, with advice like John Brinsley's in *Ludus Literarius* that ink should be "thin, blacke and cleere" (29). Many manuscript recipes do, however, provide evidence of correction and adaption, with, for example, Roger Twysden of Kent copying some ink recipes in 1615 and 1626 along with changes to make them fit for his own hand; writing "yf it write not black enough *th*e want is in *th*e galls" and "ink made of water is apt to freeze" but "wyne [...] never will" (1r, 4r). Twysden's itinerate process, where adaptations were made after his making attempts, demonstrates how flexibly basic ink components were used by makers to make ink that suited their own writing style and needs.

Experimentation with ink recipes was a practice of self-expression, precisely because it was not necessary for individuals to make their own ink, as it was available for purchase in stationers' shops, through itinerant sellers, and at marketplaces.[4] Although Adrian Johns has argued that before the mid-seventeenth century there was little evidence for an ink-making industry with makers, particularly printers, wanting to keep recipes secret, it is clear from account books across various geographical locations and writing spaces – from households to corporations and to parishes – that individuals and institutions bought ink for handwriting as a ready-made substance (105). To choose to make ink at home was to create a tailored material to form a liquid more suited to a writer's needs than that which was available to purchase (Daybell 38).

Davis's ink recipes are particularly important for understanding his individual experience of making and self-fashioning because they were written in the first person, using the freshly made ink, along with a date and his signature: for example, "This ink was made ye 11th March 1625" (78r, p. 46). By signing his recipes, Davis reinforced the relationship between writing, the self and his making processes, providing both a verbal and material record of his ink-making where the reader might judge the success of the recipe from its appearance on the page (DiMeo and Pennell 11). By recording processes of interest to him and by reflecting on his ink-making practices, Davis situated himself within a social context of individuals who marked their identities in writing. Through his compiled content, he also established himself as a man with leisure time to pursue interests like perfuming, brewing, poetry, card games, and ink-making. Seen through Adam Smyth's understanding of commonplace books as writings that "reveal the degree to which a compiler's identity was [...] formulated [...] through a process of alignment with other figures, narratives and events," Davis framed his identity as a man interested in the leisure pursuits of those who perhaps shared his social status (156). Although it is difficult to form a clear biography of Davis, the compilation of a poem in Somerset dialect perhaps suggests he was resident there – his name was very common in North Somerset and Bristol – and his interest in malt-making, his copying down of a legal document relating to a field, and a recipe for horse medicine, perhaps suggest that he was of at least comfortably middling status and potentially a yeoman (Lilley, Chapter 4).[5]

Davis's making took place over many years and was recorded at intervals. Indeed, it would not be surprising if the recipes he recorded only represent a small number of those he tried, as ink-making was borne out of repeated practice to generate knowledge of the craft.[6] Writing was a process secondary to the practical, artisanal, fleeting moments of making in which Davis partook. An inscription in his homemade ink therefore gives access to a world of associations, embodied actions, and material-spatial understandings; the tangible material trace that can be read in his manuscript is linked to the intangible and ephemeral matter from which it emerged. In this sense, ink can be seen in Jonathan Gil Harris' terms as "a complex polychronic assemblage of material *agents*" – a "palimpsest" that constantly refers outwards to ephemeral actions and the domestic consumables utilised by Davis (17). This palimpsest goes beyond the manuscript's paper and visible traces and into the components of the ink that inscribes it.

The Ephemera of Ink-Making

To uncover Davis's relationship to ink-making, this section thinks through the itineraries of the objects he mentions, understanding them as significant to his process, but simultaneously "embedded in a multitude of contexts" with their own "pathways" through time and space (Hahn and Weiss 1). Measuring pots and ink ingredients are analysed to explore Davis' embodied making experiences: what these objects connoted in the making process and, more broadly, as mobile things that moved through spatial contexts. I therefore build a conversation between the personal associations generated by objects in use and the broader public significance of those things. Notably, the ingredients of ink-making – wort, copperas, galls, and gum arabic – can be considered *ephemera* in the sense that they were used in large quantities across multiple contexts to generate consumables like inks, dyes, and beer, but (apart from the iron ore from which copperas was drawn) had a short lifespan.

The first set of objects Davis noted were measures, and these included valuable items like brass weights and pewter pots, whose metals were often reused over time through a process of melting down and remaking, but also semi-durables like earthenware (see Hunt). These earthen pots were unlikely to survive extensive use over time due to their breakability, and they were of fairly low economic value, easily replaced and mass-produced, making them a category of household ephemera that were essential to storing, dining, and making.[7] Davis mentioned "2 lyttle black stone pots" which were "*the* waight of a q*uarter* of a pint of water" and a "blew stone pot" which was a "quarter of a pint of water which water waighes 4oz & half & half q*uarter*" (47r). These pots would have been small and represented non-standard measures for containers, or else he would have referred to them as "quart," "pint" or "pottle" pots, like those that conventionally appeared in probate inventories. As such, their intended purpose may have been for storing ink or ointments, like the stone pot in Figure 8.1. Stone pots were very common items in the early modern home and were imported into England from the Netherlands and Germany in huge quantities during the seventeenth century (Allan 119; Hamling and Richardson, *A Day at Home* 78). Archaeological evidence for stoneware suggests that it was more common in locales proximate to ports, and research on Exeter has indicated that a small

Figure 8.1 Stone Ointment Pot, Seventeenth Century. STRST: SBT 2013-1/1. © Shakespeare Birthplace Trust.

group of local merchants had it imported to the town from London, suggesting that a significant group of middling individuals were driving the demand in the town (Hamling and Richardson, *A Day at Home* 78). If this model were repeated in other port towns like Bristol, which was probably the closest to Davis, then it suggests he had access to imported earthenware, and his attention to its "blue" and "black" hues indicates he could acquire the colourful stoneware increasingly prevalent over the seventeenth century.[8]

Alongside these stoneware measures, Davis also utilises a pewter standish to measure water: "8 of the little pot 'full of water' of my pewter standish which is a pint" (78v). This standish was likely to have looked like the Shakespeare Birthplace Trust example in Figure 8.2, with a pewter stand surrounding a small lidded earthen pot in which the ink was stored. This pot would have been of higher value because of pewter's durability, and it is significant due to the fact it was an item

Figure 8.2 Pewter Standish, Seventeenth Century. STRST: SBT 1993-31/3.
© Shakespeare Birthplace Trust.

only used by those who could write and was thus a material signifier of an individual's literacy. By using the standish pot in the process of ink-making, Davis also performs a circular process, where the inkpot used to measure the liquid elements of his ink then became a container for the finished product. These three pots' significance to Davis as measures developed through practice and it is in use that he discovered their affordances (intrinsic properties) (Ingold, "Back" 40).[9] By deploying stone pots, and describing them as such in his manuscript, Davis also situated himself within a privileged group of middling individuals who could afford to purchase a variety of stone pots and some metal items in order to perform complex domestic making processes.[10]

Another insight into Davis's identity as it was carried in the ephemera of ink-making comes via his use of wort (a sugar water used in beer brewing) as the liquid base. Wort was a common ingredient in ink and was prevalent within middling to elite households, who produced beer at home and were most likely to have included literate individuals (Overton et al. 35–35, 38; Hamling and Richardson, *A Day at Home* 62). Davis was a domestic brewer: he shows a strong interest in malt making, copying a satirical piece on the "moral, allegorical, litteral, tropologicall" significances of the word "malt," and describing taking "a pint of woorte of the first shut" in a 1646 recipe (12v). Further, women often carried out domestic brewing and, if this were the case in Davis's home, we can imagine him consulting his wife on which vessel to extract wort from (Hamling and Richardson, *A Day at Home* 62). By writing of wort "first shut" (the oldest), Davis also demonstrates technical knowledge about brewing, with contemporary printed texts like Gervase Markham's *The English House-wife* instructing brewers to put wort in "cleane washt and scalded" hogsheads stopped (or "shut") with clay (245). Although, in practice, it is difficult to know whether Davis's process was the same as Markham's, it is clear from Bristol inventories from the 1620s that domestic brewers used a variety of tubs, vessels and barrels for the process, and Davis selected the matured wort by choosing the "first shut." It is presumably through experimentation that he discovered that this produced the best quality ink. By deploying a liquid produced domestically, Davis utilised a material he had to hand, entwining his ink-making with another household process. Both brewing and ink-making were markers of his status as a man with space to process malt and make beer domestically and also to communicate these acts in writing. Davis's decisions were linked with space and the very ink he wrote with was imbued with a substance that he produced in enough quantity to use in both ink and beer, connecting the two practices. So Davis's reaching for the wort "first shut" demonstrates the interrelatedness of ink-making and brewing within his domestic environment, and he clearly had expertise in both. The connections between ink-making and brewing may have generated for Davis a coherent sense of his identity as a middling man with the space and skill for large-scale ale making and writing.

The other ingredients Davis mixed with the wort to make ink were bought into his home. Galls and gum arabic were imported during the sixteenth and seventeenth centuries, though there was limited domestic gathering of galls. The domestic copperas industry fulfilled the majority of the demand from the mid-sixteenth century into the seventeenth century. It was, again, a substance that was produced, in part, with the labour of women as copperas pickers (Allen, Cotterill, and Pike 100). Davis was likely to have purchased these ingredients from an apothecary for the purposes of making ink. Port books demonstrate how materials like copperas, galls, and gum arabic made their way through Europe to the Netherlands and then across the channel to diffuse across English ports (see Dietz ix–xx). Apothecaries' inventories and price lists illustrate a market for these ingredients, with some stocking all three (see U269/E80/2 and MS 7646 132v). An example of this trade in the provinces comes from the inventory of Chester mercer Kenricke Eyton, who sold a lot of imported artisanal and medicinal goods. He had 8 3/4li of gum arabic in stock at his death worth 7s 5d, 18li copperas worth 1s 6d and 6li of "gaueles" at 3s 6d (WC 1623 Eyton). With Davis only employing ounces (usually a maximum of 2), rather than pounds, of ingredients in his ink recipes, Eyton's stock levels were comparatively high, suggesting good demand for these substances (though some were likely to have been used in dyes and pigments too).

The furthest travelled of these three ingredients was gum arabic (also known as gum acacia and gum Senegal), an essential ingredient in aiding the binding of writing to a substrate, which was imported into Europe from the Southern edge of the Sahara, first from East Africa, and then later from the West, through Senegambia (Curtin 215–21). Although the trade in gum arabic, an ephemeral substance, has been overlooked in favour of valuable materials like ivory, ostrich feathers, and gold, our written heritage was built, in part, upon it. It is substances like this, which demanded a large labour force to meet European consumption, that connected households such as Davis's with human exploitation through slavery. As Ousmane Traoré has observed, "gum arabic, in parallel fashion to the slave trade, was under the monopoly of the Trarza and Brakna Moor tribes who lived on the north bank of the Senegal river" (60), with Philip Curtin further explaining that "gathering was done by slaves belonging to the moors" (216). Despite the fact that this substance was not very valuable compared to other substances traded through North African merchants, it passed through the hands of slaves, into merchant trading networks, and then into middling and elite households for its qualities as a binding agent (Austen). When the utilisation of gum arabic is seen within this context, as connected in its labour source to the slave trade, the consumption of ephemeral matter can be seen as an act of control over the world's resources; a bolstering of the English middling household's power. Although Davis may not have thought of the origins of his gum arabic whilst dissolving it into his ink, in taking an itinerant perspective on this substance, its conflicting significance to other audiences – from the exploited slaves to the European merchants – can be layered up to give this substance depth beyond its immediate use, in a dynamic world of movement, power relations and the legacy of exploitation that is inscribed into iron-gall ink documents.

Tracing the itineraries of some of the domestic ephemera that were used as ingredients and tools in Davis's ink-making has been valuable for the exploration of how material narratives can be used to texture literate identities. By writing down his use of stone pots and ink ingredients, Davis situated himself as a man with middling status: he had space to brew beer at home and did so in multiple vessels; he owned imported stone pots in which to complete complicated preparation processes at home; and utilised ingredients like gum arabic, which connected his home to global trade networks and his consumption practices to slave labour. The ephemera of black ink-making, in this sense, created an image of status which was not only granted in the privileged ability to write and have the need for good ink for this purpose, but also in the very matter that went into the substance. Following the itineraries of some of the ephemera Davis used reveals a history of ink where the remaining trace of a quill on a substrate is underpinned by a dynamic global network whose lines touch exploited and hidden workers. Davis's ink-making, then, tells strands of a non-verbal autobiography built through his relationship with the surrounding material environment. In order to get to grips with this further, and explore Davis' fleeting practices whilst making ink, this chapter now follows the ingredients just discussed as they are used in embodied making through practice research.

Practice Research and Ephemeral Actions

Over the course of a year, I made one of Davis's recipes twice. The first time was in a lab environment where I could draw upon the equipment and knowledge of the lab technicians whilst making the recipe, and the second was by myself. The attempts had divergent results due to the changeable material qualities of the natural ingredients and improvisational processes used in following the text. Practice research (PR) experiments can further our understanding of Davis' recipes, and allow the researcher to bring together all of the itinerant material strands that make up a craft process in order to think through embodied actions and the relationship between text, person and materials. This way of approaching instructional texts has been exemplified by the *Making and Knowing* and *Artechne* projects, with the *Making and Knowing* team describing the method as a way of gaining "a stronger sense of a Renaissance understanding of materials and the ability to transform them" (Smith, "Historians" 215). In reconstructing the ink recipe, I acknowledge my distance from the past, using tools and materials available in the present to reconstruct the process, using making as an exercise in creative reading and reimagining in order to explore the interpretive possibilities carried by Davis' descriptions.

When making the ink, my aim deviated from the *Making Knowing* team's objective to "work through the variables and resistances of materials to bring about a successful (and replicable) result" (Smith, "Historians" 219), which suggests that practical knowledge develops into a fixed understanding of a technique. Instead, I took an approach in line with recent discussions of PR in performance, which accepts that theatre is, in Andy Kesson's words, a "speculative contingent thing" and therefore always changing (n.p.). Ink-making performed by me or by Davis would vary every time, making a reproducible process difficult to achieve. Davis himself acknowledges the impact his environment had on his making; his example of completing an action in mid-December "before it was quite cold" shows how much impact aspects outside the maker's control can have on a process – especially in early modern homes, which were hives of interrelated activities and variable climates.

From the outset, it has been clear that Davis's recipes were recorded after the event, and not even to remember the process, but as a means through which he could test the ink. As explored earlier in this chapter, Davis's recipes are often in the form of lists of ingredients rather than descriptions of actions. Making one of Davis's recipes gives a sense of the dynamic world of his domestic ephemera in action, bringing his words to life, and it therefore engages with the idea of the multi-temporal object itinerary that Joyce and Gillespie argue has the "potential to resist the imposition of a boundary between a thing and representations of it, allowing us to ask when a reproduction or translation of a thing remains actively connected to it" (12). In seeing my own making as being "actively connected" to Davis's, I create a palimpsest where practice is layered on practice, ink-facsimile on manuscript, and where the words Davis recorded are linked with materials past and present. Davis's ink recipes as texts therefore juxtapose the ephemerality of the ingredients listed within them in their performance across time.

The recipe I followed was the most detailed included in Davis's manuscript, and thus the one that provided slightly less room for experimentation than his lists of ingredients but more possibilities for interpreting practice:

> The 19th of Jan: 1646 ^being Saturday^ I tooke a q*uarte*r of a pint of woorte of the first shut letting it stand until the eveinging to settle & then powred out the cleere from the groundes wh*i*ch cleere woort being a iust quarter of a pint I put into a very cleane earthen pott and put therto half an oz of galls grossly bruised and stirred it very well thrice a day for 3 daies togather then upon the 12th day in the evening being Tuesday I put therto a quarter of an oz of copp*era*s and stirred it very well thrice a day for other 3 daies vizt untill Friday in the evening at w[hi]ch time I put into it a quarter of an oz of gome arabick and stirred it very well other 3 daies thrice a day and now this present Tuesday being the 19th of Jan: it is fytt for use. (67v, p. 44)

The first observation was that the recipe demanded eighteen days of attention, and the substance needed stirring three times a day. This suggested that ink-making had a routine that fitted with the passage of the day, and that Davis's making process began on January 1st which held significance as the liturgical New Year which marked a fresh start, just as the mix of ingredients that made black ink materially metamorphosed in the process. In the lab, we used an electric stirrer to lessen the need for thrice daily travel, but at home, I was able to stir the mixture (at varying times) three times a day. The wort, on both occasions, was sourced from Canterbury Brewers in a gesture to Davis's local sourcing of materials.

In the process of making, an issue with specifying material qualities and actions became clear, challenging how terms could be translated into specific results. For example "grossly bruised" (in reference to the oak galls) could have multiple connotations, with "grossly" giving applicable meanings like "coarsely" and "roughly" but no obvious quantifiable way of describing a "grossly bruised gall" ("grossly" adv. *OED*). As a result, rather than making them into a powder, I broke them open with a pestle and mortar to get an uneven sample. In this instance, the galls

I used were still slightly soft – not quite dry – and so fairly light. This meant that the ratio of galls to liquid proved surprising, being almost equal, and that the resulting mixture was very thick. The second time I made the ink at home, the galls I used were dry and dense, meaning that there were far fewer galls than there was wort; this clarified the kind of galls Davis used in his recipe, which would have been hardened and dried, perhaps imported and bought from his local apothecary, rather than gathered by Davis and used soon after. Other adjectives came to life during the making process with, for example, the meaning of "cleere" before "wort" becoming obvious only after seeing the wort full of particles and sediment that had to be left to settle at the bottom before "pouring out the cleere from the groundes" (67v, p. 44). With natural ingredients used within the early modern home in great quantities, but not surviving due to natural decomposition, re-making can give access to the material qualities of ephemera and clarify their stage of life.

The process also exposed temporalities of making over the eighteen days: both a sense of how checking on the substance would have punctuated Davis's routine, and also how labour-intensive, and therefore important to Davis, this was. Due to the lack of heat used in the recipe patience was essential, as the liquid slowly evaporated, thickening and becoming harder to stir over time – a quality only revealed in the haptic experience of making. Its material quality transformed from loose galls mixed with wort to one where the galls broke down and muddied the distinction between solid and liquid. In the first lab iteration the substance went mouldy, suggesting again, I discovered in my second attempt, that I had used too-fresh galls. The spectacular moment of transformation from brown to black upon adding the copperas (or, in my case, its purer modern form Iron II Sulphate), and the chemical, slightly sterile scent arising from the ink on its addition, was a moment where I realised my control over *how* the ingredients interacted was limited by their properties, ones that provoked the necessary reaction that created the desired colour – the way in which my actions were entangled with the sometimes linked, sometimes separate agencies of materials. At the moment the ink turned black, I also thought of the synergy between Davis's making and my own – the transitory instant in which the process created ink and how this was ephemeral and difficult to describe both for him and me. However, this transitory instant was also contained in the new form of the black ink, giving an insight into what Ingold calls the "rhythm" of movements involved in making, which leave traces on the materials and maker that act as 'memories' of a process (Ingold, *Making* 115).

Making therefore revealed how the adjectives for describing processes created interpretive challenges, even with the ingredient in hand. Making is important to understanding how a verbal record interacts with its material world. Finally, when looking at my own resulting ink – black and shining like the substance of Shakespeare's sonnet – the very ephemerality of the manuscript text and its inscriptions became clear. Davis's writing has faded to brown over time – the result of decay – whereas interventions like rebinding and paper preservation have aimed to slow the passage of time.

Conclusions: Ephemera and Identities in Black Ink-Making

In an article on "human-thing entanglement," archaeologist Ian Hodder writes that "in most of the work in the social and human sciences in which it is argued that human and things co-constitute each other, or fluidly mix together, there is, oddly, little account of the things themselves" (157). In taking an "object itineraries" approach to the ink used to produce the textual evidence upon which the disciplines of history and literature have been built, I have sought to think through some of the entanglements between humans and things and uncover not only the processes Davis as a maker and writer performed in the making of ink, but also some of the journeys and associations of the materials he used. In doing so, I have uncovered a network of "entanglements," or, to recall Pamela Smith's similar phrase, a "material complex" between humans and things that is broadly depicted in Figure 8.3: from sub-Saharan Africa, to the apothecary's shop, before Davis' own encounter and then, 400 years later, my own.[11] Many of the materials that went into ink can be considered domestic ephemera because they have a limited lifespan and survive as makers transformed them into new substances. The traces

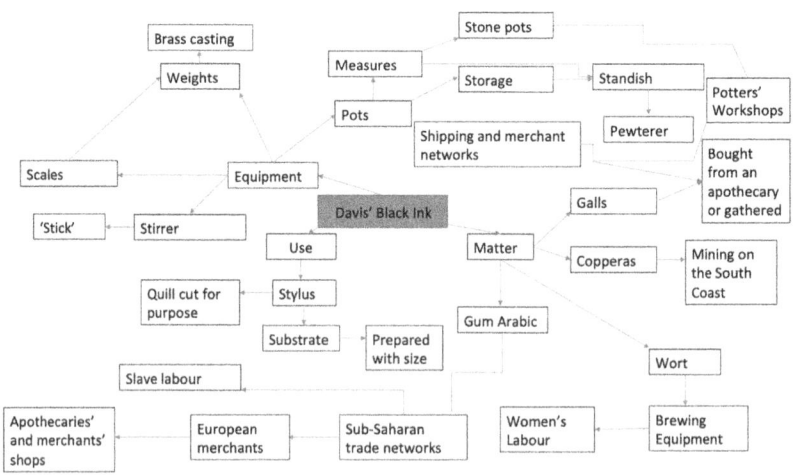

Figure 8.3 Diagram of 'entanglements' in Davis' black ink (inspired by Hodder, 158).

of ink have been shown to reveal material absences, dynamic narratives of ephemeral actions by Davis as a maker, and the itinerant matter that went into ink.

Ink-making has also been established as a means of identity crafting. The act of writing down a process as a memorialising, autobiographical, and therefore legitimising activity seems to have been an important motivator for Davis. Ink-making and process recording demonstrated his ability to write and his domestic practices and utensils, which expressed his yeoman middling status. Writing was interrelated with Davis's other activities as a means of self-situation and expression within his domestic environment and, in choosing to make a manuscript in which to record his ink experiments, Davis gave an insight into the importance of memorialisation to his life and daily practices. Davis' recipe writing was entwined with other processes in his household, part of a set of activities that, in the case of his ink-making, were in conversation with his social status and literacy. The inscription of the ink on the pages of his miscellany exhibited his writing ability and careful making practices to future readers. By choosing to make ink rather than buy it, Davis invested time, energy, and money in craftsmanship, and therefore actively performed his literate, yeoman identity as it was related to a variety of ingredients and objects.

This chapter has uncovered the itineraries of ingredients, equipment, and practice in order to illustrate a dynamic perspective on a slice of domestic ephemera which went into the making of black ink. I have sought to lift ink from the page and separate it into its parts to think about the significance of ephemeral substances for the construction of a literate identity in early modern England. Through pots, gum arabic, and wort, Davis's embodied processes were given life and significance at each stage of the making cycle, from the buying of these ingredients to their origin stories, which go on to inform how we might read them today. Like Callan Davies's "bioperformative apple" in this volume, which held "significance and agency" as a prop despite its prolific presence and propensity to decay, ink's ingredients, and the tools and actions of its making, held their own affordances and "agencies" as matter: from the reaction between the galls and copperas that made the ink black to the volume of Davis's pots. Further, despite gum arabic's neglect as a traded substance, in comparison to the ostrich feathers, ivory, and gold that travelled the same route, its disappearance into the inks and pigments which built documentary cultures should not hide its power as a substance that was used to write the legal and political records that were a cog in the mechanics of colonisation. By inscribing ink recipes into his manuscript, then, Davis set off layers of association, which actively situated him within a world of domestic ephemera, the components of which had their own itinerant narratives and significances before they reached the tip of his stylus.

Notes

1 Many studies of early modern ephemera focus on print and paper, see for example, Russell and Michael Harris.
2 A paper book was a "pre-bound blank book" (Gibson).
3 'Ephemeris', n., 3a. *OED*. By nature these were an ephemeral text as the predictions would only apply for a certain period.
4 See Blount's description of stationers as those who sell "paper, paper books, ink, wax &c" (598), while Cordier mentions ink available to buy at a market (199).
5 A potential candidate of the right location and social status would be a Thomas Davis who lived in Easton in Gordano near Bristol (see Somerset Heritage Centre, PROB 11/329/571; DD\X\WI\24; Q\SR\72\87).
6 For "embodied reasoning," see Smith, "Knowledge" (110).
7 These items rarely appear in probate materials but are well represented in archaeological deposits (Hamling and Richardson, *A Day at Home* 78).
8 For early-1620s Bristol, the probable closest metropolis to Davis, embellished pots were more likely to be mentioned: John Butcher, alderman, inventoried in 1623 had "three stone cups with silver covers guilt" (EP J/4/18, bundle 1623).
9 Tim Ingold, 'Back to the Future with the Theory of Affordances', *HAU: Journal of Ethnographic Theory*, 8:1/2 (2018): 39–44 (40)
10 Hamling and Richardson state that the market in stone pots was "driven largely by middling groups" (*A Day at Home* 79)
11 Diagram inspired by Hodder (158).

Works Cited

Allan, John. *Medieval and Post-Medieval Finds in Exeter, 1971–1980*. Exeter Archaeological Reports, Vol. 3. Exeter U and City Council, 1984.

Allen, Tim, Mike Cotterill, and Geoffrey Pike. "Copperas: An Account of the Whitstable Copperas Works and the First Major Chemical Industry in England." *Industrial Archaeology Review* 23:2 (2013): 93–112.

Austen, Ralph A. "Marginalization, Stagnation and Growth: the Trans-Saharan Caravan Trade in the Era of European Expansion, 1500–1900." *The Rise of Merchant Empires: Long Distance Trade in the Early Modern World 1350–1750*. Ed James D. Tracy. Cambridge UP, 2011. 311–50.

Banik, Gerhard. "Ink Corrosion – Chemistry." *Irongallink*. 1998. Online. Accessed 8 Sep. 2021.

Blake, Liza. "Pounced Corrections in Oxford Copies of Cavendish's *Philosophical and Physical Opinions*; or, Margaret Cavendish's Glitter Pen." *New College Notes* 10:6 (2018): 1–11.

Blount, Thomas. *Glossographica: Or A Dictionary Interpreting All such Hard Words of Whatsoever Language now Used*. London, 1661.

Brathwaite, Richard. *Times Treasury, or, Academy for Gentry Laying Downe Excellent Grounds, both Divine and Humane, in Relation to Sexes of both Kindes*. London, 1652.

Brinsley, John. *Ludus Literarius*. London, 1612.

Cockeram, Henry. *The English Dictionarie*. London, 1623.

Cordier, Marthurin. *Corderius Dialogues Translated Grammatically*. London, 1636.

Curtin, Philip D. *Economic Change in Precolonial Africa: Senegambia in the Era of the Slave Trade*. U of Wisconsin P, 1975.

Davies, Callan. "Playing Apples and the Playhouse Archive." *Practices of Ephemera in Early Modern England*. Eds Callan Davies, Hannah Lilley, and Catherine Richardson. Routledge, 2023. 191–209.

Davis, Thomas. Lansdowne MS 674. MS. British Library, London.

Daybell, James. *The Material Letter in Early Modern England: Manuscript Letters and the Culture and Practices of Letter-Writing 1512–1635*. Palgrave Macmillan, 2012.

DD/XJ/WI/24. MS. Somerset Heritage Centre, Somerset.

Dietz, Brian, ed. *The Port and Trade of Early Elizabethan London*. London Record Society, 1972.

DiMeo, Michelle and Sara Pennell. "Introduction." *Reading and Writing Recipe Books 1500–1800*. Eds Michelle DiMeo and Sara Pennell. Manchester UP, 2013. 1–22.

Eckhardt, Joshua and Daniel Starza Smith, eds. *Manuscript Miscellanies in Early Modern England*. Ashgate, 2014.

EP J/4/18, bundle 1623. MS. Bristol Archives, Bristol.

Gibson, Jonathan. "Casting Off Blanks: Hidden Structures in Early Modern Paper Books." *Material Readings of Early Modern Culture: Texts and Social Practices 1580–1730*. Eds James Daybell and Peter Hinds. Palgrave Macmillan, 2010. 209–28.

Hahn, Hans Pewter and Hadas Weiss. *Mobility, Meaning and the Transformations of Things*. Oxbow, 2013.

Hamling, Tara and Catherine Richardson. *A Day at Home in Early Modern England*. Yale UP, 2017.

———. "Introduction." *Everyday Objects: Medieval and Early Modern Material Culture and its Meanings*. Routledge, 2016. 1–27.

Harris, Jonathan Gil. *Untimely Matter in the Time of Shakespeare*. U of Pennsylvania P, 2009.

Harris, Michael. "Printed Ephemera." *The Book: A Global History*. Eds Michael F. Saurez and H. R. Woudhuysen. Oxford UP, 2013. 205–19.

Harris, Mitchell M. "The Expense of Ink and Wastes of Shame: Poetic Generation, Black Ink, and Material Waste in Shakespeare's Sonnets." *The Materiality of Color: The Production, Circulation, and Application of Dyes and Pigments, 1400–1800*. Eds Andrea Freeser et al. Routledge, 2016. 65–81.

Hodder, Ian. "Human-Thing Entanglement: Towards an Integrated Archaeological Perspective." *Journal of the Royal Anthropological Institute* 17 (2011): 154–77.

Hunt, Katherine. "More Lasting than Bronze: Statues, Writing, and the Materials of Ephemera in Ben Jonson's *Sejanus His Fall*." *Practices of Ephemera in Early Modern England*. Eds Callan Davies, Hannah Lilley, and Catherine Richardson. Routledge, 2023. 111–27.

Ingold, Tim. "Back to the Future with the Theory of Affordances." *HAU: Journal of Ethnographic Theory*, 8:1/2 (2018): 39–44.

———. *Making: Anthropology, Archaeology, Art and Architecture*. Routledge, 2013.

Johns, Adrian. "Ink." *Materials and Expertise in Early Modern Europe: Market and Laboratory*. Eds Ursula Klein and E. C. Spary. U of Chicago P, 2010. 101–24.

Joyce, Rosemary A. and Susan D. Gillespie. "Making Things out of Objects that Move" *Things in Motion: Object Itineraries in Anthropological Practice*. School for Advance Research P, 2015. 3–20.

Kesson, Andy. "Acting Out of Character: A Performance-as-Research Approach to *Three Ladies of London*." *Three Ladies of London*. Online. Accessed 8 Sep. 2021.

Lansdowne MS 674. *British Library Online Catalogue*. Online. Accessed 11 Oct. 2021.

Lilley, Hannah. "Interpreting Practice: Scribes, Materials and Occupational Identities 1560–1640." Diss. U of Kent, 2019.

Manso, Marta et al. "The Mysterious Halos in Iron Gall Ink Manuscripts: An Analytical Explanation." *Applied Physics A*. 118:3 (2015): 1107–11.

Markham, Gervase. *The English House-wife*. London, 1631.

Meyer, Morgan. "Placing and Tracing Absence: A Material Culture of the Immaterial." *Journal of Material Culture*. 17:1 (2012): 103–10.

MS 7646. MS. Wellcome Library, London.

Overton, Mark, et al. *Production and Consumption in English Household 1600–1750*. Routledge 2004.

Pennell, Sara. "Making Livings, Lives and Archives: Tales of Four Eighteenth-Century Recipe Books." *Reading and Writing Recipe Books 1500–1800*. Eds Michelle DiMeo and Sara Pennell. Manchester UP, 2013. 225–46.

Polanyi, Michael. *The Tacit Dimension*. U of Chicago P, 2009.

PROB 11/329/571. Prerogative Court of Canterbury. MS. National Archives, Kew, London.

Q/SR/72/87. MS. Somerset Heritage Centre, Somerset.

Russell, Gillian. *The Ephemeral Eighteenth Century: Print, Sociability, and the Cultures of Collecting* Cambridge UP, 2020.

Shakespeare, William. "Sonnet 63." *The Oxford Shakespeare: The Complete Sonnets and Poems*. Ed. Colin Burrow. Oxford UP, 2002. 50.

Sloane 1203. MS. British Library, London.

Smith, Pamela H. "Historians in the Laboratory: Reconstruction of Renaissance Art and Technology in the Making and Knowing Project." *Art History* 39.2 (2016): 210–33.

———. "Itineraries of Materials and Knowledge in the Early Modern World." *The Global Lives of Things: The Material Culture of Connections in the Early Modern World*. Eds Anne Gerritsen and Giorgio Riello. Routledge, 2016. 31–61.

———. "Knowledge in Motion: Following Itineraries of Matter in the Early Modern World." *Cultures in Motion*. Eds Daniel. T. Rodgers, Bhavani Raman, and Helmut Reimitz. Princeton UP, 2014. 109–33.

Smyth, Adam. *Autobiography in Early Modern England*. Cambridge UP, 2010.

Traoré, Ousame. "State Control and Regulation of Commerce on the Waterways and Coast of Senegambia ca. 1500–1800." *Navigating African Maritime History*. Eds Carina E. Ray and Jeremy Rich. Liverpool UP, 2009. 57–80.

Tullett, Will. "Extensive Ephemera: Perfumer's Trade Cards in Eighteenth-Century England." *Practices of Ephemera in Early Modern England*. Eds Callan Davies, Hannah Lilley, and Catherine Richardson. Routledge, 2023. 210–28.

Twysden, Roger. U48/Z1. MS. Kent History and Library Centre, Maidstone, Kent, UK.

U269/E80/2. MS. Kent History and Library Centre, Maidstone, Kent, UK.

Vine, Angus. *Miscellaneous Order: Manuscript Culture and the Early Modern Organisation of Knowledge.* Oxford UP, 2019.

WC 1623 Eyton (Kenricke). Inventory. MS. Chester Record Office, Chester.

Wendy Wall. "Literacy and the Domestic Arts." *Huntington Library Quarterly* 73:3 (2010): 383–412.

9 Things That Last

Ephemerality and Endurance in Early Modern England

Helen Smith

On folio 5v of Ann Bowyer's commonplace book, someone has recorded a miraculous survival. An inscription copied from the tomb of Thomas Grey, 2nd Marquess of Dorset (1477–1530), tells a story of unlikely preservation. Grey had died in 1530, but his remains needed to be re-located in 1608, "by reason of the fall of the church and ye ruine of ye chappell whearin it was layed" (Ashmole MS 51 5v). Despite the passage of time, and the dissolution of the church buildings, Grey's corpse was found to be "perfect and sound, the flesh of ye bodye nothing perished nor hardned, but in colour proportions and softness like to any ordinary corps." Grey's body, in this account, is anything but ephemeral. The in-scription, as copied in Bowyer's book, offers a plausible explanation for Grey's remarkable post-mortem history, noting "the strong embalming and for that the vault wherein his corps lay was flowing with water." Reinterred, Grey's remains are reimagined within the vast timescales of the resurrection: the body "heare doth Rest expecting the coming of ye last Day." Seventy-seven years may be an extraordinary period for a body to endure, but, in the context of the end of time, it is nothing at all.

This brief history of interring, revelation, and remembering ties to-gether the themes that run throughout this chapter, which explores the material affordances of ephemerality and how the evanescent might be used to imagine multiple temporalities and to hold them in tension. Against the habit of thinking of solidity and endurance as coterminous, the writers I explore in this chapter imagined substance and persistence in an inverse relationship: material things fade, immaterial things en-dure.[1] Transience was, paradoxically, a mode of conceiving of another kind of time: one that extends beyond the limits of time itself. This mode of thinking both contributes to, and pushes at the limits of, our under-standing of the relationship between "world time" (the timescales of human activity) and "earth time", or geological time, as explored in recent accounts of the Anthropocene and its ethics. In an influential ar-ticle, Dipesh Chakrabarty suggests that Christian theology contributed in decisive ways to how we conceive of geological time, "a class of time that has always been seen (long before geology) as opposed to the sense or scale of temporality of human history" (22). Ephemerality was one

DOI: 10.4324/9781003058588-12

way of understanding the extraordinary duration of the world's transformations; at the same time, it was used to conceive of endurance as
something which belonged properly outside both world and time.

Ephemeral things, in the early modern period, as now, were things
that were markedly short-lived. "*Ephemera*," noted John Maplet, "is
a fish which ariseth in the Sea water euen as the Bubble doth, where as
much raine is. Whome *Iorach* in his Booke *de Animalibus* reporteth
after thrée houres of the day to die" (M4r). Both bubble and fish are evanescent, forming spontaneously in water, and as quickly dissolving. But
for early moderns, it was not just fish or froth that were destined to fade,
but all earthly things. The Bible exhorted early modern English readers:
"Lift up your eyes to the heavens, and look upon the earth beneath: for
the heavens shall vanish away like smoke, and the earth shall wax old
like a garment, and they that dwell therein shall die in like manner"
(*KJV*, Is. 51:6). This verse epitomises the period's pervasive conviction
of the ephemerality of solid things. At the same time, it exemplifies a
mode of thinking that sought points of comparison in the everyday experience of ephemerality: the earth fades and thins like a well-worn piece
of clothing.

Within this theological tradition, the most ephemeral thing of all was
man: a blip or bubble within the expanse of eternity. Man's "fraile and
tickle [*sic*]" life, reflected Elizabeth Grymeston, in her *Miscelenea. Meditations. Memoratiues* (1604), is

> a vapour that soone vanisheth, a drie leafe carried with euery winde,
> a sleepe fed with imaginarie dreames, a tragedy of transitory things
> and disguised persons, that passe away like a poste in the night, like
> a ship in the sea, like a bird in the aire, whose tract the aire closeth.
> (C3r)

Invocations of ephemeral phenomena – bubbles, smoke, shadows,
grass – had one eye on the vulnerability of man, and the other fixed on
eternity. Conversely, dwelling on those things which could not last was
also a mechanism for imagining things which would endure: as Isaiah
51:6 concludes, "my salvation shall be for ever, and my righteousness."
The timescales of ephemerality did take in the brief existence of the mayfly, "always playing at the River side," but, as Bruce Boehrer notes in
this volume, they simultaneously embraced the mayfly's evanescence as
a measure for the existence of man and the persistence of the divine
(Barker A4v). As Grymeston demanded, "canst thou sit by the riuer side,
and not remember that as the riuer runneth, and doth not returne, so is
the life of man?".

Gillian Russell argues movingly that "Ephemerality ... also represents a poetics: an intensified sense of presentness and the evanescence or quickness of time; of the difficulty of holding on to and

preserving what we momentarily know and experience" (29). In the seventeenth century, I contend, not only knowledge and experience but existence itself was recognised as vivid, full, and fleeting. This period's theology of the ephemeral was tightly entwined with a corresponding poetics that took ephemeralness as its theme, attempting both to represent and hang onto the fleetingness of existence. In a neat formulation relating to the still-life paintings characteristic of seventeenth-century European art, Margreta de Grazia, Maureen Quilligan, and Peter Stallybrass argue that "while bringing to mind the passing of things, these paintings also give those things the permanence of art" (1). In the examples I trace in this chapter, it is ephemerality itself that writers (rather than painters) seek to make present as an enduring truth.

The first part of this chapter asks what it meant to stockpile conceits that took ephemerality as their subject. Bowyer's commonplace book, written between c. 1590 and c. 1617, is one example of the vogue that saw snippets of verse and other writings brought together in new forms by readers and copyists. It forms a thread that runs throughout the chapter, twining together the flexible strands of a culture that was energetically of the view that virtually everything, properly regarded, is ephemeral. My second section centres around Samuel Purchas's *Purchas his Pilgrim Microcosmus* (1619), a sustained meditation on the ephemerality of man. I take Purchas's text as exemplary of a passionate – and hyperbolically prosy – commitment to demonstrating mankind's ephemerality in the face of biblical time. Despite the evident differences between Purchas's lengthy printed book and Bowyer's slender manuscript, both are products of a commonplacing culture: his relentlessly, copiously degenerative, hers a thing of scraps and patches; his monumental and memorialising, hers conditional and responsive; his explicit about the theme of evanescence, hers a site where transience glitters as one occasional theme among many.

My short, final section turns to the specific temporalities of printing and writing. I am alert to the material record, as well as the transience, of text production: the specific modes in which ideas of ephemerality and immortality were articulated and sometimes erased, what it means that these concepts were both arrested and set in motion in script and print. Bowyer's slim bundle of pages and Purchas's hefty book not only contain meditations on the theme of transience, they also present compelling instances of the material expression of those ideas and the multiple temporalities of writing, marking, and remembering. Throughout the chapter, I aim to demonstrate how an attention to man's vanishing existence was thought through via a concern for natural and artificial mutations and material effects. Man's ephemerality and the vanishing nature of material things were commonplace in a double sense. They were favoured *topoi*, picked up and varied by writer after writer, and they were rooted in a supple, collective regard for the everyday: the shared ground of use, experience, and loss.

"Good Things": Commonplacing the Ephemeral

Ann Bowyer, as Victoria Burke has documented, was the daughter of a Coventry draper. Like other surviving commonplace books, hers is a collection of sententiae, notes, proverbs, aphorisms, verses, and more, compiled by one or more owners or copyists as a resource for future use (see especially Moss; Smyth). Multitudes of books like it once existed; many are now lost. This is especially true for women's papers, frequently dispersed, disposed of, or even burnt on the occasion of their owner's or writer's deaths (Wolfe; Travitsky).

There is an etymological connection between the act of commonplacing – the creation and use of a book like Bowyer's – and ephemerality. "Ephemera" derives from the Greek εφημερίδες, lasting only for a day, and shares its derivation with "ephemeris": a diary, calendar or daybook. In *A Dictionary in Spanish and English* (1599), John Minsheu defined "Ephemeri" as "day-bookes, or registers of euerie seuerall day" (K5v), while in a sermon delivered on Easter Sunday, 1629, John Donne reflected that God is ready to record men's sins: "in his Ephemerides, his journals, he writes them downe under that Title, sins, and he reads them every day, in that booke" (Y1v). Donne's God is a diligent commonplacer: owners of commonplace books were encouraged to select apt headings for their pages, or even to buy books pre-printed with suitable categories. Early modern uses of the term "ephemerides" are marked by a fascination with the connection between fast-passing time – the actions of a single day – and the extraordinary duration of biblical chronologies. Thomas Jackson, dean of Peterborough, for instance, reflected that God's "written Oracles," communicated through Moses, constituted "an absolute Ephemerides of all things that had bin since the first moment of time" (N3r). Each day is transient, but the act of recording amasses a history that reaches back to the creation of the world.

On one page of her commonplace book, Bowyer pieced together several couplets from Michael Drayton's *England's Heroical Epistles* (the 1602 or 1603 rather than the 1597 edition). Among these pithy extracts stand the lines:

> Good thinges while wee posses wee neuer hould them dear
> bout when ther gonn wee know how good ye wear. (6r)

This couplet is not from Drayton and is plausibly Bowyer's own addition. The lines reflect on the relationship between ephemerality and loss, memory and value. "Things," a capacious category taking in everything from objects to relationships, which are "held," in the sense of being possessed, handled, or stored, cannot at the same time be valued or appreciated, "held dear." A reader of these lines might embrace a double view of ephemerality, recognising the mundane experience of loss, alongside the inevitability of dissolution. As Richard Rogers reminded readers in 1603:

> all things in this world are transitorie, vaine and soone flitting away, and we our selues with them daily drawing vnto our end. Thou hast caused this to be published in our hearing, that all flesh is grasse, and the glory and beautie of it, as the flower of the field that fadeth: and that all things below the more they haue bene delighted in, the more deeply they shall sting and vexe vs when they forsake vs. (Nn5r)

Bowyer's couplet is an instance of the stings of transitoriness, a lament over the particulars of a given, but unspecified, loss that simultaneously generalises transience as a commonplace experience.

In Bowyer's couplet, the vagueness of the noun phrase "good things" creates a compelling poetics of loss: it is impossible to identify Bowyer's meditation with a specific object, and so the reader is invited to reflect upon the condition of ephemerality and to substitute their specific "good thing" for the general category. Within the larger context of Bowyer's commonplace book, "good things" are positioned in contrast to material accumulation: in an unattributed couplet, adapted from Spenser's *The Shepheardes Calender*, Bowyer observes "Goodes ar no goodes if the be not spend/god giues them vnto vs for noother eand" (4r). Cling to your goods and you become a miser, stale and unproductive; distribute your "good things" and you realise their value in losing them. As Joni Mitchell put it some centuries later, "Don't know what you got till it's gone."

There is a delightful pun embedded in Bowyer's erratic orthography: "wee know how good ye wear." That final word – "were" but also "wear" – emphasises the past tense of the lost object, asking the reader to reflect on what it was before the time of reading or recollection. The sentence contains within itself the act of erasure: the routine "wear" that transforms an object, altering its constitution to the point of losing gloss, colour, or lustre, of thinning, breaking, fading away.[2] It highlights the ubiquity of ephemerality, any good thing's vulnerability to use and encounter. "Wear," the result of touch and use, is one of the things that renders material things ephemeral. It may also be one of the things that renders them "good," adding to their emotional affordances and physical effects.[3]

Bowyer's lines make for an abbreviated meditation on the nature of commonplacing: what does it mean to possess "good things" in the form of a sentence? What does the act of quotation say about the urge to accumulate both words and sentiment? Bowyer's lines propose that the practice of commonplacing is self-defeating: the fact of possessing "good things" renders the commonplace mundane, something that, in being collected, cannot be valued. In a sentence culled from "FB" (possibly a family member), and copied earlier in her book, Bowyer reflects on the process of maturation that transforms the commonplace into a resource for use: "Words ought to be well filed in the hart / Befor by the tonge the bee outered [uttered]" (2v). "Filed" could mean, as it does now, to collect documents or papers, and, by extension, to collect and store ideas and memories (*OED*, 'file', *v. 3*, def. 1a.). It also meant, in another term both practical and metaphorical, "to remove the roughness of; to smooth, polish, elaborate to perfection. Also, to wear *down*; to bring *into* (a certain condition) as if by filing" (*OED*, 'file', *v. 1*, def. 1b.). This is the sense in which Ben Jonson commands the would-be writer, wrestling with unwieldy words, to "bring all to the forge, and file, againe; tourne it a newe" (R2r; for more on Jonson's conceptions of writing material, see Hunt in this volume). The purpose of commonplacing is two-fold: it allows the user to file information in the sense of storing it, and it allows them to hone sentiment, making it handleable, useable, and "outerable". "Outerable" too benefits from Bowyer's idiosyncratic spelling, which articulates the public, "outer" manifestation of words matured within the confines of the heart.[4]

On the same page as Bowyer's meditation on "good things," a couplet is crammed against the outer margin, at ninety degrees to the bulk of the writing:

> mans wit doth build for time but to deuoure
> but vertue free from time & fortunes power (6r)

This text is taken from Drayton's *England's Heroical Epistles*, where it forms part of a verse letter from a fictionalised Lady Jane Grey to her husband, Lord Guildford Dudley, written as though during the couple's imprisonment in the Tower of London (K8r; also extracted in Bodenham, D8v). Next to this couplet, and in the same orientation, Bowyer has added an attribution to Henry Howard, Earl of Surrey. On the page, the citation appears to be attached to this verse, though it in fact refers to different lines. Whether we read this sententious rhyme as voiced by Grey, Drayton, Bowyer, or even Howard, the couplet, along with the slender book in which it is copied, presents a telling study in non-ephemerality – or preservation, as it is more usually known. The verse is concerned with the fleetingness of "mans wit": its aptitude to be consumed by time. Yet the poetic products of Drayton's wit persist through writing, enduring not only until Bowyer's historical moment, but also – thanks to Bowyer's commonplace book, as well as the other textual witnesses to Drayton's poem – until our own. Bowyer's notebook appears to have escaped destruction thanks to the relentless compilatory project of her son, Elias Ashmole, whose collections formed the basis of the Ashmolean Museum. Caught up with numerous other papers, books, and writings, Bowyer's scrappy collection of thoughts and forms is, in some sense, a foundational document in the history of the modern museum as both concept and institution.[5] It illuminates the dual temporalities of commonplacing, presenting itself on the one hand as an ephemeral assemblage, on the other as an intention to preserve.

Drayton's theme, and hence Bowyer's, is the contrast between the ephemerality of man's witty effervescences – those dazzling snippets so beloved of the commonplacing reader – and the endurance of virtue. This split resonates in the translator and devotional writer Thomas Tymme's popular guide to achieving everlasting salvation, *A silver watch-bell* (1605), in which Tymme points his reader to "two wonderfull and monstrous things." The first is

> that man being scarcely borne, dieth, when as notwithstanding, he hath a forme & shewe of immortalitie: other thinges how long they retaine their forme, so long they remaine: A house falleth not all the time that his forme and fashion lasteth: The bruite beast dieth not, except first he forgo his life, which is his forme. But man hath a forme which neuer is dissoluing, namely, a mind endued with reason, and yet he liueth a very short time. (A6v)

For Tymme, reason (the foundation of virtuous living) is subject neither to time nor to the vicissitudes of forms: the taking on and dissolution of the shapes that materialise things in the world. It is, in other words, free from the processes of generation and corruption which characterise mortal affairs. Other things last as long as their shape endures, but man's body is peculiarly corruptible, in contrast to the constitutive, eternal form which is his rational mind.[6]

Man's besetting vice is his passion for the ephemeral: he knows that the "life to come shall neuer haue end, and yet neuerthelesse setteth his whole mind most carefullie vpon this present life, which is to day, and to morrowe is not: but of the life which is euerlasting, he doeth not so much as thinke." This stands in contrast to a couplet that appears towards the end of Bowyer's book. The back of her book is written in a much more formal hand, featuring a narrow strip of text at the top of each page, where practice alphabets, letter shapes, and epistolary conventions are interspersed with moralising *sententiae*. One reflects: "Commendable are the Deedes of charitie the remebraunce therof & reacheth vnto the heauens: the commendationn of itt Remaneth on Earth emongst the poore: But the Lorde rewardeth the deedes euer:" (15v). Here, Bowyer attempts to reconcile the specifics of earthly materiality with the *longue durée* of eternal life. To hoard good things is miserly; to give them away has an eternising function on earth as well as in heaven.

Tymme's formulation compresses and dilates time within a single sentence, reducing man's years on earth to one day, and setting them against eternity. The Church of England clergyman, Samuel Purchas, offers a similar vision. In place of Tymme's despair at man's fascination with life's immediate vicissitudes, Purchas offers a picture of the "sound Christian." The true believer *"desires to be dissolued*, not to be this Man; that when hee hath put off these Ragges, hee may put on those Robes of Immortalitie, which are future, and therefore *now are not"* (Ff6r). Tymme's devotional instructions, like Purchas's contrast between the ephemeral rags of this life and the glistening robes of a post-apocalyptic future, emphasise the timescales of ephemerality, and demonstrate how fleeting things were understood as analogues for man's short duration and as a means of conceiving of the unimaginable timescales of a Christianised cosmos.

In Tymme's account, it is man's reason that enables him to understand that only immortal things persist, and recognise "that his life is like vnto a shadowe, to a dreame, to a tale that is tolde, to a watch in the night, to smoake, to chaffe which the winde scattereth, to a water bubble, and such lik fading things". Tymme's rhapsodic collection of similes patches together a set of biblical verses that were regularly invoked as emblems of ephemerality. The speaker of Psalm 90 laments:

> For a thousand years in thy sight are but as yesterday when it is past, and as a watch in the night.
>   Thou carriest them away as with a flood; they are as a sleep: in the morning they are like grass which groweth up.
>   ...
>   For all our days are passed away in thy wrath: we spend our years as a tale that is told. (Ps 90.4, 5, 9)

These verses too were commonplaces: part of the mobile, flexible stock of phrases, sententiae, and ideas that were picked up and reworked by early modern writers across genres and contexts. Like Bowyer's commonplace book, they point to an enduring concern for ephemerality; a desire to preserve fleeting things for the individual reader and for generations to come.

"Man Vanished into Smoake": Ephemeral Humans

For the theologically orthodox early modern English man or woman, nearly all things, properly considered, were fleeting. All that was material was ephemeral; it was the immaterial that endured. As the surgeon and author John Hall reflected in one of his biblical paraphrases, it is only God's word "which dures and doth not fade":

> For mountaynes they shall moued be
> With water from their springes,
> And in thy sight harde thinges shal melt,
> As wexe and liquid thynges.
>
> And yet to them that doe thee feare
> Thy mercy doth extende:
> From the fyrste tyme to this present,
> And euer without ende. (H1v)

Hall's is one of the gentler apocalyptic visions of the period: other writers revelled in the global violence of the end of days. God's wrath, crowed the clergyman Lancelot Dawes, "will licke vp the sea like dust, and melt the mountains like waxe" (H4r).[7] But all shared the conviction that God alone was immortal, infinite and capacious; everything else was fleeting, mortal, bound by time.

Paying attention to immortality offers a way to rethink the relationship between materiality and ephemerality. Extraordinary duration, for us, is pinned to physicality: as Chakrabarty puts it "There remains a *material* side of time for geologists, for there is no geological time without geological objects" (22). Ephemerality, in contrast, is readily associated with a certain tenuousness, an uneasy relationship to the solid. It has a charged imaginative connection with touch: ephemerality is a property of things that are inherently fragile, miniature, or both, at least in the categories of insects and of paperwork which demarcate our primary analytical relationship to the concept (see especially the chapters by Boehrer and Anna Reynolds in this volume). Ephemeral things are vulnerable to handling. For early moderns, the relationship between that which is solid and that which is fleeting was different; the examples I chart in this section capture a willingness to conceive of things that are durable as inherently friable and to embrace the imperceptible and immaterial as fixed and lasting.

In 1619, Samuel Purchas published a follow-up to his popular *Purchas his Pilgrimage* (1614). Where *Purchas his Pilgrimage* was the culmination of almost twenty years of collecting oral and written accounts of global travel, *Purchas his Pilgrim Microcosmus, or the Historie of Man* took a different tack, promising on its title-page to instruct each reader in the "*Wonders of his* GENERATION, *Vanities in his* DEGENERATION, *Necessities of his* REGENERATION." The text is an extended meditation on mortality, prompted by a series of personal losses, including the death of Purchas's daughter in 1619. "Vanity" is a recurring term, and Purchas uses it in its strongest sense:

"that which is vain, futile, or worthless; that which is of no value or profit" (*OED*, 'vanity', *n.*, def 1a.). In his 1598 Italian-English dictionary, *A World of Words*, John Florio defined "Vaneggia" as "vanity, folly, lightnes, fondnes, doting in words or deeds. as Vanità. Also a voide place or grasse plot in a garden" (Oo3v). Thomas Wilson's *A Christian Dictionary* (1612) makes the ephemeral import of vanity clear: it is "A thing of no force, vse, or continuance. ... The Creature is subiect to Vanity; that is, to a vanishing and fleeting estate" (Kk3v). Transience was both emblematised and lamented within the vanitas tradition: the artistic and literary convention devoted to reminding readers and viewers of the lustre but also the impermanence of earthly pleasures, and the urgency of repentance (see Reynolds' chapter in this volume).

Purchas's project for much of the *Microcosmus* is to explore what a feeble, fleeting thing man is. According to the Table of Contents, Chapter 33 describes "Mans degradation beneath all profitable Beasts; comparing him with Beasts unprofitable, infectious, wilde, & beasts of prey". Chapter 34 goes further, promising readers a vision of "Man degraded beneath foure-footed Beasts, to the likenesse of venomous Serpents, and fabulous Monsters". Working down the Aristotelian hierarchy that privileged reason above animal life, and animism above vegetable existence, Purchas descends through the "vegetative" and ends by comparing man to things lacking sense or life: "Mans Retrograde pursued to Hay, Chaffe, Heath, Metals, Drosse, Stones" in chapter 37; "Mans successive degradation to Rocks, Bricks, Potsherds, Clay, Dung, Sands, Mortar, Dust, Ashes" in chapter 38.[8] As the book expands upon its themes, man becomes ever more evanescent: chapter 39 describes "Man vanished into Smoake, Darkenes, Tempestuous Clouds, Water, Froth, Vapours, Sleepe, Dreames; a Tale, Shadow, Nothing, lesse then Nothing" (A3v-A4r). Alert readers will recognise Purchas's source: like Tymme, he invokes and reworks Psalm 90, an enduring sequence of *topoi* or commonplaces of the ephemeral.

Purchas's style is to test and then exceed his sources: he reflects that even a tale "after the telling, leaues some impression, hath a being in vs, if not in it selfe; whereas Man is a *Shadow*" (Bb4r). Where the Psalm positions both stories and man as ephemeral, Purchas insists that fictions persist. This is a reality made manifest in Purchas's hefty patchwork of biblical citation, in which popular biblical verses are preserved and manipulated to new ends. Purchas's emphasis on the "impression" left by tales illustrates early modern attitudes to comprehension: readers and listeners were understood to receive sense impressions from the texts they read (or heard) and to be vulnerable to their effects.[9]

A couplet in Bowyer's commonplace book invites us to reflect further on influence, using the lingering presence of smell to imagine the enduring effects of education, whether virtuous or vicious.

What Lickar first the veselle doth reseue
The sent thereof bee^hind Lonnge time it Leavs AB (2r)

Early impressions endure, like the scent that lingers in a container. These lines rely on the reader's familiarity with the phenomenon of persistent smells: a shared, embodied memory. Often imagined as ephemeral, smell is the one sense experience that remains when a bottle's or jar's contents have long been used up or discarded (on smell, see Dugan). Like the perfumer's trade cards explored by William Tullett elsewhere in this collection, this couplet invites an imaginative sensory engagement from the reader. Bowyer's lines reflect on the influence of that which is taken in first, and the enduring effect of that which seems ephemeral, in ways that again act as a double-edged comment on her own practice of commonplacing.

In Purchas's account, Man has too high an opinion of himself by far. The stuff of which he is made "was not deriued from the Sunne, Starres, or any part of the AEthereall superiour World; no, not from the higher and nobler Elements; but from this lowest and basest of all, the Earth … [which] is but a point, and in manner as nothing to the Vniuerse" (C3r). The comparison of ephemeral and universal time is translated here into physical terms, invoking the same extremities of scale. In an extraordinary, baroque riff on the biblical commonplace that man is made of earth, Purchas reflects that Man is made of "*Dust*, the lightest, vnstablest, and most contemptible of her Possessions; and that, whereof the very Birds make their Nests, which the Beasts tread vnder their feet, the Creeping things dispose at pleasure, euery blast of Wind hurrieth and whirleth quite away, and euery plash of Water turns into myre" (C3v). This is a theme to which Purchas returns. Even sand persists, he insists in chapter thirty-eight, "Sands also are vsed for Mortar; but we *dawbe with vntempered Mortar*; we vse (as the Builders of Babel) *Slime in stead of Mortar*: wee are fruitlesse, heauie, easily diuided; but not strong & great, as the Sands: wee are liker the *Dust*, that yeelds not Mortar, but Myre" (Aa7v). The *Microcosmus* is relentless: man is not even "moister, weightier, fertiler Dust" but "Dust, in Originall; Ashes, by Corruption: for Sinne, as a Fire from Hell, hath consumed that *quondam* Originall Man into the Ashes of himself; he is now but Ruines, Rubbish, Dust, Cinders, and Ashes" (Aa8r). This drawn-out, conspicuously copious sentence is characteristic of Purchas, who spends a great deal of time dwelling on things that don't last. His expanding, hyperbolic prose brings into view the temporality of writing, highlighting the writing and reading hours required to convey just how evanescent mankind is.

In print, Purchas's list of nouns ("Ruines, Rubbish, Dust, Cinders") takes on a still more relentless quality. The compositor has set the commas between these words without spaces. It is not clear why: in the first vernacular English printing manual, published in parts between 1683 and 1684, Joseph Moxon suggests a lack or reduction of spacing is an aesthetically regrettable but forgivable response to a lack of space on the page.[10] But that explanation makes little sense here, where the following line is notably short ("ders, and Ashes") and is followed by a significant space before the start of the next chapter. Whatever the reason for this peculiarity of layout, the effect is twofold. It adds urgency to the rush of plural nouns and it reminds us of the passing time of the printing house: the window of human activity in which decisions are taken, or mistakes made, which can endure for centuries in print.

As he works his way down the hierarchy of being, Purchas emphasises at every turn the vanishing nature of man's existence. Riffing on the Old Testament sentence, "All flesh is grass" (Is. 40:6), a commonplace frequently engraved on English ledger stones and church monuments, Purchas instead translates "the vulgar Latin," *Omnis caro fœnum* as "*all flesh is Hay*, not *Grasse*, nor *Flowres* in the *fading*, but *already faded and vanished* from all degrees of life, cut downe and withered" (Z7r). In characteristically hyperbolic mode, Purchas pushes beyond the popular truism that life is ephemeral to argue that it is over before it has begun: we are not vital grass but dry hay. It is, ironically, in the comparison with those things that are least ephemeral – minerals – that Purchas enters most fully into his theme. "We haue the imperfections, the torpiditie, but not the perfection of stones, for strength and beautie" (Aa3r-Aa4v). Comparing humans negatively to stones, Purchas contrasts the perfections of polished and hewn stone against the roughness of "vnfashioned *Rocks*." But to reinforce man's lack of durability, he turns to crafted minerals, products of art: "We are meaner then *Bricke*, for this is durable: wee are like *Potters Uessels*, easily broken" (Aa6r). A marginal note directs the readers to Isaiah 64.8, "But now, O LORD, thou art our father; we are the clay, and thou our potter; and we all are the work of thy hand" (*KJV*).

The phrase "potter's vessels" invokes Isaiah 30.14, which develops a complex metaphor of the Egyptians' iniquity as a high wall, cracked by a breach: "And he shall break it as the breaking of the potters' vessel that is broken in pieces; he shall not spare: so that there shall not be found in the bursting of it a sherd to take fire from the hearth, or to take water withal out of the pit" (*KJV*). Purchas riffs upon the brittleness of clay, contrasting the perfection of divine creation with the reality of earthly wear and tear: "*Thou art our Potter, and wee the worke of thine hand*, may be spoken of our first and best estate: but we are now fallen, and broken in the Fall." The biblical comparison of man to clay or earth was pervasive in this period, invoked in sermons and devotional writings,

Figure 9.1 Tin-glazed earthenware plate with a hard white glaze and central inscription in blue: You & I are Earth 1661. © Museum of London.

poetry and commonplaces, and a host of other contexts.[11] It was reproduced on pottery like the 1661 plate in Figure 9.1, which reminds users "You & I are Earth."[12] In Purchas's writing, as elsewhere, the biblical commonplace and the everyday experience of pottery's propensity to break reinforce one another, creating a compelling poetics of the ephemeral as both materially and temporally frail.

Purchas's emphasis on "degeneration" and "corruption" reminds us of the physical purchase of these terms: corruption refers to "the destruction or spoiling of anything, *esp.* by disintegration or by decomposition with its attendant unwholesomeness; and loathsomeness; putrefaction," while degeneration refers specifically to the dissolution of formed matter: it is both the antithesis and the destined end of generation, the epitome of ephemerality on the grand scale (OED "Corruption, *n.*" def. 1a.; see Hunt in this volume for the manifestation of these processes in bronze statues). The physical force of "degeneration" is only partially captured in the definition offered by the *Oxford English Dictionary*: "The process of degenerating or becoming degenerate; the falling off from ancestral or earlier excellence; declining to a lower or worse stage of being; degradation of nature" ("degeneration, *n.*", def. 1a). For Purchas's readers, the term would axiomatically have invoked Aristotle's theories of matter, expressed in part in his *De generatione et corruption*, which explores the causes which constitute any given thing: the continual process of the shaping and dissolution of matter. In Latin (as in many modern Romance languages) the necessary link between existence and ephemerality is reinforced by the combination of noun and preposition: degeneration is inherent in "de generatione." Earth time is a continual, material process of creation and degradation; Purchas's articulation of its transformations anticipates Chakrabarty's view that the earth, "the stable and unshakable ground from which all human thoughts ... arose actually has always been a fitful and restless entity" (31). At the same time, the insistence of Purchas and his contemporaries on the ephemerality of earth time within the context of timeless divinity unsettles the yoking together of physical substance and passing time.

Erratic Ephemera

Purchas's preface, which describes the motivation behind his "more serious view of Humane Mortalitie, and all the Vanities thereon attending," underlines the role of the printed text, and books more generally, in preserving memory (¶4v). Against Purchas's recollection of his dying mother, a printed marginal note records "M. Anne *Purchas, March,* 13. Last"; a note below glosses the death of Purchas's daughter, *"MARIE Purchas* aged fifteene yeeres, *April* 15. 1619." William Sherman has explored how book users registered family events and kin or social relationships in the margins and blank spaces of books, recording and extending genealogies and networks (esp. Chapter 3). Here, Purchas reproduces that practice in print: the deaths of loved ones are not an addition to the printed text but the germinal force of the book. These printed marginal notes establish Purchas's personal misfortune as part of the larger record of human loss, a tissue of recollection, citation, and recording networked across the margins and endpapers of early modern England.

Every element of Purchas's book is conscripted to the project of reinforcing the fleetingness of man. In a note "To the Reader" that precedes a short errata list, Purchas reflects "That Man in his best is Vanitie, hath thus many witnesses, these Vanities, escaped in the Impressions of this Booke, my best diligence in perusing the same from the Presse, notwithstanding" (A8v). Errors of the press, and mistakes that have slipped through unobserved, become emblems of man's constitutive errancy. At the same time, Purchas's note reminds the reader of the ephemerality of error: "Some are in some cases mended," he reassures us, referring to the practice of stop-press correction in which mistakes spotted after a small number of sheets had been printed could be corrected in the forme before the printer completed the remaining sheets. This is a version of what Wendy Hui Kyong Chun terms the "enduring ephemeral": the material trace of deleted digital material, "neither alive nor dead, neither quite present nor absent" (133). In some copies of Purchas's text, errors that once existed have been removed, persisting only insofar as they are memorialised in Purchas's brief errata note.

A diligent reader of the Petyt Library copy of Purchas's text has responded to Purchas's plea – "Be intreated to amend these, to pardon all" – and gone through the text correcting the errors listed at the front of the book (University of York Library, Rare Books Collection, Petyt Collection SC 7-7-8-17). These manuscript emendations remind us that error has a vexed relationship to ephemerality: even when mistakes have been erased and corrected, they frequently endure, remaining present and legible. They resonate with Jonathan Gil Harris's account of the Archimedes Palimpsest, which both "capture[s] and cancel[s] Greek philosophy, preserving it in the present yet banishing it to the past by overwriting it with Christian liturgy". In a palimpsest, defined by the functions of erasure and overwriting, the "under-text … retains its legibility, albeit faintly" (15). Error has the potential to be ephemeral, caught, and corrected during the printing process. It also has the capacity to endure under erasure, formally cancelled while still wholly or partly present.

Bowyer's book too is a document of erasure as well as compilation. A preliminary draft of a list of inks, written on f. 6v in the same hand as the record of Grey's reinterment, has been scribbled out but remains legible, in part because of the different colours and intensities of the inks used to write the list and to blot it (on the affordances of ink, see Hannah Lilley's chapter in this volume). Along with the undeleted list of "Inckes. Or Colours" which follows (7r), this erased list offers a further permutation of the relationship between language and ephemerality: it aims to capture the distinctiveness of colours in ways that endure beyond, or allow for the reproduction of, their ephemeral existence. Bowyer is interested in ingredients: "red lead," for example, or "smalte," which is listed under blue, or "verdigreae," under green. This is a list of materials and effects, as much as of particular shades. "Lambe blacke" offers a puzzle. It is probably an idiosyncratic spelling (or mishearing) of "lamp black," a carbon produced by the incomplete combustion of heavy petroleum products. As a pigment or ink, lamp black is designed to endure, though as a polishing or blackening agent for domestic use, it attests to the constant processes of wear. "Lamb black," though, conjures something else entirely: the striking colours of young livestock, destined to grow and lose the intensity of their visual charm. Bowyer's concern for preservation is manifested as her list digresses into instructions "To bind any picture that is cut in Satine," before veering back to browns. After "Spanish Browne, & Red lead" and "Gambooch," a spice, the list of colours concludes with the indented words, "Love & Loyalty," possibly a heraldic reference to accompany these shades.

Bowyer's text, like Purchas's, speaks to memory as a material and temporal (and perhaps ephemeral) practice. Her commonplace book contains evidence that Bowyer marked *sententiae* for emphasis and as an aid to memory, sometimes with a stubby manicule, sometimes with a pin, evidenced by the holes that remain in the page.[13] The page of Bowyer's book which records the fate of Grey's body has been bookmarked: its bottom left corner retains a crease, a remnant of the quasi-ephemeral marking technique that is dog-earing. Within a single page, time expands and contracts, taking in everything from the ephemerality of the fold to the timeless future of the resurrection, along with the transience and persistence of all things in between.

> In her *Miscelenia*, Elizabeth Grymeston reminds readers:
> Life is a bubble blowen vp with a broath,
> Whose wit is weaknesse, and whose wage is death (C3r)

These lines illustrate Grymeston's own commonplacing practice: they are adapted from Spenser's *The Shepheardes Calender*, replacing his idiosyncratic "youngth" with the generalising "life" (Spenser B1r). Either Grymeston or the print-house compositor has made an apt mistake, transforming Spenser's "breath" to "broath." Readers might spot the mis-rhyme with "death" and make a mental correction; they might instead be prompted to link the transience of life with the familiar thick bubbles of soup at the point of boiling. Grymeston's verse epitomises many of the themes of this chapter: the temporality of copying, print, and error; the transformations of commonplacing; the experience of natural or artificial phenomena; and the evanescence of life. In accounts of ephemerality, and reflections on the transience of things, early modern English readers were asked to understand their existence as an exercise in momentariness, a bubble. Yet it was in meditating on ephemerality that theologians, writers, and readers could imagine the possibility of something immaterial, persisting not just to the end of, but beyond, time.

Notes

1 My division between the material and immaterial is shorthand for a much more complex set of ideas. The materiality of God, the heavens, angels and other divine things was a topic of extensive debate. See, for example, Joad Raymond, *Milton's Angels*, esp. Chapter 7, and James Kearney, *The Incarnate Text*, esp. Introduction.

2 Sara Pennell notes the reluctance of many studies of material culture

> to engage fully with ephemerality in the (material) historical record, and how non-durability has a part to play in that record. ... [O]ur preoccupation with the surviving, whether document or dish, leaves us little historiographical space to consider the discarded, the non-surviving (30).

3 As Catherine Richardson notes, attending to wear and use encourages us to "think ... of the individuality of things and the way they relate to the body – my old leather doublet, with its unique marks of wear and the length of its association with my changing body whose shape it bears" (18).

4 On interiority and privacy, see Orlin.

5 The first Ashmolean Museum, built on Oxford's Broad Street to house the cabinet of curiosities Ashmole presented to the University of Oxford in 1677, was opened in 1683. See MacGregor. On the collecting impulses of the early modern period, see especially Findlen.
6 On connections between mind, soul and reason in the early modern period, see Park.
7 Cf. Micah 1:4, "And the mountains shall be molten under him, and the valleys be cleft, as wax before the fire, and as the waters that are poured down a steep place" (*KJV*); Psalm 97:5, "the hills melted like wax at the presence of the LORD, at the presence of the Lord of the whole earth" (*KJV*).
8 On the tripartite soul, see Park, 'Psychology'.
9 On the psychophysiology of reading, see Craik; Smith, *Grossly Material Things*, chapter 5.
10 "*Thin-spaces*," insists Moxon, should be used to help justify lines, rather than between words (where a letter space should be used), "yet do some *Compositers* too often commit this error, rather than put themselves to the trouble of *Spacing* out a *Line*" (207–08).
11 On the use of biblical commonplaces and sententiae across a wide range of domestic and public surfaces, see Morrall.
12 On the ephemerality of pottery, see Pennell.
13 On marking and marginalia, see Sherman; Acheson (ed.). See also blog posts by Giscombe and Duroselle-Melish, which illuminate the use of pins in books.

Works Cited

Acheson, Katherine, ed. *Early Modern English Marginalia*. Routledge, 2019.
Ashmole MS 51. MS. Bodleian Library, Oxford.
Barker, Thomas. *The Art of Angling*. London, 1653.
Bodenham, John (attrib.). *Bel-vedédere, or, The Garden of the Muses*. London, 1600.
Boehrer, Bruce. "Time's Flies: Ephemerality in the Early Modern Insect World." *Practices of Ephemera in Early Modern England*. Eds Callan Davies, Hannah Lilley, and Catherine Richardson. Routledge, 2023. 44–64.
Burke, Victoria E. "Ann Bowyer's Commonplace Book (Bodleian Library Ashmole MS 51): Reading and Writing Among the 'Middling Sort'." *Early Modern Literary Studies* 6.3 (2001): 1.1–28.
Chakrabarty, Dipesh. "Anthropocene Time." *History and Theory* 57:1 (2018): 5–32.
Chun, Wendy Hui Kyong. *Programmed Visions: Software and Memory*. Harvard UP, 2011.
Craik, Katherine A. *Reading Sensations in Early Modern England*. Palgrave, 2007.
Dawes, Lancelot. *Gods Mercies and Jerusalems Miseries*. London, 1609.
Donne, John. *LXXX Sermons Preached by that Learned and Reverend Divine, John Donne*. London, 1640.
Drayton, Michael. *Englands Heroicall Epistles*. London, 1597.
Dugan, Holly. *The Ephemeral History of Perfume: Scent and Sense in Early Modern England* John Hopkins UP, 2011.
Duroselle-Melish, Caroline. "A Pin's Worth: Pins in Books." *The Collation*. August 4th 2015. Online. Accessed 21 Jan. 2022.

Findlen, Paula. *Possessing Nature: Museums, Collecting, and Scientific Culture in Early Modern Italy*. U of California P, 1994.

Florio, John. *A Worlde of Wordes*. London, 1598.

Giscombe, Jane. "The Use of Pins in Early Modern England." *The Book and Paper Gathering*. 31st May 2018. Online. Accessed 21 Jan. 2022.

de Grazia, Margreta, Maureen Quilligan, and Peter Stallybrass. "Introduction." *Subject and Object in Renaissance Culture*. Cambridge UP, 1996. 1–16.

Grymeston, Elizabeth. *Miscelenea. Meditations. Memoratiues*. London, 1604.

Hall, John. "Judith 16." *The Courte of Vertue*. London, 1565.

Harris, Jonathan Gil. *Untimely Matter in the Time of Shakespeare*. U of Pennsylvania P, 2009.

Hunt, Katherine. "More Lasting Than Bronze: Statues, Writing, and the Materials of Ephemera in Ben Jonson's *Sejanus His Fall*." *Practices of Ephemera in Early Modern England*. Eds Callan Davies, Hannah Lilley, and Catherine Richardson. Routledge, 2023. 111–27.

Jackson, Thomas. *The Eternall Truth of Scriptures, and Christian Beleefe*. London, 1613.

Jonson, Ben. *The Workes of Benjamin Jonson*. London, 1641.

Kearney, James. *The Incarnate Text: Imagining the Book in Reformation England*. U of Pennsylvania P, 2009.

Lilley, Hannah. "Uncovering Ephemeral Practices: Itineraries of Black Ink and the Experiments of Thomas Davis." *Practices of Ephemera in Early Modern England*. Eds Callan Davies, Hannah Lilley, and Catherine Richardson. Routledge, 2023. 128–47.

MacGregor, Arthur. *The Ashmolean Museum: A Brief History of the Museum and its Collections*. Ashmolean, 2001.

Maplet, John. *A Greene Forest, or A Naturall Historie*. London, 1567.

Mitchell, Joni. *Big Yellow Taxi*. Song. 1970.

Morrall, Andrew. "Domestic Decoration and the Bible in the Early Modern Home." *The Oxford Handbook of the Bible in Early Modern England, c. 1530–1700*. Eds Kevin Killeen, Helen Smith, and Rachel Willie. Oxford UP, 2015. 577–97.

Moss, Ann. *Printed Commonplace-Books and the Structuring of Renaissance Thought*. Clarendon, 1996.

Moxon, Joseph. *Mechanick Exercises on the Whole Art of Printing (1683–1684)*. Eds Herbert Davis and Harry Carter. Dover, 1978.

Orlin, Lena Cowen. *Locating Privacy in Tudor London*. Oxford UP, 2007.

Park, Katherine. "Psychology: The Organic Soul." *The Cambridge History of Renaissance Philosophy*. Eds C. B. Schmitt, Quentin Skinner, Eckhard Kessler and Jill Kraye. Cambridge UP, 1990. 464–84.

Pennel, Sara. "For a Crack Or Flaw Despis'd: Thinking about Ceramic Durability and the 'Everyday' in Late Seventeenth- and Early Eighteenth-Century England." *Everyday Objects: Medieval and Early Modern Culture and its Meanings*. Eds Tara Hamling and Catherine Richardson. Ashgate, 2010. 27–40.

Purchas, Samuel. *Purchas His Pilgrim Microcosmus*. London, 1619.

Raymond, Joad. *Milton's Angels: The Early-Modern Imagination*. Oxford UP, 2010.

Reynolds, Anna. "What do Texts and Insects have in Common?; Or, Ephemerality before Ephemera." *Practices of Ephemera in Early Modern England*.

Eds Callan Davies, Hannah Lilley, and Catherine Richardson. Routledge, 2023. 25–43.

Richardson, Catherine. *Shakespeare and Material Culture*. Oxford UP, 2011.

Rogers, Richard. *Seuen Treatises Containing Such Direction As Is Gathered Out of the Holie Scriptures*. London, 1603.

Russell, Gillian. *The Ephemeral Eighteenth Century: Print, Sociability, and the Cultures of Collecting*. Cambridge UP, 2020.

Sherman, William H. *Used Books: Marking Readers in Renaissance England*. U of Pennsylvania P, 2007.

Smith, Helen. *Grossly Material Things: Women and Book Production in Early Modern England*. Oxford UP, 2012.

Smyth, Adam. "Commonplace Book Culture: a List of Sixteen Traits." *Women and Writing, c. 1340–1650: The Domestication of Print Culture*. Eds Anne Lawrence-Mathers and Phillipa Hardman. York Medieval, 2010. 90–110.

Spenser, Edmund. *The Shepheardes Calender*. London, 1579.

Travitsky, Betty S. *Subordination and Authorship in Early Modern England: The Case of Elizabeth Cavendish Egerton and Her "Loose Papers"*. Arizona Center for Medieval and Renaissance Studies, 1999.

Tullett, Will. "Extensive Ephemera: Perfumer's Trade Cards in Eighteenth-Century England." *Practices of Ephemera in Early Modern England*. Eds Callan Davies, Hannah Lilley, and Catherine Richardson. Routledge, 2023. 210–28.

Tymme, Thomas. *A Silver Watch-Bell*. London, 1605.

Wilson, Thomas. *A Christian Dictionarie*. London, 1612.

Wolfe, Heather. "Reading Bells and Loose Papers: Reading and Writing Practices of the English Benedictine Nuns of Cambrai and Paris." *Early Modern Women's Manuscript Writing: Selected Papers from the Trinity/Trent Colloquium*. Eds Jonathan Gibson and Victoria E. Burke. Ashgate, 2004. 135–56.

Part III
Environments/Buzzing

10 Toy Coach from London

Michael Lewis

Deposition, survival and recovery are key stages in the "life cycle" of archaeological finds (Robbins 27–37), offering clues about how they were used, valued and curated in the past. These items entered the ground as a result of casual loss, disposal or ritual activity etc., leading to a variety of archaeological interpretations, depending on context (including spatial and topographic), as well as understandings of human society and culture through time (Gilchrist 216–51).

The River Thames is a graveyard for finds of all periods, with its foreshore offering rich pickings for those (mostly mudlarks) scavenging for archaeology (Cohen and Wragg; Maiklem), particularly since these items can be well preserved (certainly surviving better than they would in the ploughzone on land) thanks to the anaerobic conditions of the river mud. Even now, Londoners use the Thames to throw away and conceal objects or to make ritual offerings on the riverbank, as they have done for centuries.

Amongst the items recovered from the Thames foreshore and recorded with the Portable Antiquities Scheme (PAS) – established to record archaeological finds made by the public – was a toy coach of late sixteenth-century date (LON-81D1C7; Lewis 328). An object of (apparent) ephemera that was once exquisite and created with care, but latterly (seemingly) thrown away, (ironically) only to survive because of its purposeful destruction.

Around the mid-sixteenth century, coaches "seem suddenly to have become much more plentiful and fashionable" (Forsyth and Egan 316), and this is reflected in their survival as "toys." Several fragments thereof have been found in London (Forsyth and Egan 316–22), as well as in the Low Countries (Willemsen, *Kinder* 261; Willemsen, "Poppengoed" 350); a complete example (of Forsyth and Egan Type 1, like the PAS example) was recorded by the Portable Antiquities of the Netherlands (PAN: 1876) from a cesspit dated to 1640, though based on form it is probably late sixteenth century.

DOI: 10.4324/9781003058588-14

Such coaches are rarely found complete, due to the fact they are usually made from component thin cast lead-alloy parts (Forsyth and Egan 316). In the case of the near-complete example from London, the item was not only discarded in the Thames, but (seemingly) crumpled first, thus ensuring that its (delicate and easily disarticulated) parts remained together. It was in this state that it was recovered through metal-detecting and then reconstructed (and resurrected) by its finder, Andy Johannesen.

We can only wonder why it was crumpled and thrown away. Maybe it was broken, perhaps by a child in a fit of anger, and then screwed up, possibly even repurposed as a ball. It seems that the object was then purposefully delivered to the Thames – though perhaps (as a ball) it was accidentally lost. The object's materiality suggests it was simple to make, and (if owned by the right sort) could be discarded with ease. Its life story therefore suggests the coach was owned by those in a social group with newly disposable incomes – perhaps a child of the middling sort (Figures 10.1 and 10.2).

Acknowledgements

Special thanks to Andy Johannesen and Mirjam Kars for help with this "paper," but also all those involved within our publication "draft party" group, including Callan Davies, Katherine Hunt, Hannah Lilley, Catherine Richardson, and Helen Smith.

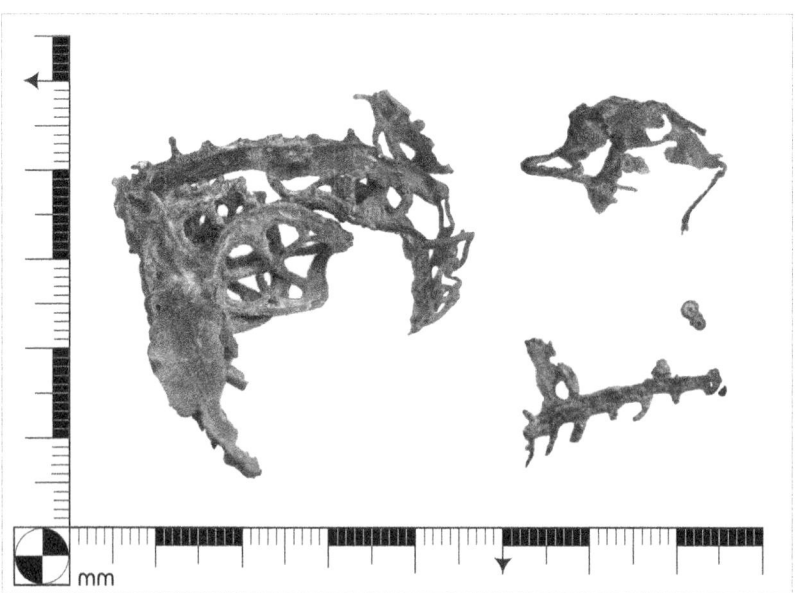

Figure 10.1 Toy carriage from London as found. LON-81D1C7. London, British Museum, Portable Antiquities Scheme.

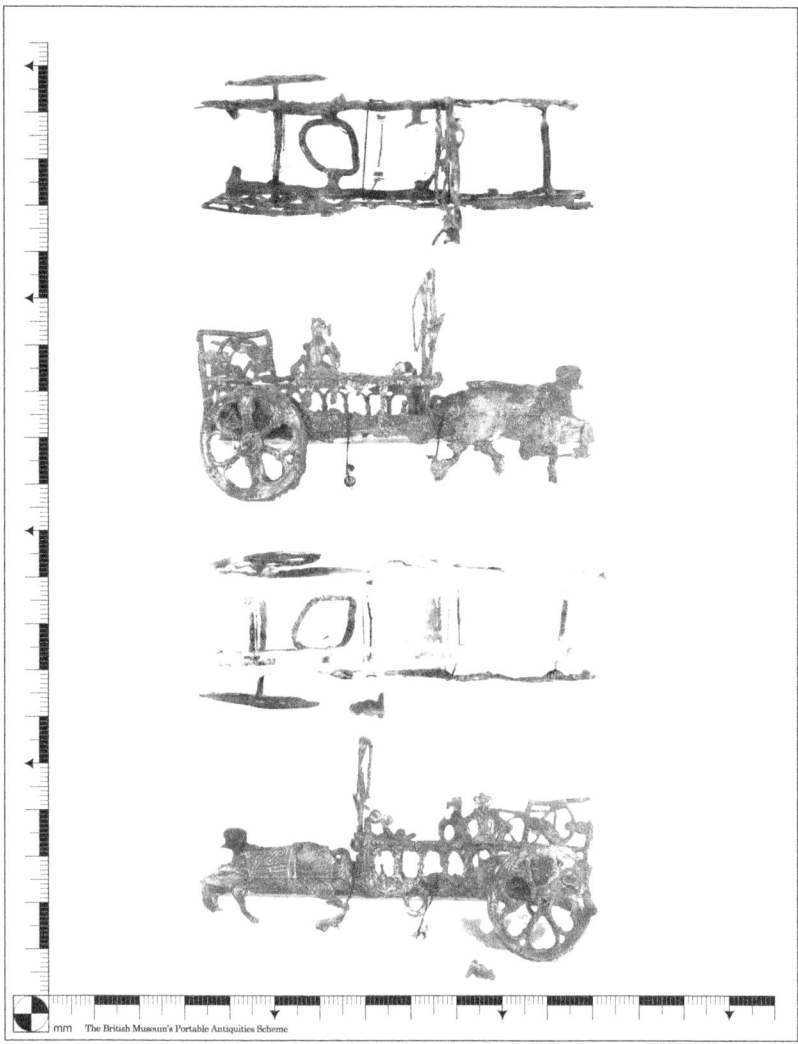

Figure 10.2 Toy carriage from London as reconstructed. LON-81D1C7. London, British Museum, Portable Antiquities Scheme.

Works Cited

Cohen, Nathalie and Eliott Wragg. *The River's Tale: Archaeology on the Thames Foreshore in Greater London.* MOLA, 2017.

Forsyth, Hazel and Geoff Egan. *Toys, Trinkets and Trifles: Base Metal Miniatures from London's River Foreshore 1150–1800.* Unicorn, 2005.

Gilchrist, Roberta, *Medieval Life: Archaeology and the Life Course.* Boydell, 2012.

Lewis, Michael, "Report of the Portable Antiquities Scheme 2009." *Post Medieval Archaeology* 45.2 (2011): 325–36.

Maiklem, Lara. *Mudlarking: Lost and Found on the River Thames*. Blooms-bury, 2019.

Robbins, Katherine Jane. *From Past to Present: Understanding the Impact of Sampling Bias on Data Recorded by the Portable Antiquities Scheme*. Diss. U of Southampton, 2002.

Willemsen, Annemarieke, *Kinder Delijt: middeleeuws speelgoed in de Neder-landen*. Nijmegen UP, 1998.

Willemsen, Annemarieke. "Poppengoed Precies Bekeken Verzameling: her-komst en functie van loodtinnen miniatuurtjes." *Lost and Found: Essays on Medieval Archaeology for H. J. E. van Beuuingen*. Eds D. Kichen, J. Kolde-weij, and J. ter Moen. Rotterdam Papers 2. BOOR, 2000. 347–55.

11 Maritime Ephemera in Walter Mountfort's *The Launching of the Mary*

Jemima Matthews

In 1632, on a voyage home from Persia, Walter Mountfort wrote a play entitled *The Launching of the Mary: The Seaman's Honest Wife*. The play explores the role of the East India Company (EIC) and its impact on three maritime communities in Blackwall. The main plot is a formal dialogue between company officials as they monitor work on the *Mary*, a company vessel in the shipyard. They debate the role the company plays in overseas trade and the maintenance of both its ships and the families of the sailors away at sea. The second plot focuses on three sailors' wives and their attempts to support themselves. It follows two wives as they wander through London sampling its pleasures whilst carrying low-value products they pass off as luxury commodities brought by the EIC ships. Their deceptive wandering is set up in opposition to a third wife who chooses to stay at home and produce silk work. The final plot concerns workers preparing the *Mary* in the Blackwall shipyard before it is launched at the end of the play. The latter two plots undermine the claims made in the main plot by company officials defending the actions of the company overseas and at home. Whilst the main plot presents a formal debate, the subplots provide an insight into the material and social conditions of the male and female riverside communities and the impact of overseas trade on their lives, livelihoods, and bodies.

Mountfort's play is a product of his work as a clerk for the EIC and it records the movement of ephemera transported from India to the eastern suburbs of London. These commodities included pepper, cloves, nutmeg, raw silk and Indigo, which had their own relatively short life cycles as well as being used as ingredients in other luxury consumables. Silk and associated silk work, which might appear to have the longest life cycle in this collection of goods, proves to be the most ephemeral material in *Launching* where the substitution made by two wives of low-grade goods for silk work means that at points on stage the silk does not just have a relatively short life cycle, in fact, its existence is itself a fiction. Ephemera arriving by ship could be easily used up, misplaced, misappropriated, or simply vanish in the commotion of the city. The three subplots in *Launching* place continual pressure on the relationship between bodies and various ephemera. One of the subplots of the play concerns

DOI: 10.4324/9781003058588-15

ship workers who embody the tools of their craft. They are called respectively Tar, Tallow, Sheathing nail, Trunnel and Oakum. These materials were deployed to make a vessel watertight and were themselves ephemeral components of the ship requiring regular maintenance and replacement. These consumables had a shorter lifecycle than the ship itself and were regularly used up or worn away. Their maintenance was crucial to prolong the lifecycle of the ship. In the play, the materials act as extensions of the identity of the workers and the labourers themselves contemplate the relationship between maritime wear and tear and their own working and aging bodies. The luxury and high-value consumables brought by the ship contrast with, but also provide a parallel to, the quotidian low-value consumables used to repair the ship.

Written at sea over the duration of his voyage, Mountfort's manuscript bears the imprint of his inked finger and additional marks made by water and travel. The page has been textured by his bodily impression and additional traces are the result of contact with his writing site on-board *The Blessing*. The surface of the page remembers both the labour of its writer and their contact with an aqueous environment. This chapter examines ephemera captured on the surface of the manuscript, ephemera encountered within the play world, and the role of travel itself as, what Joshua Fisher has termed, an "ephemeral act" (139). It does so by considering the points of contact between the luxury items brought from India, the ephemeral materials used to resurface the ship, and the associated working bodies that make ephemera legible on the page and stage. I argue that attention to these surfaces (page, object, body) reveals a set of new entangled histories about maritime ephemera in the 1630s. In the context of long voyages undertaken by maritime communities these entangled histories begin and end with the bodies of those on board. Bodies and their labour were essential to the process of preservation of perishable and permeable ephemera carried within or coating the outside of individual vessels. Mountfort's third plot concerning ship workers highlights that the bodies which carried, packed, repaired or deployed tools and materials were also altered, changed, used up, or worn away. These bodies and their ephemeral surfaces are also part of this history. This chapter begins by examining the role of travel as an "ephemeral act" and the etymology of "ephemera"; after that it turns to the ephemeral surface of the text before shifting to the ephemera inside Mountfort's playworld. The ephemera within the play fall into three categories: the listed item, the circulated object, and the embodied material.

"Ephemeral Acts" and Ephemeral Etymology

Mountfort's play is preoccupied with "things" and yet when speaking of the play as a whole his prologue claims that "[t]he sea made this" (14). Mountfort suggests that the sea has shaped the text's import and substrate, implying that both are formed by the aqueous terrain and travel upon its surface. In his study of travel literature and ephemera, Fisher has observed "[b]y its very nature, travel is an ephemeral act. The transitory process of seeking out and desiring place is defined by mobility and unfixity" (139–40). Travel can be traced in the etymology of the word "ephemera" itself through different modes of "mobility and unfixity" and it is undoubtedly this connection and overlapping etymology which underlies Fisher's definition of travel as an "ephemeral act" even if this is not made explicitly clear in his argument. This etymological layering also, I would argue, underlies Mountfort's assertion that the "sea made" his play.

In order to demonstrate this etymological layering it is necessary to trace the definitions not only of the word "ephemera," but also of the interconnected cluster of words through which "ephemera" itself is defined. To illustrate this, I have set them out in sequence below. The *Oxford English Dictionary (OED)* defines "ephemera" as:

> **ephemera, n.2,** 2. transferred and figurative. One who or something which has a **transitory** existence. (*OED*, "ephemera" n.2, 2.)
>
> **transitory, adj. and n.** 1. Not lasting; **temporary**; brief, **fleeting**; 2. Of the nature of a **passage** or **transition**; **transitional**. (OED, "transitory" adj. and n. 1, 2.)
>
> **fleeting, adj.** †1. Floating; of a fish: Swimming. Obsolete. †2. That moves constantly, shifting, unstable, wandering; hence of a person or his attributes: Changeable, fickle, inconstant, vacillating. Obsolete. 4. **Passing** swiftly by. Chiefly of life or time. 5. **Passing** or gliding swiftly away. 6. Existing for a brief period; not permanent or enduring; **transitory, passing, fading.** (OED, "fleeting" adj. 1, 2, 4, 5, v.)
>
> **temporary, adj. and n.,** 1a. Lasting for a limited time; existing or valid for a time (only); not permanent; **transient**; made to supply a passing need. (OED, "temporary" adj. and n., 1a.)
>
> **transient, adj. and n.** A. adj. 1. a. Not lasting; temporary; brief, **fleeting**; †3. **Passing** or flowing through; **passing** from one thing or person to another. Obsolete. 4. a. **Passing** through a place without staying in it, or staying only for a short time. (OED, "transient" adj. and n. A. adj 1a., 3, 4a.)
>
> **transition, n.,** 2.a. A **passing** or **passage** from one condition, action, or (rarely) place, to another; **change.** (OED, "transition" n.2a.)
>
> **passage, n.** 1. a. The action of going or moving onward, across, or past; movement from one place or point to another, or over or through a space or medium; transit. (OED, "passage" n. 1.a.)
>
> **passage, v.2,** 1. a. intransitive. To travel, esp. in a boat or ship; to go or move onward, across, or past. Also figurative. b. transitive. To travel across or by way of (a body of water). (OED, "passage" v.2, 1a, 1b.)

> passing, adj., prep., and adv. A. adj. 1. a. Of time, or things bound or measured by time: that passes away or elapses; that is in the process of **passing away; transient, fleeting; ephemeral.** (OED, "passing" adj., prep., and adv. A. adj. 1.a)

These interlinking definitions of ephemera highlight four broad but distinct issues: time, movement, fragility, and change. Observing these OED definitions together reveals some surprising additional preoccupations. Associations with mobility and travel especially by water recur, all implicating the role of movement. "[M]obility and unfixity," which are according to Fisher the key preoccupations of travel, neatly encompass these four issues. Each of the definitions cited above incorporates one or more of these components. Movement is essential to the deployment of ephemera in Mountfort's play. Ephemera are associated in the OED definitions, and in the play itself, with what is "transient," "passing," and an anticipated or observed "transition" from "one condition, action, or [...] place, to another." In Mountfort's play ephemera is bound up in larger movements of trade or local negotiations and exchanges, including, in the case of the sailor's wives, the fraudulent substitution of low-grade goods for high-value commodities. Ephemera, as these definitions highlight, are inherently changeable either diminishing in perceived value or requiring replacement through diminishing quality or simply becoming interchangeable. The sailor's wives in *Launching*, as I will show, highlight the ephemerality of commodities brought by the EIC by rendering them easily interchangeable or even demonstrating that their very existence may in fact be fiction. Moreover, their wandering associates their own identities with the instability of the goods they carry. Ephemera are present in the play at the level of description, as physical properties on stage, and as action, or movement. Mountfort's play is not in fact about *his* travels, instead, it is about various forms of "ephemeral act" and it is constructed around moments of "mobility and unfixity" involved in tracing traveling maritime ephemera as it moves through the city and the shipyard. Before we turn to the play, however, I would like to linger for a moment at the surface of the manuscript.

Ephemeral Page

Written on board a ship on its voyage home to London, this play was exposed to a variety of writing conditions. The surface of Mountfort's page plays witnesses to numerous "ephemeral acts" over the course of his travels. We are now more attuned to the material nature of manuscripts and the value of minutiae on the surface of the page. Mountfort appears to have used "at least three different inks" a "brown," a "blackish," and a "paler ink" (Walter viii). Written over the course of a year the colour of the inks clearly represents different batches or inks of different compositions or sources. It may even suggest that some were less reliable or even made on board the vessel. As Hannah Lilley has shown, the ink-making process was lengthy and might be shaped around daily routine. In his prologue, Mountfort suggests "He did yt, wch did doe yt to reviue/his stupid sences" (12–13). Mountfort argues that the "sea made this" (14) and on long voyages ink making as well as play writing may well have been one of the activities structuring time and "reviu[ing]" both body and mind. He compares the process of playwriting to the practice of a chemist:

> The limbecke of our author hath distilld salt water into fresh. Each scene is filld wth various distillations. To extract fresh out of salt (though Comon) is an acte of a good Chymist: This was done at sea on land tis facile. (6–11)

Matteo Pangallo has commented on the unusual ability of Mountfort's page to record the voyage itself. Pangallo observes that it is possible:

> to consider the physical manuscript of the play as a chronicle in microcosm of Mountfort's voyage back to London in 1632. The variation of the ink on the folio pages suggests it was written over a long period of time, sometimes perhaps by candle-light in a cabin, but often out upon the deck. There seem to be water stains on some pages and, as the Malone Society editor of the play, J. H. Walter [1933], observed, '[i]t seems possible that one of the inks used was very susceptible to sea air' and had begun to fade even while the document was being written, requiring the author to write over some words in a darker ink at a later date. ("Seldome Seene" 6)

The intriguing surface of the page encourages Pangallo to imagine writing moments and moments of encounter during the voyage. The idea that these passing changes, ephemeral moments, might be traced in the manuscript suggests that the object itself is transitional, "characterised by or involving transition or change." It is "something intermediate or undergoing a transition; something temporary or passing" (OED, "transitional" adj. and n. A. adj a., B. n.,). As it is "intermediate," it has the capacity to illustrate passing phenomena from the voyage such as changes in light, air, salt, ink composition, and so on, on its surface. The surface or substrate of this manuscript is transitional, prepared in transit it captures ephemeral marks of travel as well as time.

It might be possible to argue that any manuscript in this period is in its very nature transitional. Unfinished, these documents are susceptible to change from successive writers, readers and archivists. The manuscript certainly contains other transitional components which do not relate to the voyage. Mountfort's text contains not only Mountfort's hand and

marks over time but also the marks of the censor, Henry Herbert, exer-
cising his right to impose cuts and reconfigure the text. The same surface
captures and holds in limbo the changing nature of the text as it comes
into contact with different working practices – at sea and in the theatrical market. It traces "layers" of engagement with and negotiation with
the censor as well as illustrating the changes made after circulating back
to the author and the additional marks of a bookkeeper (Pangallo, *Playwriting* 79–81). The manuscript can be thought of as a "thing" in process, undergoing change, with suggested alterations, substitutions, and
modifications by multiple actors human and non-human visible on its
surface. The aspects of the text which should be removed are, however,
still visible in their annotated-for-excision form. It is in this sense an
object held in transition, passing but not passed, and changing but not
changed. The surface of the manuscript accounts for its past encounters
with the ephemeral environment of the ocean and the future absence of
sections of its text deemed inappropriate or impractical for performance.
It is suspended in transition. The object is not inert but a traveling site
of communication.

Furthermore, the transitional nature of this manuscript is remarkable
in terms of its connection to travel and the body. The changes in the ink
when Mountfort wrote in different ink, or light or exposed the paper
to 'sea air' results in a surface in and on which it is possible to observe
the passing ephemeral environment of the journey itself: in Pangallo's
terms a "chronicle" or "microcosm." The inks on its surface trace passing time, changing writing conditions, and indeed increasing distance
travelled on the voyage ("Seldome Seene" 11). Nevertheless, the manuscript also captures transient contact with the author himself, his writing
practices, and his body. In fact, the manuscript also includes:

> another unusual, perhaps unique feature in this manuscript that
> seems to date from this round of revisions and that also represents
> the author 'writing' himself into his work: literal fingerprints. On
> several pages it appears that Mountfort has accidentally placed his
> thumb into blots of ink and left his thumbprints on the paper (on one
> page, there are two prints squarely opposite each other in the mar-
> gins, indicating precisely how he held the leaf) ("Seldome Seene" 11)

The surface of the page becomes the archive of contact between body
and environment whilst writing. The writer's bodily contact with a
text is one of the physical encounters between text and body which are
rarely captured and held by the text itself but offer a tantalising glimpse
of the arrangement of body and page whilst writing. These accidental
marks are representative of the essential role of the ephemera in his play.
The notable absence or presence of bodies in relation to the ephemera
discussed, displayed or exchanged in Mountfort's playworld becomes

important in terms of the play's explicit praise but implicit criticism of the EIC. In order to illustrate how this works, it is necessary to trace the play's three modes of engagement with ephemera in three different plots. *Launching* is preoccupied with ephemera in three states: the listed item, the circulated thing, and the embodied or anthropomorphised material. In the subsequent three sections of this essay, I will explore ephemera which is listed, carried, and circulated or embodied by the workers employed on the ship.

Mercantile Lists and Tables

In Mountfort's play, the plot focusing on the EIC officials concerns the defence of the company against criticism of its waste of money and resources. As critics like Bradley Ryner have noted, this plot is largely based on mercantile treatises and, in particular, sections of the dialogue are paraphrased from Thomas Mun's, *A Discourse of Trade* (1621) (Ryner 18; Pangallo, *Playwriting* 79). Certain sections of the play text present a table found in Mun's text comparing the price of goods brought from India and Aleppo (398–407). A table is, as Ryner notes, a mercantile mechanism created in order to present multiple transactions and designed to show the "aggregate" rather than the "individual" sale (19). City comedy reduces multiple ephemeral transactions within the metropolis into a few salient examples. Mountfort's play takes this concept a stage further and presents an attempt to integrate a mercantile tool into what is, at least in part, a city, or suburban, comedy. Mountfort's characters ventriloquise Mun's page, making it "speak" (Ryner 16). Nevertheless, Mountfort does not manage the transfer from written text to performance especially effectively. Ryner argues that the economic metaphors used in the plot concerning Doretea, the eponymous seaman's wife, are effective, whilst the debates concerning the company's trade through the integration of lists are not. "[T]he stage," he suggests, "might function to question, rather than simply transmit economic models" but when it is expected to simply "transmit," as in the case of the table from Mun, it is much more problematic (19). In fact, a table like the one comparing prices of pepper, cloves, mace, nutmeg, and indigo brought from Turkey and Lisbon to those from India (1769–1804) is marked up by the censor or playhouse reviser for removal (Ryner 17). Mountfort sets out the table in this manner:

		H
	400000H. of pepper at 3^s. 6^d. the H. mony.	70000. 0. 0./
In Turkie/	40000. of cloues. at. 8^s.	16000.
	20000. of mace. at. 9^s.	9000.0-0-
	160000. of Nutmeggs: at: 4^s. 6^d.	36000.
	150000. of Indico at. 7^s.	52500. 0-0-
	Sume Totall.	183500^H.0.0/

In England thus. a little more or lesse./.

	H	S	d
400000H. of pepper at. 20^d. PH. mony.-	33333.	6.	8.
40000. of Cloues . at 6^s.	12000.	0.	0.
20000. Of Mace at. 6^s.	6000.		
160000. Of Nutmeggs. at. [4^s. 6.] 2^s. 6^d.-	20000.	0.	0.
150000. Of Indico. at. 5^s.	37000.		
sume totall.	108333.	6.	8.

(1773–1785)

Its very ineptitude for the stage is something that makes it intriguing for a discussion of the relationship between ephemera and the body, precisely because the body is absent from and not required by a table or list other than to recite it. In her discussion of the use of lists in early English travel literature, Kelly Wisecup notes that "objects influenced actions and communications in cross-cultural encounters" and "lists" are the "outcomes of cross-cultural negotiations about the meanings of objects" (267, 266). Wisecup does not consider Mountfort's play but many of the items listed in Mountfort's play are the result of an enormously complex set of "cross-cultural encounters" and cross-cultural "negotiations." Whilst the table focuses on the relative value of goods from India or Aleppo, the cross-cultural encounters and negotiations, which are the context for these items, are written out of Mountfort's play. The company officials dismiss the charges concerning the death of seamen and the poverty of their wives and children. In fact, one of the few mentions of the complex and fraught social context of their trade is the conflict between the Dutch East India Company and the EIC (1624–1637) and the Amboyna massacre of English merchants (1076–1125). This is included by Mountfort but then marked by the censor for omission. Pangallo notes that there is evidence of Mountfort trying to work around the censor, adding in enough material so that his audience can work out the context from the discussions between the workmen (*Playwriting* 81–85). Nevertheless, the reality, or human cost of this global trade is written out by the censor (Christensen, "Absent" 118). What is also pertinent to my argument is that the potentially violent and exploitative cross-cultural encounters which lie behind these items, calculations and figures, or the bodies which carry, transport, pack, and unpack these goods are not noted. What a table or list is very effective in achieving is writing out the human, bodily element. This technique is unusual in a play that elsewhere, as I show, is obsessed with the relationship between ephemera and the ephemeral body.

Wisecup notes as a general principal that "[l]ists are defined as antithetical to narrative" and this antithetical nature is undoubtedly part of the context for the decision to remove the table (265). The reviser appears to think the table is unsuitable partly because of the impact on performance. Unless actors were required to carry the items onto the stage as the list was read, then the table would be cumbersome to read out item by item (Christensen, "Absent" 120). Its use may suggest an author who is familiar with working with mercantile tools or reading mercantile treatises and who has observed but not written plays previously (Pangallo, *Playwriting* 2). In her study of the impact of lists on early modern travel literature Wisecup notes some general principles:

> [...]lists represent experience as an 'itemised terrain', that is as data or as things distanced from individual experience, and [...] writing provides the necessary technology and accompanying forms of thought necessary to render the past as 'thing-like'. (276)[1]

A list becomes a vehicle for thinking about the role and nature of an object and although shaped by the cross-cultural circulation of those items it simultaneously erases those encounters. The list setting out the value of goods from Allepo and India in Mountfort's play is concerned with relative value and charts the different trade routes in terms of financial profit. "[I]ndividual experience" is missing from Mountfort/Mun's table which simply provides an "itemised terrain." Although Mountfort's play might leave out the cross-cultural context and "individual experience" behind these tables, it does focus on the local negotiations of those engaged both in furnishing the ship and selling commodities and this will be the focus of the next section of this chapter.

Circulated Item

The ephemera in this play occupy a series of states from list to circulated objects and to bodily anthropomorphised embodied materials. *Launching* tracks the movement of commodities coming from India into Europe such as "drugs, spices, rawsilke, Indico:/& Callicoes" (266–67) and *Launching* is preoccupied with the constant stream of materials being delivered to the ship to furnish it for its departure. In Act 1, the admiral marvels at the delivery of:

> Ad: - [...] such anchors, tymber, plankes, masts, yards, sayles, Cordage, [& to Conclude, what not] truñells, okum, nayles, brasse shiuers, shiuers Coakte, blocks greate & small, Oares, deales,: greate ordnance, powder, fire workes, Shott, Crosbarre, Chayne shott, [Ch] Clappe shott, langrell, round, musketts, swordes, targetts, Crosspitts, halberts, pikes, Beefe, porke, bread, [meale] beere, wine, sydar, oatemeal, pease, [Chees] meale, butter, Cheese, rice, vinegar, sweet oyle, A surgeons Chest well furnisht, & what not that eyther shipps or men may stand in need of? (160–69)

These materials range from the fabric of the ship to its ammunition, to supplies in terms of food, drink, and finally medical supplies. The ship is understood here as a storehouse composed of materials, resources, and ephemera with various life cycles and ephemeral to different degrees and under different conditions. By contrast, taverns are a site for acquiring ephemera in the play. This time the focus is on the consumption of the luxuries brought by ships such as the *Blessing* or the *Mary*. In the tavern space the results of the company's cross-cultural trade mix with the more quotidian local produce. The sailor's wife Nutt announces that

> To daye I must meete, 3· or 4· Grocers prentises at a tauerne in west Smithfield, they bringe sugar & nuttmegge, wch wee infuse into white wine & rosewater, & then a barell of pickelld oysters to rellish our liquor, & soe wee are mighty merrie an houre or two & awaye, roundly for Ratcliffe./(988–94)

The movement of consumables is matched by the use of perfume which circulates both in the tavern of the play world and the stage space of the theatre. Act three ends with music and perfume:

> musicke   Enter the drawer, hastily wakinge the women./
>   who startinge vp, & layinge hold on the
>   bottome of the basketts, out falls the
>   bricke batt, & the peecs of painted clothes./
>   wch they (as yf no body sawe them) put vp
>   agayne./ exeunt. then enter boye agayne
>   takes bush & all awaye. perfumes the
>   roome. – exit./. (2012–19)

The sailors' wives Nutt and Sparke have proceeded to drink their fill in a local tavern and after falling asleep, one of the ship workers Trunnel, riffles their baskets revealing that, rather than containing silk and the ephemera transported by the company's ships, they in fact contain a brick and a piece of painted cloth. These carried items are part of a disguise for their real motivation, the seduction of apprentices, and their enjoyment of the ephemeral pleasures of the city. Ann Christensen points out the "extreme fragility of women's reputations" that the play repeatedly underlines (*Separation* 198). This female trade has an interesting parallel to the male traffic or the "socially and sexually anarchic potential of the emerging global market" (Christensen, "Absent" 117–36). Whilst the workers on the ship are busy readying their shipborne household, the wives circulate beyond the bounds of the home and engage in subsistence via the substitution of low-value materials for high-value silk work. Whilst searching their baskets, Trunnel exclaims:

Now ys my tyme to search the baskettes: (pluckes a new bricke batt
out) good people I am a little hasell eyde, I praye you tell me is this
silke, ? yf there Came no other silke from Persia, the m'chants would
make but a poore trade. what sayes the other baskett: (pluckes out
·4· or 5· peeces painted Cloth) These be Cappes & sleeues for Children./. the diuell in a painted Cloth Ile put them vp agayne but so,
that when they awake, they shall shew themselues what they are.
(1982–88)

After the drawer wakes the wives, accidentally revealing the true contents of the baskets, Trunnel revelation uncovers the way in which female bodies and the maritime ephemera from the ships are both aligned.
Christensen describes the "sham" contents as "(non-)labor" ("Absent"
125). Building on this it is possible to argue that the silk work is shown
to be the most ephemeral item in the play because it does not in fact exist
and it has already been replaced.

The baskets facilitate the movement of the wives throughout the city,
serving as a token of their licence to mobility and working as "metonyms
for women's labor, class, gender and geographic location" (Christensen,
Separation 202). Responding to accusations from the virtuous wife of
the play, Doretea, who does carry out legitimate silk work, Nutt and
Sparke retort,

> Spa: X [...] but what thinkst thou Nutt yf fryar Bacon weare now
> aliue that could make dumbe thinges speake. what would my bas-
> kett saye at first word?/
>   dor: Some shameles language I dare pawne my life those needful
> basketts serue[s] your needles vse for –
>   Nutt – for what M^ress Minx. S'life I haue seene as good a woman
> as you Carry a hand baskett: (943–50)

This imagined moment of anthropomorphism, which provides a parallel to the trick played on the sleeping women is, I suggest, significant.
Anthropologist Ian Hodder talks about the way in which "things" or
objects can be "part of a chain of obligations and desires as things circulate" (*Entanglements* 22). Whilst Hodder is concerned with gifts, the
same can be said of the ephemera that circulate through the city. The way
the wives manipulate this circulation, translating the material exchange
into a bodily one, is meant to suggest to the audience that the virtue the
wives possess is just as ephemeral as the commodities they are supposed
to be trading. The luxurious silk is replaced with a heavy brick and
instead of delicate work there is simply painted cloth. Here both bodily
and material substitutes are made, simultaneously highlighting not only
the transitory existence of EIC ephemera but the set of social obligations
and desires which underlie trade and exchange. This in turn suggests the

materials are almost irrelevant and can certainly be easily substituted. This is also an example of what Hodder calls "enchainment," which "is created because of the 'hau' of things – that, is their need to be moved on, to be mobile" (*Entanglements* 22). The sheer mobility of the ephemera in the play, both globally and locally, is intentionally astounding. It is meant to be a source of both wonder and anxiety. As Paula Findlen has noted, early modern "Things multiply across time and space. [...] Virtually every society vacillates between the euphoria of its materialism and episodes of introspective anxiety" (5). In Mountfort's play the city, the ship, and the EIC more broadly are caught in a moment of wild "vacillation" between euphoria and anxiety. The transient wives represent that vacillation through their own circuitous movements and the exchange of their wares. Through this substitution, the travelling commodities seem even more ephemeral as they are not in fact represented on stage and do not in fact occupy their baskets. The baskets themselves signal their transient identity by their absence. Sparke's humorous suggestion that the basket might be able to "speake" is, however, one of the many moments at which things and humans become productively entangled in the play.

Launching includes luxuries but is also stuffed with mundane domestic "things" such as rose water which appear alongside nutmeg or sugar. These items generally exist as part of the dialogue of the play and it is not clear if they deck the stage or simply exist in the minds of the audience. If it is the latter, it contributes to the sense of the transient trade in maritime ephemera which is always out of reach – part of the narrative spun by the company and not part of the tangible material reality of the working world and its stage. In contrast, the material props used in the play include a brick and painted cloth, timber, ship supplies, and mechanisms associated with ship repair, shipbuilding, and ship launching. The play is preoccupied with their transportation, consumption, durability, perishability, and state of repair. What is even more significant is that just as the baskets stand in for the identity of the transient wives, as a token of their hard labour and virtue, just as their female bodies replace the legitimate sale of female silk work; so too do the identities of the male ship workers bind bodies to the materials of their trade in some interesting and surprising ways.

Bodily/Embodied

Mountfort's play is full of things that are to be fetched, carried, supplied, loaded, unloaded, or, in the case of the ship itself, launched. The movements of workers associated with the ship, whether described or performed, contribute to the play's presentation of "travel as an ephemeral act." The bodies of the wives, as we have already seen, are aligned with the goods to be sold and the ephemera to be traded within the city port. Female and male labour mimic each other and each is marked by movements that figure forth and embody the points at which trade and travel collide. As the last section illustrated, Sparke and Nutt the sailors' wives circulate consuming local and international luxuries – purporting to be selling silk work but in fact indulging in the pleasures of the town. The play repeatedly aligns ephemera associated with the trade of the EIC with a human cost, underlining the fact that humans are far more ephemeral than the materials they are engaged in selling, transporting, and constructing.

The relationship between bodies and maritime trade, however, was far more entangled than simple movements or circulating ephemera might suggest and this can be seen if we pause briefly on the bodies of sailors offstage and their relationship to foodstuff on board during a voyage. The admiral in Mountfort's play marvels at the goods arriving at the ship, many of which include food. When we consider the absent sailors it is necessary to remember that at sea their bodies were almost constantly under threat from the elements or from dearth and disease. In her study of the work of Hugh Platt, Ayesha Mukherjee notes that "[s]peculations about causes of decomposition, efficient storage, and health – especially the health of itinerant persons exposed to dearth and disease – were intricately linked" (41). Through his experiments with foodstuff, which he then sold to Drake and ships' captains, Platt was able to draw on his research into common practices at sea and his own observed practice. As a result of this work, he was able to conclude that:

> In the context of dearth, especially useful features of sailors' and soldiers' food were durability and easy transportation. [...] Other foods, recommended for consumption during dearth, appeared on lists of sea victuals. Sodden oatmeal, seethed with clarified butter and spices like mace and cloves, had the advantage of being easily warmed by a candle or the heat of one's body: it was placed 'in ones boosome or breaches'.(Mukherjee 41)

In this example, we see the intermixing of everyday familiar foodstuffs with the luxury and unusual items procured through travel. In this moment of surface-to-surface contact, the heat of the bosom or breaches acts to warm the ephemeral foodstuff of oatmeal and spiced butter.

In encounters at sea, attempts to survive and thrive involve surface-to-surface contact between the body and the thing. The heat of one warms the other and the consumable nourishes the body. Travel itself may be an ephemeral act but it also included within it multiple ephemeral acts.

The role of surfaces here is intriguing if we note, as the recent movement of surface studies suggests we should, that "humans, ourselves a body of surfaces, meet and interact with a world dressed in surfaces" (Oakley-Brown and Kileen 1).[2] Furthermore, Lucy Razall has traced the early modern etymology of the word "surface" to reveal that it includes the "'visible outside part of a body' or 'outermost boundary of any material object'" (see *OED* 2016), as well as being a technical geographical and mathematical term (Razall 7). It seems apt, therefore, that in encounters with new geographies, the travelling body, and travelling object collide in new ways becoming, to use Hodder's term, ever more "entangled." Or perhaps we should say an entangled set of surfaces. Whilst these moments of connection outlined by Platt highlight a mode of "entanglement," other moments of connection take on quite a different shape.

In order to travel in a world that assaults the senses and the barriers of the body itself, mariners needed to protect and coat their outer boundaries against the elements. Dan Brayton, in his recent study of the later figure of maritime travel Jack Tar, notes the early modern use of tar to make the boat and sailor's garments watertight:

> sailors spent much of their time at sea tarring the standing and running rigging of sailing vessels, which was composed of perishable materials – linen, wool, hemp, canvas – and softwood spars that would quickly rot when exposed. Mariners' clothing and bodies were habitually covered with the redolent substance, detectable by its distinctive odour. (515)

Early modern sailors were "marked by a [...] indelible tactile and olfactory presence that is at once cultural and material, familiar and foreign." As Brayton suggests, the tar covering the outer surface of their "hats, trousers and foul weather coats" duplicates the techniques and effect of the tarring of the ship itself (515). Sailor and ship were waterproofed in the same manner and the ephemeral surface of tar needed to be maintained, replaced, and patched regularly.

In Mountfort's play "Tar" becomes the name of one of the workers labouring on the ship rather than a sailor. These workers are synonymous with the tools of their labour. Tar is not the only character whose name professes his trade, he is accompanied by Sheathing Nail, Oakum (a material made from rope), Tallow, and Trunnel. In this group, it is Tallow, not Tar, who is known by his "vnsauourie smell" (2708). This comes into focus in one of the sets of disputes between the workmen:

> Tarre./ why although he vse none amongst us, yet he may be a regratour of witt, that ys, he may buy a little in one place< & sell yt in another, where he ys vnknowne,:
>   Shea: Goe too, goe too, he hath neyther beene wrunge so hard, nor layne in the sunne so longe, but I am sure there is some waight in him & though yt be but little, yet yt < will serue for some small purpose or other./

Oku. witt or no witt, saye what you will, but I will mayntayne
there as much neede of me, & my helpe ys as much require<d
in buildinge & repayringe of shipps, as any of all yours
I could tell you Tallow, of your vnsavourie smell, -- & you Tarre,
of your shortnes, & brittleness, but alas I haue no witt to decypher
all your knaueries, : should some knowe, what I knowe – but I haue
no witt, I haue no witt – to – (2698–713)

Even wit is a commodity to be exchanged and, as the workmen vie
for who is of more value in shipbuilding and repairing, it is clear that
their material characteristics are both human and thing-like. Tar is too
"shor[t]" and "brittl[e]" whilst the oakum has been rung too hard and
exposed to the elements for too long. This aligning of the verbal and
physical is also found earlier in the play where Oakum himself explains,

Okum: This boyes tongue runnes as slippery as a rope newe tal-
lowde, quicke & nimble, yfayth, quicke & nimble – –
Tallo: You had best take a pott & wett your selfe, neighbour
Okum, for you are euer as drye as a spunge, :
[...]
Trunnell./. Of all impossibilities, yt ys most impossible to please
all men/ and yet me thinkes wee (beinge almost of one facultie)
should neuer displease one another: for the m'chants Canne finde
fault (fast ynough) wth us all.
for one sayes the Tallow stinkes, another sayes, the Tarre hath
water & soote in yt: another says the Okum ys to wett: a fourth
says the sheathing nayles are to short, A fift says the Trunells are
neyther longe ynough nor round ynough: & euery one of us haue
one [fuolt] fault or other, & yet wee Cannott winke at one anothers
faults. – (1055–72)

In this passage Oakum is accused at one moment by his fellows of being dry as a sponge and needing to "pott & wett" himself; then in the
context of complaints from merchants, he is described as being too wet.
The workmen joke about the exacting merchants who find fault in their
workforce and the products of their labour for they are one and the
same. Here, Tar is found to have imperfections, Tallow to stink, and so
on. This inspection of their work and the alignment of their working
bodies highlights the crucial role of shipbuilding and ship repairing in
the preservation of the vessels themselves and the ephemera entrusted to
them.

In Act I the workers congratulate themselves on their labour caulking
(plugging the gaps) checking auger holes, sheathing the ship, and greas-
ing her sides with tallow. They settle down to drinking and discuss the
impact of their labour on their working bodies:

> Trun: Here neighbours, wee are all mortail, God knowes wch of us
> shall dye first, I am so malld euery daye, that I feele my very soule
> Cr{}ckt:
> Tarre X [fayth] & I am so heat wth fire, & scortchinge flames, that
> all my fatt fades awaye like [stinkinge] Tallow agaynst the Sunne/.
> Tallo: And why like Tallow goodman Ruface: you might haue
> made other similitudes then of a mans name, Ile for sweare the
> Companie of all such pitch [kettles] potts as – thou art, for this, that
> I will./
> Okum./Why goodman Tallow, doe not frett so in your owne
> grease, I knowe my neghbour Tarre meant neyther sence nor reason
> against you [...]
> Oku: fill tother·3·full potts, & wee are gone, : tis well boye: neigh-
> bour Truñell, you haue a longe breath, and deepe swallow, & for
> your bore, [Ike] knowe yt ys an Inch & ½ · diameter, take you there-
> fore that full pott, & wee
> 4: will dispatch the rest, (78–111)

In this scene, the workmen contemplate their own mortality and the
impact of their hard labour on their bodies. The impact is measured in
material terms, according to their specific trade, whether that be scorch-
ing of tar, melting fat, or the specific measurements of a borehole. The
ephemeral surfaces of bodies so essential to the process of preservation
of the vessel itself, its workers could be worn away by that labour just
as the perishable and permeable ephemera carried within or coating the
outside of individual vessels were also degraded by or used up during a
voyage. The ephemeral and replaceable nature of their internal and ex-
ternal materials is significant in the survival of each and the 'entangled'
relationships are, as Mountfort's play illustrates, a matter of entangled
surfaces.

Conclusion

In his theory on objects, Hodder asserts for quite different reasons
that "things are not inert" ("Human-thing" 1). Wisecup takes this a
stage further to indicate that objects acquired during travel are a form
of "communication" ('Wisecup, "Encounters" 275). We can trace both
these ideas in the three plots of the play from the mercantile tool of the
table, to the baskets which may or may not speak but are certainly used
as a tool of communication, to the workmen who embody materials.
Hodder has claimed that things and humans are "enchained" and entangled. In Mountfort's play, this is taken to the extreme in the case of the
workmen as they embody the tools of their craft and speak in a language
that interprets the world and their own bodies in terms of the specific

qualities of those materials. Furthermore, they understand their own mortality and ephemerality in social and material terms by expressing them in terms of the physical characteristics of ephemera.

Mountfort continually underlines the fact that in this human/thing entanglement it is the human element that is the most vulnerable, the most ephemeral, the most transient, mobile, and unfixed. In the case of the listed items from Mun's treatise, in the calculation of the value of items from India or Aleppo the human cost and indeed labour is absent. In the case of the massacre its human cost is written out by the censor. In the case of the sailors' wives, the fraudulent substitution of brick and painted cloth facilitates their circulation and consumption of the ephemeral pleasures facilitated by trade. In the plot concerning the workers on the ship, the materials are replaced repeatedly over the life cycle of the ship and the working bodies are ephemeral and subject to decay. These workers, the play appears to suggest, are themselves replicable, replaceable, and ultimately the most ephemeral. As I have illustrated throughout this chapter, the play shows an awareness of the layered etymology of ephemera. It is preoccupied with time, movement, fragility, and change, not just of the goods transported by the company, but of the whole playworld of the ship and the shipyard. Caught between euphoria and anxiety, the playworld traces the wild vacillations of those employed by or associated with the EIC. Through a series of "ephemeral acts" Mountfort's play travels continually and yet, like the eponymous ship which is only launched at the end of the play, most of the frenetic movement circulates around a very contained and local spot. It is held together by Trunnel, Tar, Tallow, sheathing nails, and bits of old Oakum.

Notes

1 Wisecup draws on the work of Ong (98).
2 Here Brown and Killeen quote from Amato (xv).

Works Cited

Amato, Joseph. *Surfaces: A History.* U of California P, 2013.

Brayton, Dan. "Enter Jack Tar: The Blue-water Mariner in the Early Modern World Literature." *The Routledge Companion to Marine and Maritime Worlds 1400–1800.* Eds Claire Jowitt, Craig Lambert, and Steve Mentz. Routledge, 2020.

Christensen, Ann. "'Absent, Weak, or Unserviceable': The EIC and the Domestic Economy in *The Launching of the Mary, or the Seaman's Honest Wife.*" *Global Traffic: Discourses and Practices of Trade in English Literature and Culture from 1550 to 1700.* Eds Barbara Sebak and Stephen Deng. Palgrave Macmillan, 2008. 117–36.

Christensen, Ann. *Separation Scenes: Domestic Drama in Early Modern England*. U of Nebraska P, 2017.

Findlen, Paula, ed. *Early Modern Things: Objects and their Histories, 1500–1800*. Routledge, 2021.

Fisher, Joshua B. "Reclaiming Ephemeral Territory in Early Modern English Domestic Travel Writing." *Encountering Ephemera 1500–1800: Scholarship, Performance, Classroom*. Eds Joshua B. Fisher and Rebecca Steinberger. Cambridge Scholars, 2012. 135–73.

Hodder, Ian. "The Entanglements of Humans and Things: A Long-Term View." *New Literary History* 45.1 (2014): 19–36.

———. "Human-thing Entanglement: Towards an Integrated Archaeological Perspective." *The Journal of the Royal Anthropological Institute* 17.1 (2011): 154–77.

Mountfort, Walter. *The Launching of the Mary*. Ed. J. H. Walter. Malone Society, 1933.

Mukherjee, Ayesha. *Penury into Plenty: Dearth and the Making of Knowledge in Early Modern England*. Routledge, 2015.

Oakley-Brown, Liz and Kevin Killeen. "Introduction: Scrutinizing Surfaces in Early Modern Thought." Scrutinizing Surfaces. Spec. issue. *Journal of Northern Renaissance* 8 (2017). Online. https://jnr2.hcommons.org/2017/5100/. Accessed 19 Dec. 2017.

Ong, Walter. *Orality and Literacy: The Technologizing of the Word*. Routledge, 2000.

Pangallo, Matteo. *Playwriting Playgoers in Shakespeare's Theater*. U of Pennsylvania P, 2017.

———. "Seldome Seene: Observations from Editing *The Launching of the Mary, or the Seaman's Honest Wife*." *'Divining Thoughts': Future Directions in Shakespeare Studies*. Eds Pete Orford with Michael P Jones, Lizz Ketterer, and Joshua McEvilia. Cambridge Scholars, 2007. 2–17.

Razall, Lucy. "'Like to a title leafe': Surface, Face, and Material Text in Early Modern England." Scrutinizing Surfaces. Spec. issue. Eds Liz Oakley-Brown and Kevin Killeen. *Journal of Northern Renaissance* 8 (2017). Online. https://jnr2.hcommons.org/2017/4861/. Accessed 19 Dec. 2017.

Ryner, Bradley. *Performing Economic Thought: English drama and Mercantile Writing 1600–1642*. Edinburgh UP, 2014.

Wisecup, Kelly. "Encounters, Objects and Commodity Lists in Early English Travel Narratives." *Studies in Travel Writing* 17.3 (2013): 264–80.

12 Playing Apples and the Playhouse Archive

Callan Davies

This chapter explores one-off entertainments in commercial venues in early modern London, which regularly sat alongside staged drama. Such occasional skits, extemporisations, or shows often focus on the display and use of transitory *things*, on props largely used up or consumed in the event itself. These items vanish, in part, with what Diana Taylor terms the live *repertoire*: "performances, gestures, orality, movement, dance, singing—in short, all those acts usually thought of as ephemeral, nonreproducible knowledge" (20). Yet they have dynamic afterlife in the *archive*: as post-performance accounts, in images, or as excavated artefacts and ecofacts. I focus here on what Lisa Woynarski would term the "bioperformative" apple, in order to consider "the biological/material and the performative effects of things" (71–72). Apples occasioned impromptu skits when they were thrown on stage by audience members or wrestled for among a playhouse crowd; they prompted and structured immersive performances when they were dropped from an exploding giant flower onto crowds below; and they marked the seasonality of both natural and theatrical worlds.

This chapter demonstrates, then, how apples could initiate or structure early modern ephemeral performance.[1] Like staged drama, ephemeral performances took place in the playing structures of inns, playhouses, and bearbaiting arenas, which were themselves overlapping institutions not always distinguished by contemporaries. The apple-shows discussed here help us understand the theatre industry in the transformative years of the 1570s to 1580s and beyond (Davies, Kesson, and Munro), in particular its imbrication with other modes and locations of "play"—a term that early modern individuals understood flexibly to encompass anything from theatrical performance to gambling activities, sport, and less easily categorised recreational activities (Wickham 32; Davies 42). The theatrical agency of apples captures how multiple modes of play and game coincided and alerts us to the wider ecology of early modern commercial performance. It also reminds us that while live performance is inherently ephemeral, the materials that make it possible continually evolve into new forms and meanings. Both the contemporary and early

DOI: 10.4324/9781003058588-16

modern senses of ephemera emerge from the inter-play of imagination, creation, and environmental process.

Indeed, a focus on "bioperformative" things and their agency and afterlives offers a fluid model of early modern playing venues and a reassessment of what exactly constitutes the theatre-historical archive. I take up S. P. Cerasano's notion of the "transitory playhouse" to suggest that apples emblematise a mutable playing infrastructure, built and transfigured by both human and more-than-human agencies. The playing apple endures through various archival traces: as seeds and as written accounts but not in its entirety. This is a strikingly similar fate to theatrical venues. I finish by exploring contemporary crowds' spectacular consumption of both goods and playhouses and by emphasising the latter's ongoing archival transmutations. The fruity performances explored here tease out forms of enquiry that look beyond "loss," "survival," or "absence" towards a theatre history open to *repertorial* narratives of transformation, decay, disintegration, and dispersal—narratives that have always been at the core of the early modern playing industry, its buildings, and its shows.

Commercial Ephemeral Performance

Pamela Smith et al. reappraise the nature of ephemeral art by focusing on elaborate performances and their furnishings (banners and pennants, backdrops, machines, sugar sculptures, temporary structures) to argue for the importance of spectacular but fleeting entertainments. Their study emphasises the collaborative creation of such forms, their participatory nature, and their political significance, and they accordingly urge scholars to think about process and materials as much as the final product (82; 126). Smith et al.'s focus on the *stuff* of artistic performance offers a productive angle beyond art-historical discourse, including English commercial theatre.

Early modern English "play" similarly depended, for its performative capacities, on natural materials. Richard Preiss warns that, because "texts were the medium by which theatre preserved itself [...] whenever we reconstruct it, we do so through their logic" (3). Preiss has importantly critiqued assumptions made about early modern performance culture by restoring the figure of the clown to the collaborative "organizing agency of the theatrical event" (6). Indeed, the form of "medley" theatre identified by Scott McMillin and Sally-Beth MacLean in the Queen's Men repertory explores the multiple registers of theatricality simultaneously present in dramatic playing venues in the 1580s. More broadly, Erika Lin has shown how, far from being "yoked" to text, commercial performance was part of the "hybrid" modes of performance associated with may games, holiday celebrations, and festivity (212; see also Bishop). Civic pageantry was likewise a form of ephemeral entertainment, not least in that the materials (speeches, decorated arches, platforms, fire-works, and other accoutrements) produced for mayoral processions, for instance, were tied to a unique occasion. Tracey Hill's study of the practice in London provides ample evidence of their dispersed creative agency and collaborative nature. I build on these critics' work to explore a different "organizing agency of the theatrical event": organic matter.[2]

I therefore take up Preiss's invitation to think beyond text, but I consider instead those one-off shows and performances driven not by people but by things. Things have been at the heart of a wealth of "material turn" studies that have expanded knowledge of and centred attention on the theatricality of early modern drama.[3] Yet these studies, for the most part, focus on objects as "staged properties" (to borrow from Jonathan Gil Harris and Natasha Korda's edited collection)—things to which agency is applied, to which actions are done. The apples discussed here demand a different relationship to theatre. While props in staged drama also held complex and active relationships with text, story, and actorly decision-making, organic materials in commercial ephemeral entertainments more squarely provided the prompt for and defined the horizons of the theatrical event. These playing apples were what Robin Bernstein calls "scriptive things"—material items that "help structure a performance" while allowing "necessary openness to resistance, interpretation, and improvisation" (68, 69). Such things, "physical and visceral as much as theological," for Julie Sanders, "inform the ways" that play "made meaning in the world" (117). Apples can therefore trouble text- and document-led forms of theatre history: they occasioned, structured, and represented the live theatrical moment (Taylor's *repertoire*) and their presence continues to perform, via various states of entropy and decay, the playhouse *archive* today.

Ben Jonson's induction to *Bartholomew Fair* (1614) offers an instructive conceptualisation of such thing-ly ephemeral performances in a commercial playing venue. In the royal prologue for court performance, Jonson claims the play encapsulates a series of "wares" that excite the wider population, including puppet plays and hobby-horses or other toys like the carriage discussed by Michael Lewis in this volume. The play's commercial performance brings these goods into its venue, the Hope—a theatre-cum-bearbaiting-arena built in 1613. The induction begins with the Hope's stage-manager complaining that Jonson has failed to capture the spirit of the real Bartholomew Fair, its "sword and buckler-man," its "juggler with a well-educated ape," or the "jig-a-jog in the booths" (Induction ll. 14–24). He nonetheless suggests an affinity between these activities and the Hope. The keeper dissolves the boundaries of the playhouse by recalling how the fair itself served as an extended stage for the famous Elizabethan clown, Richard Tarlton. The entrance of the book-holder (carrying the text) and a scrivener ready to draw up a contract between the audience and the performance interrupts these opening musings. The scrivener continues the conflation of theatre and street entertainment by insisting that jigs, jugglers, fencers, and monkeys have counterparts in the drama and that Jonson's "ware is still the same" (Induction ll. 159–60). The ephemeral entertainments of the fair—its human-animal-object "wares"—are brought within the compass of the playing venue.

While *Bartholomew Fair*'s induction at the Hope implies a textually-imposed performance structure for its transitory things (its "staged properties"), bioperformative material in the playhouse simultaneously holds its own "scriptive" agency. The book-holder snootily banishes the stage-keeper by questioning his artistic "judgement": "for what?", he asks, querying the seemingly text-less keeper's authority to pronounce on cultural matters, "Sweeping the stage, or gathering up the broken apples for the bears within?" (Induction, ll. 49–50). The lines suggest that apples remained littered around the Hope yard and perhaps its stalls or galleries following an entertainment event, where they seeped into the fabric of the playhouse. Indeed, Lupold von Wedel's account of a "play" at a bearbaiting arena in the 1580s, discussed in detail later in this chapter, suggests apples were features of human performance and blood sport, and that they could be both a prompt for and residue of an entertainment event. Jonson's induction puts the fruit in contrast to the apparently learned authority of a textual script, personified by the book-bearer and the pen-wielding scrivener. Like the dramatic framing device of the induction itself, though, the apple here provides a bridge between forms of ludic activity; it represents a different performance—the residue of or sustenance for bearbaiting and its surrounding theatrics—and the broken down organic matter also performs in this incipient dramatic show.

I follow Jonson's (and the Hope's) logic of situating manifold ephemeral entertainment practices within the multipurpose playhouse and take up, like the stage manager, the broken apples. I therefore employ the category of "commercial ephemeral performance" to refer to nonreproducible shows in playing venues that were not dependent on set text or speech but occasioned or were structured by "scriptive" materials partially used up in performance. Asking after such performances presents obvious challenges analogous to those set out by Smith et al.; I similarly seek to recover the material journeys made within and across playing structures by narrowing down to one object of focus: where does a "playing apple" come from, how was it used, what collaborative participatory processes are involved, and where does it end up?

The Apple in Play

In order to understand the material processes of commercial ephemeral performance, I explore in this section three instances of the apple's instrumentality for such shows: the apple "in play" (as an object of both performance and competition) among audiences; two skits by comic performer extraordinaire Richard Tarlton; and a high-octane account of a "play" at a bearbaiting arena by German visitor Lupold von Wedel in 1584. In each instance, the fruit acts as a "scriptive thing," helping delineate and structure performance, and its wider contexts open up fresh ways of appreciating what a "play" might mean for early modern audiences.

The Audience Apple

Jonson's induction to *Bartholomew Fair* helps transport us into the audience, where we find ourselves standing among and smelling bruised and half-eaten fruit. Playhouse refreshments, Hillary M. Nunn explains, were a central economic feature of the playhouse as well as a "vital part of the theatre-going experience" (101). Apples were "the most commonly mentioned playhouse refreshment," with numerous plays building what was on sale to audiences into the drama on stage (101). There is a telling irony in Robert Wilson's prologue to *The Three Ladies of London*, which claims that the play's performers "play not here the gardener's part, to plant, to set and sow, / You marvel then what stuff we have to furnish out our show" (Prologue ll. 13–14, l. 11): agricultural labour was indeed the stuff of drama. Wilson includes a varied list of "country toil" (husbandry, milking, threshing) surprisingly (it is implied) absent from his city comedy. The fruits of the countryside were expected narrative and material encounters for spectators in a playing venue—a journey from rural food production to urban consumption discussed later in this chapter. Nunn explains how apples in dramatic productions of this period had an "array of meanings," which make

> clear that the use of playhouse concessions onstage served more than crassly commercial purposes. The similarities between the foods appearing on- and offstage allowed the plays and audience members to consider, together, profound questions about the nature of hunger, temptation, and human desire. (105, 117)

There are also moments, however, when apples generate their own ephemeral performance worlds, and their presence in wider early modern leisure culture pushes us to think about fleeting performative possibilities beyond the thematic concerns and narratives of playtexts.

When Paul Hentzner travelled to England in the 1590s, he observed that, amid the grim "spectacle" of bearbaiting arenas, men watched the entertainment and smoked tobacco profusely, while "fruits, such as apples, pears, and nuts, according to the season, are carried about to be sold" (Walpole 30). Randall Channock was perhaps one such carrier.

His deposition in a church court in 1611 suggests that these forms of leisure consumption made common commercial partners: his fields being spoiled, he "hath bought and sold apples and tobacco" to make a living, and came to the city of Chester to "play at the town ditch at the tables" and to "buy tobacco, apples, starch, and tracle" (*Intoxicants* ZQSF 59/31). Indeed, such a coupling of "play" and "apples" is a feature of inn and alehouse culture. William Sampson paints a picture of sociable leisure time for non-elite individuals in 1585. He dined with his wife at five o'clock before departing to Widow Warmingham's alehouse "to pass away the time." While there, he ate and then "fell to play and then [...] [Mr] Ince and he played at the cards for ale and apples for 2 hours space" (*Intoxicants* ZQSF 36/32). We might imagine somebody like Channock, fresh from the alehouse, entering a playing venue to sell his goods to spectators or to the bearwards to feed the bears, or Sampson as one of urban England's many apple-consuming gamers.

Apples accordingly formed an entertainment currency both inside and outside of theatrical venues, structuring forms of game and play—here at the cards or the tables. Gina Bloom claims that commercial theatrical venues in London established themselves in negotiation with a pre-existing culture of games like those played by Channock and Sampson ("Games" 196). The apple's association with gambling in these instances indicates its circulation within a wider betting industry that encompassed cards, bowling, and of course bearbaiting. Bloom's contention is that the London stage, eager to affirm its participatory possibilities for paying spectators, borrowed strategies from its "ludic competition" (*Gaming* 3). At the same time, though, that competition *was* inherently theatrical, with bearbaiting arenas hosting plays (as discussed below) and "spectatorship" being central to gambling more generally—as John Earle describes the bowling alley, "The best Sport in it is the Gamesters, and he enioyes it that lookes on and bets not" (H2v). The theatrical and the ludic operated simultaneously and often in the same venue. Ephemeral games and performances that centred on the circulation of an inexpensive perishable fruit reveal a culture that, at least sometimes, "strategically collapsed" theatre and games (Bloom, *Gaming* 3).

The adversarial or competitive nature of gambling provides context for the agency of apples among playhouse audiences. Jonson is hardly the only playwright who sees spectators wading through fruit remains. When a crowd gathers to watch Queen Elizabeth's christening towards the final stages of Shakespeare's *Henry VIII*, the palace porter scoffs at the assembly, "do you take the court for Paris Garden [...] These are the youths that thunder at a playhouse and fight for bitten apples [...]" (5.4.2, 5.4.39). His reference again draws together gambling crowds at the bearbaiting arena Paris Garden and playhouse spectators. The envisaged activity suggests apples generate a discrete performance in the playhouse pit, providing a parallel or alternative site of drama and a different form of material engagement than that offered by the controlled "stage properties" of the scripted play. Bloom might recognise this as "participatory" theatre: "real interactivity comes from the audience-users' ability and encouragement to play *with* the objects and narratives presented via the interface. [...] Interactivity emerges in the theater when audiences don't simply consume, but *play*" (*Gaming* 5). Both Jonson's stage-keeper and Shakespeare's thundering youths map out imagined performances in which readily available commercial snacks for consumption can quickly turn into "scriptive" playhouse things, dissolving boundaries between the Globe and Paris Garden, bearbaiting and theatre, organic matter and the stuff of play.

Tarlton's Apple

The image of Shakespeare's audiences fighting for bitten apples is a rhetorical one, but the notion is far from fanciful. Not only were apples widely sold in playhouses, their cores scattered about the floors, and, as Nunn's readings demonstrate, thematically and sensorily incorporated into stage drama, but audiences also used them to generate and manipulate play. Throwing rotten fruit at the stage is a popular shorthand for a discontented crowd (Nunn 111), but a look at one of the memorable jests of Richard Tarlton suggests wider possibilities for such actions. Tarlton was a towering theatrical figure in mid-to-late Elizabethan London. He was an actor with the Queen's Men, performing some of its larger-than-life roles, as well as something of a soloist and adept at music and dance; he was also an innkeeper and a master of defence, able to train and test new fencers (usually in playing venues) and admit them into the society. His skills therefore straddled a number of the entertainment offerings of the late sixteenth century.

Numerous of Tarlton's comic turns are recorded in a posthumous jest book, *Tarltons Iestes* (1613; much reprinted). This collection presents readers not only with his verbally inventive quips but with their curious exposition, bringing into focus the prompts and materials that occasioned and sustained them. We therefore learn how the apple sold, eaten, or gambled at an in-house playing venue can generate participatory theatre:

> *Tarltons* Iest of a Pippin [a sweet apple].
> At the Bull in Bishopsgate street, where the Queenes Plaiers often-times played: *Tarlton* comming on the Stage, one from the Gallerie threw a Pippin at him, *Tarlton* tooke vp the Pip, & looking on it made this sodaine iest.
> Pip in or nose in, chuse you whether,
> Put yours in, ere I put in the other:

> Pippin you haue put in, then for my grace,
> Would I might put your nose in another place. (B2r)

The spectator in the gallery was seemingly put out by this violent retort; he waited for the stage drama to start and, when Tarlton was kneeling for a part in the play,

> the fellow threwe an Apple at him, which hit him on the cheeke:
> Tarlton taking up the Apple made this Iest:
> Gentlemen, this fellow with his face of Mapple.
> In stead of a Pippin hath throwne me an Apple:
> But as for an Apple he hath cast a Crab,
> So in stead of an honest woman God hath sent him a Drab.

At these apparently devastating lines, "The people laughed heartily, for he had a Queane to his Wife" (B2r-v).

The succession of these two apple "jests" confirms the Bull as a site of extratextual material play. David Wiles recognises the value of these anecdotes given how little survives of the ephemeral art of solo clowning, "because performances were given extempore" (16). He identifies such throwaway exchanges as capturing something of Tarlton's skill, which depended upon "making spectators feel like participants" (16). Yet the line between the two dissolves in this sketch of an afternoon at the Bull. As with the bitten apples on the playhouse floor, the apple and pippin facilitate interactive play and allow patrons in the playing venue to "manipulate rules and technologies for their own enjoyment" (Bloom, *Gaming* 6). The apple makes the spectator the participant and upends divisions and hierarchies between performer and audience member, a division almost entirely absent from the textual account.

It is ironic, of course, that such ostensibly transitory extemporal acts find themselves recorded in text. Wiles insists "*Tarlton's Jests* helps us to reconstruct the comedian's technique," (16), though Preiss acknowledges its inevitably apocryphal elements and warns that written figurations of Tarlton promote textual preservation and perpetuation over theatrical "actuality" and erase the agency of the clown (120). While this written archive of performance inevitably obscures the dynamism and skill of live comic performance, it also provides the means for looking beyond text (of all kinds—the "eyewitness" textual account, supplementary texts used by Tarlton, and any supposedly-governing performance script). These anecdotes are rooted in materials—in their processes and resources. It is via these items that the "script" for extemporal exchanges is generated and physically enacted. Physical prompts like an apple remind us of the material agency of these jests; they direct us away from the textual performance fragment towards the dynamic objects that "scripted" ephemeral entertainments like these. Indeed, Tarlton's word-play with apples depends upon exchanges between humans, food, and household items: the offender's face is like "Mapple," a rag or cleaning cloth; the apple is also a "crab" (a bitter apple that also means a base and sour person); and in the first anecdote, the pippin and the spectator's nose are in a continual process of "putting."

The broad semiotic range of the playing apple stretches out these encounters into wider forms of "putting" and exchange that reframe the whole leisure industry as something of an "appleshop." Tarlton's ditties riff on the sexual connotations of the fruit. Indeed, apples are especially associated with perhaps the most ephemeral of early modern London's commercial forms, the sex trade. "Applesquire" was a familiar slang term for a male bawd (Florio O1v), while other posthumous writing about Tarlton suggests the commercial presence of apples across inn, playhouse, and brothel. Henry Chettle's Kind-hart notes in 1593 that, despite the ghost of Tarlton extolling the virtues of players, there is currently a widow who "complains against one or two of them, for denying a Legacie of fortie shillings summe." Should she secure the portion, "she intendes to set vp an Appleshop in one of the Innes" (G4v-H1r). This is quite likely, in part, to be a reference to Margaret Brayne, who, as the widow of its joint builder John Brayne, claimed co-ownership of the Theatre playhouse as well as associated dues from a profit-sharing arrangement with the Curtain playhouse. She also inherited her late husband's East London inn, the George. The Burbage family disputed her playhouse claims, and Brayne found herself in a protracted legal battle to assert her proprietorship. In the year of Chettle's pamphlet she was still at suit over her moity. Chettle suggests on the one hand that Brayne would use her proceeds to run a brothel, but the misogynist double-entendre is finely balanced; in referencing her prospective Apple shop, Kind-hart also recognises implicitly Brayne's theatrical proprietorship and perhaps acknowledges her commercial savvy. The journeys of apples around playing venues were the very business of early modern theatre. They functioned as scriptive things in ephemeral comic performance while also acting as a metonym for a playing culture that stretched from innyard food to playhouse lawsuits.

The Bearbaiting Apple

The pippin-wielding spectator models one form of interactive participation in a brief performance encounter. Such spectators, according to Jonson, Shakespeare, and eyewitnesses like Hentzner, would have been legion at animal-baiting events. Another European tourist, the German Leopold von Wedel, wrote probably the most full and lengthy description of a sixteenth-century commercial ephemeral performance, although it is also perhaps the most enigmatic. His extraordinary account of a visit in 1584 to a bearbaiting arena on Bankside provides a rare clue to the multiple forms of "play" spectators might experience:

> These dogs were made to fight singly with three bears, the second bear being larger than the first and the third larger than the second. After this a horse was brought in and chased by the dogs, and at last a bull, who defended himself bravely. The next was that a number of men and women came forward from a separate compartment, dancing, conversing and fighting with each other: also a man who threw some white bread among the crowd, that scrambled for it. Right over the middle of the place a rose was fixed, this rose being set on fire by a rocket: suddenly lots of apples and pears fell out of it down upon the people standing below. Whilst the people were scrambling for the apples, some rockets were made to fall down upon them out of the rose, which caused a great fright but amused the spectators. After this, rockets and other fireworks came flying out of all corners, and that was the end of the play. (von Bülow 230)

Just as with the textually mediated nature of *Tarltons Iestes*, so von Wedel's summary presents challenges of translation as well as the understandable difficulties of articulating the customs of another culture, even in one's own language. Nonetheless, his climactic, list-like description implies a reasonably thorough chronicle, and it appears in a journal or diary of his travels written up from more immediate handwritten notes.

His visitor's account should therefore query our sense of what exactly constituted a sixteenth-century "play" and whether English spectators, used to visiting the bearbaiting arena in question, would also have seen this as a theatrical performance. In the absence of nearly any other evidence of theatrical shows in bearbaiting arenas, his puzzling account helps defamiliarise the period's entertainment for theatre historians today and can prompt us to ask what "play" occurred at bearbaiting arenas, with what regularity, and what other traces might survive of it. After all, if playhouses regularly hosted physical combat in the form of fencing prizes (Sloane MS 2530; Berry), why should animal-baiting arenas not host human theatre in the form of ephemeral performance? And if, but for the chance survival of two brief legal documents about stage-building (one not privy to historians until 1983 [Loengard]), we nearly "lost" knowledge of the playing structure known as the Red Lion in Mile End, then might we not be missing whole performance practices within them? These are questions we may never be able to answer, but they encourage us to resist hierarchies of evidence forms and artistic value.

Von Wedel's apple, pear, rose, bread, bear, dancing, and firework show (for want of a snappier title) carries with it a radically participatory model of performance. The description of "people" in his account makes no distinction between those involved in the "play" and those in the audience, all of whom seem showered by the performance materials. Indeed, the experience has strong affinities with a retrospective description of play-going by Edmund Gayton written in the mid-seventeenth century and reflecting on the late Elizabethan and early Jacobean entertainment culture. In a florid and fanciful passage, Gayton explains how plays were frequently disrupted from a desired five-act structure, especially during holiday times, when they would end either in "six acts, the spectators frequently mounting the stage," or by forcing the players "to act what the major part of the company had a mind to; sometimes *Tamerlane*, sometimes *Iugurth*, sometimes the Jew of *Malta*, and sometimes parts of all these" (271). On the most lively occasions, Gayton recalls, unsatisfied individuals might riot and almost dismantle the playhouse, before heading

> to the Bawdy houses, and reforme them; and instantly to the Banks side, where the poor Beares must conclude the riot, and fight twenty dogs at a time beside the Butchers, which sometimes fell into the service; this perform'd, and the Horse and Jack-an-Apes for a jigge, they had sport enough that day for nothing. (271–72)

Gayton's account is playful and hyperbolic, but his send-up still tells us something about the perceptions and practices of early modern entertainment. The journey of play he whimsically retells merges playhouse and bearbaiting arena and incorporates animals, organic materials, and humans in a fashion perfectly aligned, it seems, with the eyewitness account of a "play" performed on the Bankside in 1584.

Both von Wedel's and Gayton's theatre histories centre on disposable, throwaway, or single-use items. They describe revelry in the ephemeral that serves as a popular equivalent to the temporary banqueting houses, marchpane sculptures, and masque scenery of the courtly set. Indeed, Gayton frames such piecemeal play in distinct opposition to "high" culture, or rather to properly textual drama—what he calls the "height of Language," such plays as "are read with as much satisfaction, as when presented on the stage" (273). For Gayton, bitty, piecemeal, and materially transient shows arising from mass participation break down both genre and structure, forcing players to "take off their Tragick habits" and leaving them "refractory" (in other words, rebellious, stubborn, or unmanageable) (271). Von Wedel's interspecies Bankside crowds also break down both genre and materials by merging consumption and theatre: the crowds look to eat the white bread, apples, and pears, while the great rose is spectacularly destroyed by the most fleeting of visual displays, a firework. Likewise, Gayton's holidaymakers go so far as to destroy the "stately Fabric" of the whole architectural structure. These immersive performances use up the materials of play and in the moment of liveness consume the theatrical *archive*—"all those items supposedly resistant to change" (Taylor 19). We might then see in these complementary performances an embrace of the fragile and the temporary, as well as a blurring of the stabilising categories (play, sport, game) with which we typically understand the period's leisure culture.

Playhouses and Apples

The consumable understanding of play presented by von Wedel and Gayton also directs us to the architectural structures that supported it. This section explores the playhouse "archive" in its physical sense by considering the relationship between the seasonal and decaying apple and the architectural playing structure. The leap between performance and physical structure is not a big one. Evelyn Tribble has demonstrated how playhouses trained their performers via a "cognitive ecology" that made a theatre building an extended technology or prosthetic of performance. That *cognitive ecology* is also a physical ecology, and I explore here the ways that playhouse materiality was seen by contemporaries to be bound up in perishable materials and natural processes.

Gayton's dissatisfied playgoers render the playhouse into pieces, in a particularly extreme act of theatre criticism. He imaginatively describes how

> the Benches, the tiles, the laths, the stones, Oranges, Apples, Nuts, flew about most liberally, and as there were Mechanicks of all professions, who fell every one to his owne trade, and dissolved a house in an instant, and made a ruine of a stately Fabrick[...] (271)

The foodstuffs commercially available in the playhouse become, in Gayton's account, part of the very "Fabrick" of the building; oranges, apples, and nuts are indistinguishable from the benches, tiles, laths, and stones. These fruit materials in fact form a considerable part of the archaeological remnants of playhouses such as the Globe and Rose and were and are indeed integral to their architectural structure. When the latter was excavated, archaeologists discovered "remains of a moderate range of potential food plans"; in one sample, "most of the material (wood, hazelnut shell, clinker) [...] was from the make-up of the floor mixed with residues of food (fruits) possibly consumed on the premises" (Bowsher and Miller 46). Playhouses were constructed from more than wood and depended on nutshells for flooring, while fruit seeds merged themselves—as they decayed, "bitten" and "broken"—into their surrounding environment. Apples therefore sat alongside a range of archival artefacts and biofacts, from bear bones and dog remains (as found at Bear Gardens and Hope, "Empire Warehouse"; Mackinder et al.) to oyster shells. In Tim Ingold's formulation, these part-repurposed materials are perpetual "substances-in-becoming": "Whatever the objective forms in which they are currently cast, materials are always and already on their ways to becoming something else" (31). Apples and other organic matter constitute the temporary existence and the ecological afterlives of these playing structures.

Such afterlives could be rather immediate. For Gayton, the skills of carpentry and joinery were also part of the "Mechanick" craft of the audience, who were not simply destructive but could skilfully "dissolve" the house "in an instant." These trades acutely understood the mutability of buildings. Cerasano summarises the "common practice of moving buildings around, of taking down a sizeable structure and reconstructing it elsewhere, a practice that was not only cost-effective but efficient and, in many cases, something that could be performed fairly quickly" (105). Peter Streete, the carpenter in charge of dismantling the Theatre and building the Globe, had form for such work (STAC 5/G17/29). He enacted precisely such a feat on the Theatre in 1599 when he "tooke yt downe but to sett yt upp [...] in an other forme." Playhouses were to some degree in perpetual conversion, shifting between one form and another and seen (perhaps partly due to complex legal contracts and clauses) as continually at risk of "dissolving."[4] The Rose's expansion in 1592 is but a large and conspicuous instance of otherwise regular material upkeep, adjustment, and offhand organic modifications (via discarded matter like seeds). The same applies to bearbaiting arenas. Henslowe and Alleyn rebuilt part of the Bear Garden in 1604 and then Henslowe and business partner Jacob Meade repurposed the space again in 1613, entirely rebuilding it as the Hope, where we have already seen how apples once more began to supplement the building fabric ("Bankside Playhouses").

If apples might be seen as one of the moving parts of an ephemeral playing structure, they also suggest parallels in their seasonality. Neil Carson divides the receipts of Henslowe's Diary from the Rose—and the playing, playgoing, and writing practices underlying them—into seasonal splits broadly along the lines of Fall-Winter/Spring-Summer. The experience of these seasons made a difference to early modern understandings of play. Plague restrictions that inhibited performance were linked to seasons, with the London Corporation concerned in late spring and summer months about "the great resorte of people in suche nombers to plays and enterlewdes in this hote season of the yere" (JORS 20, fo. 61v). Winter had an opposite problem. In 1584, the Queen's Men petitioned to return to central inn playhouses, pleading "helpe and relief in o{u}r poore lyuing the ceason of the yere beynge past to playe att anye of the houses w{i}thout the Cittye of London." Authorities acknowledged that "in winter the dark do cary inconuenience: and the start time of day after euening prayer do leaue them no leysure: and fowlenesse of season do hinder the passage into the felds," and so they added caveats for their return to playing within the city (Lansdowne MS

20, fo. 30, 38). Playhouses, like fruits, had seasonal variations and came into "convenience" at different points of the year.

Such a relationship between London and the "fields" represented a wider ecological fragility increasingly recognised across early modern England. Bruce Boehrer has charted the rise in early modern ecological consciousness resulting from "environmental degradation," from deforestation to increased reliance on coal for fuel (21). Weather problems resulted in spoiled harvests and high grain prices, and so the "inconvenience" of the way for the Queen's Men speaks to wider social issues. In 1583, for instance, Thomas Day set out an Elizabethan picture of climate change through a providential lens: "The Lorde hath forewarned us a great while [...] by his creatures, and miraculous tokens, strange monsters, blazing comets, unwanted enumbrations of waters, strange fishes, perilous wars, earthquakings, and last of all, fiery constellations" (A3v). These natural occurrences had a direct impact on the playing industry in London. Laurie Johnson has demonstrated how severe floods in 1594 forced the Admiral's Men to depart for eleven days to the Newington Butts playhouse in the south while repairs were made on the Rose. The inconvenient journey for players and audiences speaks, therefore, to environmental shifts and further represents the transitory nature of playing structures and their susceptibility to natural processes of change or destruction. Bearbaiting was also affected by these shifts. Not only did the Paris Garden structures collapse in 1583, but the sewer system designed to alleviate flooding across Southwark also had more mundane ramifications for the leisure industry. When Richard Reve purchased the Bear Garden in 1592, he inherited fines for the disrepair of its sewer portion and wharf, which led to his "great hinderaunce and almost vndoing" (SKCS 18, fo. 184r). Just as plague in the heat of summer or floods in winter prompted players to depart to alternative venues, so bearbaiting proprietors had to navigate climate consequences, too, and there is an entertainment industry parallel between commercial and environmental "undoing."

The Newington Butts playhouse provides a contrast with riverside venues thanks to the nature of its extra-urban environs, which combine the site of fruit production and consumption. The venue was built on the same plot of land as and looked out into "Jerome Savages orchard corner" (Ingram 162). Journeys to Newington Butts therefore emphasised connections between the city and seasonal agriculture, taking spectators away from the wind- and rain-damaged banks of the Thames towards the semi-rural playing destination of an appleyard—one that may itself at the time have been suffering from the inclement weather. Performances at the playhouse would make especially acute early modern drama's staging of "the imagined end-product of London's consumption of the countryside" (Boehrer 38), given that Jerome Savage's "appleshop" is both an orchard and a playhouse. Back in a suburb like

Bankside, where natural resources "are slowly, unevenly, but inexorably assimilated in the conditions of London life" (Boehrer 6–7), the apple's appearance in commercial ephemeral entertainments gestures to this wider environmental context of movement, exchange, and resource consumption. Von Wedel's bearbaiting "play," for instance, generates theatrical liveness from ecological damage. The sulphuric destruction by firework of a giant rose, blown apart to release its agricultural bounty to the hungry city, emblematises London's environmental relations. When the spectators scramble for scattered bread, the performance raises a sober warning amid the seemingly festive spirit—one especially acute when seen retrospectively from the even more "hungry" 1590s. The mass participation of this Bankside show and its theatricalisation of ephemerality, therefore, suggest shared complicity in and responsibility for ecological relations. Apples of the orchard and the appetites of the city converge on the playing structures of Newington Butts and the bear-baiting arena of Bankside, where, as we have seen, acts of both literal and theatrical consumption eventually come to bear on the fabric of the buildings themselves.

Coda: Playhouses and Archives

Apples do more than remind us of the ephemeral performance cultures at play across early modern London's different leisure venues. They emphasise the "scriptive" agency of natural materials in the period's theatrical *repertoire*, and they accordingly have consequences for its *archive*. Playhouses were not only associated with apples but were physically comprised of nuts, fruit seeds, and shells that still remain beneath the ground or in archaeological repositories and reports—both in deliberate building practices like lining the floor, as well as via accumulative absorption into their structures by way of audience consumption and disposal. They therefore challenge the bounds of the theatre-historical archive and embrace ecofact as much as artefact, fruit as much as document. The distinctions between such categories are themselves a fiction. Miles Ogborn reminds us that even the most textual archive, like memory itself, is "chemical and biological" and depends on "managing the nature of old and stretched animals' skins, pulped and reshaped woods or rags, and chemical compounds." In short, the archive is an ecology "where the materials of remembrance are living, dying, and being devoured" (240). The apple is an ideal example of theatre history's dependence on this rich and mutating archive. In performance terms, it endures as a scriptive thing, continuing to decay, disperse, or shift as "untimely matter" (Harris). It therefore represents the ceaseless demands of doing history, which necessitates revisiting and reposing questions of and assumptions about a past that itself is never static. Organic performance matter is therefore one site, familiar from Taylor, that bridges *repertoire* and *archive*, reminding us (as archivists and archaeologists well know) how the archive is always in processes of physical transformation, unfolding slowly through eco-logical "gestures, shows, performances...." (Taylor 20).

Other early modern performance networks might be discovered by following a similar line of thinking. In 1575, a "counterfeit well" was taken from the Bell in Gracious Street to the court (AO3/907/5 172). Such a journey has a great deal to tell us about the relationship between theatrical matter and the watercourses of early modern London, from conduits to river transportation, and the ecological contexts of perfor-mance that include those Bankside sewers and floods. The well itself likely arrived via river, as did so many of the other materials supplied that year to court, suggesting (like the orchards at Newington Butts and the apples on show and sale) a confluence of representation and reality centred on forever-moving or transforming organic substances. Jemima Matthews has noted, for instance, how "the working world of the river" informs and contextualises performance "events" such as *Merry Wives of Windsor* at Whitehall in 1604 and the "wider set of movements" that surround them (412–13). Plenty of the period's bioperformative (and bio-allusive) props and objects might therefore indicate the significance and agency of natural resources and their theatrical expressions and afterlives. These repertorial things emphasise the powerful imaginative current of organic ephemerality—across foodstuffs, insects, cuttings, or compounds discussed elsewhere in this volume.

Playing apples finally gesture to the deep roots of playtext-less perfor-mance in commercial venues and so offer a means for theatre historians to approach a period for which the archive might seem, on the surface, to be lacking. No plays from the commercial theatres survive, for instance, from the 1570s, prompting Andy Kesson to remark on the decade's "distinctive evidential basis" (21–22). The materials of ephemeral per-formance insist we look beyond the language of "survival" and "loss" and towards an alternative understanding of evidence. A methodology focused on material process and decay offers a lens for approaching a pe-riod for which largely no text survives before the 1580s (and after which print publication is only ever fractional). In the absence of any substan-tial textual corpus, we might look instead to the journeys of bioperfor-mative and scriptive things mapped out here for ephemeral commercial entertainment to imagine other performance models for a mutating play-ing industry and the culture that sustained and transfigured it.

Notes

1 George Peele's *The Arraignment of Paris*, a play contemporaneous with the performances discussed here, offers a playtext-led parallel to some of the apple theatrics in ephemeral performance.

2 Lisa Woynarski's conception of "ecodramaturgy" acknowledges "more-than-human performances through drawing attention to embodied ecologi-cal relationships, emotions, ideologies and political effects" (72).

3 Andrew Sofer explores the relationship "between text and performance," where "stage properties occupy an uneasy position," while Catherine Richardson notes how such properties "are capable of playing a role in the drama and playing themselves—their offstage lives—at the same time" (31).
4 For more on conversation as a paradigm for playhouse building, see Davies, "Bowling Alleys and Playhouses."

Works Cited

AO3/907/5. MS. The National Archives, Kew, London.

"The Bankside Playhouses and Bear Gardens." *Survey of London: Volume 22, Bankside (The Parishes of St. Saviour and Christchurch Southwark).* Eds Howard Roberts and Walter H Godfrey. London County Council, 1950. 66–77. *British History Online.* 25 Nov. 2020.

Bernstein, Robin. "Dances with Things: Material Culture and the Performance of Race," *Social Text* 27.4 (2009): 67–94.

Berry, Herbert. *The Noble Science: A Study and Transcription of Sloane MS 2530, Papers of the Masters of Defence of London.* U of Delaware P, 1991.

Bishop, Tom. "Shakespeare's Theater Games." *Journal of Medieval and Early Modern Studies* 40.1 (2010): 65–88.

Bloom, Gina L. "Games." *Early Modern Theatricality*, Ed. Henry S. Turner. Oxford UP, 2013. 189–211.

———. *Gaming the Stage: Playable Media and the Rise of English Commercial Drama.* U of Michican P, 2018. escholarship.org. Online. Accessed 7 Sep. 2021.

Boehrer, Bruce. *Environmental Degradation in Jacobean Drama.* Cambridge UP, 2013.

Bowsher, Julian and Pat Miller. *The Rose and Globe: Playhouses of Shakespeare's Bankside.* Museum of London Archaeology, 2009.

von Bülow, Gotfried. "Journey through England and Scotland Made by Lupold von Wedel in the Years 1584 and 1585." *Transactions of the Royal History Society* n.s. 9 (1895): 223–70.

Carson, Neil. *A Companion to Henslowe's Diary.* Cambridge UP, 1988.

Cerasano, Susan P. "The Transitory Playhouse: Theatre, Rose, and Globe." *The Text, the Play, and the Globe: Essays on Literary Influence in Shakespeare's World and his Work in Honor of Charles R. Forker*, Ed. Joseph Candido. Fairleigh Dickinson UP, 2016. 95–120.

Chettle, Henry. *Kind Harts Dream.* London, 1590. *Early English Books Online.* 7 Sep. 2021.

Davies, Callan. "Bowling Alleys and Playhouses, 1560–1590." *Early Theatre* 22.2 (2019): 39–66.

Davies, Callan, Andy Kesson, and Lucy Munro. "London Theatrical Culture, 1560–1590." *Oxford Research Encyclopedia of Literature.* 28 Jun. 2021. Online. Accessed 9 Jul. 2021.

Day, Thomas. *Wonderful Strange Sights.* London, 1583. *Early English Books Online.* 7 Sep. 2021.

Earle, John. *Microcosmographie.* London, 1628. *Early English Books Online.* 7 Sep. 2021.

"Empire Warehouse, Bear Gardens." Archaeological Evaluation Report, 2008. London Borough of Southwark. archaeologydataservice.co.uk. 7 Sep. 2021.

Florio, John. *World of Words*. London, 1578. *Early English Books Online*. 7 Sep. 2021.

Gayton, Edmund. *Pleasant Notes Upon Don Quixote*. London, 1654. *Early English Books Online*. 7 Sep. 2021.

Harris, Jonathan Gil. *Untimely Matter in the Time of Shakespeare*. U of Pennsylvania P, 2011.

Harris, Jonathan Gil and Natasha Korda. *Staged Properties in Early Modern English Drama*. Cambridge UP, 2002.

Hill, Tracey. *Pageantry and Power: A Cultural History of the Early Modern Lord Mayor's Show*. Manchester UP, 2010.

Ingold, Tim. *Making: Anthropology, Archaeology, Art, and Architecture*. Routledge, 2013.

Ingram, William. *The Business of Playing*. Cornell UP, 1992.

Intoxicants and Early Modernity, 1580–1740. Chester Record Office, ZQSF 36/32. *Intoxicants and Early Modernity, 1580–1740*. www.dhi.ac.uk/intoxicants. Online. 7 Sep. 2021.

———. Chester Record Office, ZQSF 59/31. www.dhi.ac.uk/intoxicants. Online. 7 Sep. 2021.

Johnson, Laurie. *Shakespeare's Lost Playhouse: Eleven Days at Newington Butts*. Routledge, 2017.

Jonson, Ben. *Bartholomew Fair*. *English Renaissance Drama: A Norton Anthology*. Ed. David Bevington et al. Norton, 2002. 961–1066.

JORS 20. 07 Nov. 1572-1 Aug. 1579. MS. COL/CC/01/01/020–21. London Metropolitan Archives, London.

Kesson, Andy. "Playhouses, Plays, and Theater History: Rethinking the 1580s." Forum, Ed. Andy Kesson. *Shakespeare Studies* 45 (2017): 19–40.

Lansdowne MS 20. MS. British Library, London.

Lewis, Michael. "Toy Coach from London." *Practices of Ephemera in Early Modern England*. Eds Callan Davies, Hannah Lilley, and Catherine Richardson. Routledge, 2023. 169–72.

Lin, Erika. "Festivity." *Early Modern Theatricality*. Ed. Henry S. Turner. Oxford UP, 2013. 212–29.

Loengard, Janet S. "An Elizabethan Lawsuit: John Brayne, His Carpenter, and the Building of the Red Lion Theatre." *Shakespeare Quarterly* 34.3 (1983): 298–310.

Mackinder, Anthony, with Lyn Blackmore, Julian Bowsher, and Christopher Phillpotts. *The Hope Playhouse, Animal Baiting and Later Industrial Activity at Bear Gardens on Bankside, Excavations at Riverside House and New Globe Walk, Southwark, 1999–2000*. Archaeology Studies Series 25. Museum of London Archaeology, 2013.

Matthews, Jemima. "Inside Out and Outside In: The River Thames in William Shakespeare's *The Merry Wives of Windsor*." *Shakespeare* 15.4 (2019): 410–27.

McMillin, Scott and Sally-Beth MacLean. *The Queen's Men and Their Plays*. Cambridge UP, 1998.

Nunn, Hillary M. "Playing with Appetite in Early Modern Comedy." *Shakespearean Sensations: Experiencing Literature in Early Modern England*. Eds Katherine A. Craik and Tanya Pollard. Cambridge UP, 2013. 101–17.

Ogborn, Miles. "Archives." *Patterned Ground: Entanglements of Nature and Culture.* Eds Stephan Harrison, Steve Pile, and Nigel Thrift. Reaktion, 2004. 240–42.

Preiss, Richard. *Clowning and Authorship in Early Modern Theatre.* Cambridge UP, 2014.

REQ 2/184/45. MS. The National Archives, Kew, London.

Richardson, Catherine. *Shakespeare and Material Culture.* Oxford UP, 2011.

Sanders, Julie. "Under the Skin: A Neighbourhood Ethnography of Leather and Early Modern Drama." *Staged Normality in Shakespeare's England.* Eds Rory Loughnane and Edel Semple. Palgrave Macmillan, 2016. 109–28.

Shakespeare, William. *Henry VIII. The Norton Shakespeare.* Ed. Stephen Greenblatt et al. 3rd ed. Norton, 2016. 3269–3352.

SKCS 18. MS. London Metropolitan Archives, London.

Sloane MS 2530. c. 1560–1590. British Library, London.

Smith, Pamela H., Tianna Helena Uchacz, Sophie Pitman, Tillmann Taape, Colin Debuiche. "The Matter of Ephemeral Art: Craft, Spectacle, and Power in Early Modern Europe." *Renaissance Quarterly* 73.1 (2020): 78–131.

Sofer, Andrew. *The Stage Life of Props.* U of Michigan P, 2003.

STAC 5/G17/29. MS. The National Archives, Kew, London.

Tarltons Iestes. London, 1613. *Early English Books Online.* 7 Sep. 2021.

Taylor, Diana. *The Archive and the Repertoire: Performing Cultural Memory in the Americas.* Duke UP, 2003.

Tribble, Evelyn. *Cognition in the Globe: Attention and Memory in Shakespeare's Theatre.* Palgrave Macmillan, 2011.

Walpole, Horace. *Paul Hentzner's Travels in England.* London, 1797.

Wickham, Glynne. *Early English Stages.* Vol. 2. 1963. Routledge, 2002.

Wiles, David. *Shakespeare's Clown: Actor and Text in the Elizabethan Playhouse.* Cambridge UP, 1987.

Wilson, Robert. *The Three Ladies of London. Three Renaissance Usury Plays.* Ed. Lloyd Edward Kermode. 1988. Manchester UP, 2009. 79–164.

Woynarski, Lisa. *Ecodramaturgies: Theatre, Performance, and Climate Change.* Palgrave, 2020.

13 Extensive Ephemera

Perfumer's Trade Cards in Eighteenth-Century England

William Tullett

In the eighteenth century, smell was understood in terms that emphasised its ability to endure across time and space. Perhaps one of the most interesting visual representations of this process comes from an article in the *Universal Magazine of Knowledge and Pleasure,* published in 1752. This article attempted to explain to its audience the workings of smell and the properties of odours and, in so doing, pointed to early-eighteenth-century attempts to mathematically compute the spatial and temporal distance that odours could penetrate (Keil 48; Nieuwentyt 869). The diagram that accompanied the article showed a rose surrounded by clouds of atoms that extended outwards from it. These clouds were separated by alphabetically labelled circumambient circles. As the accompanying text explained, the strength of a smell was linked to its density, and that density decreased "in proportion to the squares of the distance from the odorous bodies" ("Of the SMELL" 172). The capacity of smell to radiate out from a central object was central to eighteenth-century understandings of smell and its capacity to shape atmospheres, identities, and social relationships (Tullett, "Macaroni's" 163).

Recent studies have emphasised how we should avoid seeing printed ephemera as atoms that radiate out from books that are located at the centre of the world of print (Russell). One way of tackling this issue is to focus on the way in which particular forms of printed ephemera were used in daily life, locating ephemeral print in the diurnal context after which it is named (Harris 218). Here the interaction between ephemera and its audiences obtains central importance. In a recent chapter on news and visual culture in Restoration London, Adam Morton has coined the term "intensive ephemera" to describe ephemera that required extended interaction, expected specific knowledge, and were leveraged to temporally specific, in Morton's case political, goals (115). In this chapter, I want to suggest that some ephemera – in this case, perfumer's trade cards – might be characterised as both "intensive" and "extensive." The perfumer's trade card – like the atoms of smell itself – created an evaporating experience in which the printed object in the consumer's hands set off circumambient journeys in their mind.

DOI: 10.4324/9781003058588-17

To some extent eighteenth-century printed ephemera was extensive by its very nature. James Raven has traced how the uniform, repetitive, regularity of ephemeral print provided the reassurance, authority, and organisational framing upon which commerce and state-building depended (56). Jemima Matthews's essay in this collection emphasises the role of ephemeral material components – such as tar, tallow, and oakum – in maintaining ships. The work of maintenance performed by ephemera could be social as well as material. Gillian Russell has demonstrated that the explosion of printed ephemera, from receipts and advertisements to tickets and calling cards, was the glue that bound spaces, practices, and networks of eighteenth-century sociability together (Russell 23). Ephemera constituted the assemblages that made abstract elements of social relationships material, sensible, and therefore durable (Smith et al. 78). Various scholars have traced how the eighteenth century saw the development of a public sphere, new venues of sociability, and philosophical discussions of "civil society." In a wonderful material metaphor, Lynn Hunt has suggested that during the eighteenth century "the space of the social thickened" (86). For the purposes of this collection, the material metaphor is apt, for ephemeral print was one form of matter that occupied this thickening material and imaginative space.

This chapter builds upon these observations by integrating the senses and the imagination into our understanding of printed ephemera. It begins by examining the overlap between the materiality of smell and the metaphors used to describe printed ephemera, demonstrating that eighteenth-century writers thought about the two in similar ways. It then tracks this analogy between smell and ephemeral print through the consumption of printed matter itself, highlighting the multi-sensory urban milieu in which such print was interpreted. This included the emanating odours of city shops – of which perfumers and apothecaries provided a prime example. The final sections focus on two ways in which trade cards attempted to encapsulate the culture of perfumery and the feeling of the perfumer's shop: the civet cat and the use of biblical imagery. I argue that trade cards – and especially perfumer's trade cards – invited an intensive sensory engagement that produced temporally and geographically extensive leaps of imagination on the part of those that handled them. Customers who engaged with the material, visual, and textual properties of perfumer's trade cards were led on a journey through the history of scent that encompassed the art of the perfumer and fragrance of the Christian past. They travelled through the perfume shop into the ephemeral, evaporating, city and out across the oceans into spaces that were distant in both space and time. This chapter therefore follows this journey out from trade cards and into the wider olfactory culture of eighteenth-century England – from natural philosophy to urban ramble narratives and from biblical tales to accounts of trans-oceanic voyages.

Olfactory Ontologies

My approach draws on eighteenth-century olfactory ontologies that emphasised the radiating, atomistic, qualities of odours. The precise materiality of smell had been a subject of considerable debate since Aristotle and Plato. Were smells material or not? Late medieval writers tended to side with immateriality, focussing on the species of odour described in Aristotelian thought (Robinson 46). Seventeenth-century writers were unsure, moving between a series of different theories about odours, but eighteenth-century writers came down on the side of materiality (Dugan 11; Tullett, *Smell* 31). Influenced most prominently by the work of Robert Boyle, eighteenth-century writers understood smell as an endless stream of atoms – or effluvia – constantly exhaling from all and any objects.

This corpuscular understanding of matter also resonated with eighteenth-century understandings of ephemeral print. In Samuel Johnson's account of the Harleian miscellany – a collection of pamphlets acquired by Robert Harley and published in eight volumes between 1744 and 1746 – he emphasised how, by gathering these texts, he sought to secure them "by combination with others; to consolidate these atoms of learning into systems." Without categorization, cataloguing, and sorting into codex form, the burgeoning lake of ephemeral print would "be dispersed in imperceptible exhalations" (Russell 38). Worries about the evaporative quality of bodies of water chimed with contemporary fears about the vaporous effluvia of marshes, bogs, and stagnant water that occupied the attention of neo-Hippocratic physicians and military medicine (Riley 31).

However, the desire to fix and consolidate the atoms of ephemeral print in codex form also bore a comparison with the treatment of smells in eighteenth-century processes of production. Here, a corpuscular understanding of matter was married to ideas about smell as the material essence of a body. According to this view, promoted by Herman Booerhave, every material body had a "*Spiritus Rector*" that could be acquired by distillation (Strother 751; Nicholson 885). Thomas Reid later described this to his readers as "a kind of soul, which causes the smell and all the specific virtues of that body" and that "being extremely volatile, flies about in the air in the quest of a proper receptacle" (23). The brewing of tea and ale, and the making of syrups, all involved trapping the virtues of materials before they could evaporate. For, as one correspondent to the Dublin Royal Society noted, "should this fragrant active Spirit be dissipated, or fly off by too long Infusion or Decoction, the ale is robb'd of all its sprightly parts" and its "grateful Smell and Flavour" (Dublin 196). It was also a useful material analogy for ephemeral print. As one article put it in 1805, ephemeral print's "volatility and divisibility" meant that there was a need to "extract" and "fix" the "particles" of ephemera that flew "like long streamers" from the houses of publishers to "all parts of the united kingdom" ("Review of The Spirit" 282). Printed ephemera required cultural chemists to distil the social imaginaries of society into convenient codices.

It has been noted that early modern ephemeral productions – print and otherwise – often worked by "encapsulating through miniaturisation" (Smith et al. 91). Smell did similar cultural work. The precise qualitative character of olfactory effluvia and how it caused smell was debated. One idea was that each corpuscle was differently shaped and that it was the shape of the effluvia that caused different sensations of smelling. This curiously tactile vision of scent further encouraged the idea that smells were a kind of world in miniature: "sour for instance, is jagged like a prickly pear; bitter, is pointed like a smith's file; sweet is round like a sugar plumb" (Waagstaffe 19). Effluvia that were widely dispersed, the idea of the spiritus rector that distilled the essence of things, and the idea of smells as the material world in miniature provided useful analogies for eighteenth-century ephemeral print.

Ephemeral Cities

One other way in which the materiality of smell and ephemeral print collided in early-eighteenth-century discourse is in the form of the advertising "puff," a term that married flatulence to the insubstantiality of printed advertisements. A "Short Dissertation on Puffs" published in 1735 linked bodily and printed puffs via the medium of hypochondria: an illness that produced both a troubled mind and bouts of crepitation. The two could be discerned by an "acute nose," which would be able to sniff past the "sweet words" of advertisers and detect "a smell not unlike that of a stinking breath perfumed." According to the learned writer of the dissertation, books were "among the most common subjects" advertised by puffs and such advertisements were, like corporeal puffs, "agitations of the air, of short continuance" (1).

The multi-sensory appreciation of printed ephemera in the "Dissertation" might have been metaphorical, but it also had a basis in urban reality. The spaces of the eighteenth-century city registered the ephemerality of advertising print in sound, sight, and smell. In his chapter in this volume, Bruce Boehrer suggests that population growth – particularly in London – during this period produced a new awareness of the buzzing, swarming, environmental ephemerality of urban space. By the late seventeenth century, the growth of population, traffic, and trade in England's largest towns and cities had also produced an increasingly vibrant, changeable, and intrusive sense-scape (Cockayne 129). Observers were, perhaps paradoxically, increasingly attentive to the ephemeral attention and stimulation that urban life produced.

Visually, the exterior and interior walls of the city were increasingly peppered with ephemeral print (Harris 207). This accretion of printed matter competed with signboards, graffiti and the whirling, crowded, sight of social life that might provide the pedestrian with useful information. The "cloudy looks and busy faces" of eighteenth-century urbanites pointed to the style of looking that constantly changing visual impressions required (Corfield 143). These modes of seeing had equivalents elsewhere in eighteenth-century culture. They married with the experimental "grammar of distraction" developed in contemporary novels that encouraged the eye to roam and the fliting, roving, delight in visual variety found in eighteenth-century aesthetics (Phillips 68; de Bolla 26). Ephemera might be the recipient of sustained forms of attention. We can see this in the careful collection, curation, and re-use of recipes on delicate slips of paper detailed in Elaine Long's contribution to this collection. However, the ephemeral print might also produce or reinforce fleeting forms of (in)attention.

The cries, bells, and later horns of newspaper, ballad, and pamphlet sellers illustrated that the transacting of printed ephemera was often a noisy business as well. The broadside ballad and the bellman's verses illustrated how ephemeral print could be an "auxiliary and stimulus" to the soundscape of the eighteenth-century city (Fox 334; Mackarill 14). But ephemeral print was also linked to a "buzzing" auditory culture that drew on the original use of ephemera to describe the short-lived mayfly (Phillips 8). As Bruce Boehrer's chapter in this collection illustrates, this insectile connection had a long and established history. The coffee house, arguably the interior urban venue most associated with ephemeral print in the early eighteenth century, had its own distinct "buzzing" soundscape to match (*Iter Oxoniense* 1; *School of Politicks* 1). This description of the soundscape of the coffee house deployed an onomatopoeic language in which text mimicked sound, thus tying ephemeral print and soundscape together (Ellis 88). By the 1770s and 1780s, the growth of the newspaper press – in the number of titles and tempo of publication – joined with the popularity of the news horn in intensifying the buzzing sound of ephemeral print on metropolitan streets. George Crabbe described the "buzzing train," "noisy throng," and "echo" of alleys as newspaper vendors trumpeted their "base ephemera" through the streets of London (Crabbe 1: 106).

The circulation of ephemeral goods within the city also made tactile impressions. In the shops of the capital, the browse-and-buy model of eighteenth-century shopping enabled customers to build up their material literacy through ephemeral moments of touch (Dyer 694; Smith 1). In markets, finding fresh food and detecting decay relied on tactile and olfactory engagement with goods (Wooley; Haywood; Johnson). Ephemeral encounters shored up more durable habits and forms of commercial knowledge. On the streets, the push and shove of the crowd created an increased awareness – and fear – of tactile contamination by bodies, trades, and street furniture (Arndt 95). The metaphorical rubbing and polishing implied by polite civic life had a counterpart in the whirl of sociability (Sweet 372). The bodily proximity of theatre audience members led to complaints about tactile, visual, and olfactory contamination: spectators were accused of "throwing about their wigs, and almost blinding you with the nauseous scents of their perfumes and pulvilios" (*Tricks of the Town* 11).

Wigs were a prime example of the process of contamination, alteration, or destruction that could befall objects that circulated in the city. Christopher Smart's 1751 memoir of a "very-unfortunate Tye-wig" elaborates on some of the dangers. After starting life atop a physician's head, the wig finds itself in the costume cupboard of a London theatre where it is "duly bedizen'd with perfum'd powder and oil of sweet almonds." However, when its stage career ended abruptly, the wig relocated to the scalp of an army officer and lost its fore-top and one of its tails in battle. The wig then ends up in the hands of a coffee-house newsmonger and – as a result of an altercation – drops into the fireplace of the Temple-Exchange coffee house where had it "not offended the company with a disagreeable stink" it "should have inevitably perished in the flames" (Smart 83). The eighteenth century witnessed the efflorescence of these "it" or "circulation" narratives that followed the stories of objects such as banknotes, coins, and quires of paper. These stories demonstrated how the constant circulation of ephemeral objects in eighteenth-century culture allowed them to build up a tactile, olfactory, and visual patina as they accumulated matter from the city around them. Through recycling and re-use, paper might end up soaking up the tactile, visual, and olfactory qualities of tobacco, brandy, rosewood, or shit (Rusticus 172). But these narratives – told from the sensory perspective of the object – also illustrated the fleeting and ephemeral nature of perception in the city, as objects felt their way through a kaleidoscope of hands, pockets, and spaces (Lake 106).

The visual and auditory assemblages that printed ephemera generated suggest a view of the early eighteenth-century city in which the sensory atmosphere was thick with the interactions between print and the urban sense-scape. The advertisers that used ephemeral print to sell their wares attempted to leverage the bombardment of sensory stimulation to their own aims. They actively encouraged consumers to use all their senses when interacting with their advertising puffs. This led to the odorous analogy used by early-eighteenth-century purveyors of quack "sympathetic" medicines such as the "Anodyne necklace" (Doherty 268). The necklace was a prophylactic and curative that operated on illnesses – especially those affecting children – by sending out corpuscles that joined with the "ailing" atoms and entered back into the body with them in order to seek out and ameliorate the disease. That such atoms constantly exhaled from objects, including the necklace, one "Dr Chamberlen" argued,

> appears from nothing in the World so clear, manifest & evident, as the Sense of SMELLING; by which everyone daily experiences Bodies at a DISTANCE, to emit and send forth more or less vast quantities of these... *Steams, Atoms,* and *Effluvias.* (Chamberlen 136)

The salesman deployed his readers' everyday experience of smells on London streets to illustrate the powers of the necklace by sensory analogy. Early eighteenth-century chroniclers of the ephemeral city offered plenty of evidence for this vernacular materiality. John Gay, who tracked the diurnal rhythms of the street in a poetic guide for the weary walker, advised readers to hold their nostrils where "chandler's cauldrons boil" and "huge hogsheads sweat with trainy oil" (Gay 184). The satirical writing of Ned Ward also linked smell's materiality to the diffuse, decaying, qualities of the ephemeral city. In his jokes about the smells of civets and shit Ward created a vision of a metropolis in a constant process of going off, exuding odoriferous particles from its fungible matter (Ward 25).

The author of the "Dissertation upon Puffs" may have only associated metaphorical malodours and noises with print advertising. However, our discussion thus far has demonstrated that ephemeral print was embedded in and understood through multi- and inter-sensory practices. The particles of print and the urban environment were in a constant state of interaction. The shifting material world of the eighteenth-century city required careful management of the senses to decode the relationship between ephemeral print and an equally ephemeral sense-scape.

The sense-scape of the early modern city was in part defined by the trades and shops that dotted its streets. The percolation of commercial scent-scapes into the surrounding street is not a new phenomenon exemplified by brands like "Lush." In restoration London, the distinctive scent of the coffee shop might guide the visitor's nose to its door (*Character* 2). In fact, there were jokes about poor men effectively "stealing" a meal by loitering in the vicinity of cook-shops and imbibing the nutritive odours (Hicks 73). Perfumers, who only began to obtain a separate occupational identity in the seventeenth century, and the druggists that they evolved from, were no different (Dugan 143). In the late seventeenth century Bernardino Ramazzini recommended that apothecaries "step out of the Shop every now and then to take the Air," lest they be overcome by the heady atmosphere of odours (59). But the perfumes percolated into the street as well. As Defoe suggested in his 1722 *Journal of the Plague Year*, the use of scented prophylactics in churches meant that "there would be such a Mixture of Smells at the Entrance, that it was more strong... than if you were going into an Apothecary's or Druggist's Shop" (239).

The scent of drugs and perfumes blurred the boundary between store and street.

The best example of this in practice comes from Bucklersbury, a small street at the junction of Cheapside and the Poultry in the City of London. Since at least the sixteenth century this area had been the centre of the trade in drugs and perfumes. Shakespeare described over-perfumed gallants who waltzed about the city "smelling like Bucklersbury in simple-time" (217). The scent was such that one early seventeenth-century pamphlet referred to a man who, "passing through Bucklersbury, fell into a kind of trance, with the sweete smels of that street" (Marbecke). By the eighteenth century, claims were also circulating that during periods of plague Bucklersbury had always been protected from infection by the atmosphere of strong smells emanating from apothecary's and perfumer's shops (Moffett, xiii). By the nineteenth century Bucklersbury's scent lingered on in texts on perfume practice. Bucklersbury became part of the history and heritage of the perfumer as they attempted to claim the status of "art" and "profession" for perfumery (Rimmel 206; Thompson 90).

But the scent of the perfumer's shop also extended beyond the boundaries of the street in which it stood. Indeed, in the late seventeenth and eighteenth centuries, overly-scented persons were frequently described as smelling like "a perfumer's shop." This was meant to communicate both the excessive power and the variety of scents that a person was wearing on their person (Tullett, "Macaroni's 'Ambrosial Essences'"). But it also communicated their insubstantiality and ephemerality. The world of the literary review in the second half of the eighteenth century – where the term ephemera was used as a descriptor with increasing frequency – illustrates the developing association between perfume and ephemerality. Perfume was among those luxuries criticised as ephemeral, as when an "ephemeral tribe" of critics was compared to a walking "box of essences" ("On Critics" 465). By the end of the eighteenth century, the products of perfumers, which could only change appearances, were described as "the ephemeral agents of the costly toilet" ("Advantages" 184).

In perhaps the most revealing comment, another writer described the contents of the perfumer's shop as a "long train of etceteras" ("Art of Being Pretty" 150). Here is where the overly perfumed body and the mingled odours of perfumer's shop collide with their representation in ephemeral print. Trade cards, which aimed to miniaturise and epitomise the perfumer's trade, had a difficult job to do. This was not just a problem of stock but a problem of language. As Dominque Laporte has noted, smell "obstinately clings to the index, where the materiality of its referent cannot be suppressed" (Laporte 86). So, in a period before the abstract names associated with modern synthetic perfumery, one response was to resort to lists. Perfumers' trade cards frequently contained lists – long lists – of the scents they stocked ("Arthur Rothwell"; "A l'Etoile"; "D. Rigge"). Over several columns, the names of scents were repeated in different material forms. For example, a 1696 trade card contained around fifteen of the following sort of entries:

Wash Balls
The Royal Chymical,
Musk, Civet, Amber,
Castile, Marble Genoa, Gre-
cian, Spanish, Camphire,
Plain…

Perfumed and Plain Powder
Musk, Civet, Amber, Rose,
Violet, Orange-Flower,
Clovergilly-Flower, Jessamin,
Marshall, Orris, Damask… ("Barnard's")

However, perfumers were also beginning to develop visual languages that attempted to epitomise perfumery. These began to move beyond the encyclopaedic format of earlier trade cards in a way that presaged the use of artful and abstract names in modern perfumery (Maxwell 24). In doing so, they linked the space of the perfumer's shop to far-off temporal and geographical locations through the extensive ephemera of the trade card.

Travelling through Perfume's History

Overly-perfumed persons were also termed "civet-cats." William Cowper turned up his nose when he smelt "civet in the room" from "a fine puss-gentleman that's all perfume" (Cowper 226). The scent of the "civetty-cat" became emblematic of the products of the perfumer in seventeenth and eighteenth-century discourse (Shadwell 16). It should therefore not surprise us then that one of the most regularly used illustrations on perfumer's trade cards – across the whole eighteenth century – was the civet cat.

Civet was a popular early modern perfume. It was obtained from the perennial gland, close to the anus, of a cat native to parts of Africa and Asia. Materially, it was a brown, unctuous, material that had a scent bordering on the faecal. In the early modern period, natural histories, medical texts, and philosophical treatises all wondered at the long-lasting and materially-expansive qualities of odour. Civet and musk were oft-cited examples, both making it clear that perfume was anything but ephemeral. Civet was one among a number of strong scents that tickled the noses and minds of natural philosophers into attempting to mathematically calculate the surprising geographical diffusion and temporal durability of smells (Keill 48; Nieuwentyt 869).

In the early modern period, civet had already taken on its role as a fixative: a material that added longevity to perfumes by decreasing their volatility. It was among a number of materials that, as Robert Boyle described them, "exceedingly heightened" and "enoble[d]" other scents (Boyle 1: 548). Civet and musk lasted a long time, lost little weight despite their atmospheric impact, and thus continued to serve their original purpose long beyond their first use. It was no accident that a London watchmaker chose to trade under the sign of the Civet Cat in the 1760s ("Brachygraphy"). Just as one wound up a watch to set it ticking again, civet was the thing that kept perfumes performing by extending their reach in time and space.

The apparently never-ending scent of civet was proving a useful analogy for contagious materiality in medical thought by the early eighteenth century. The Marseille plague of 1720 produced a flourishing medical discourse in Britain on the qualities and nature of contagious matter (DeLacey 154). Musing on the ability of contagion to travel across time and space, the physician Richard Mead drew an analogy with scent:

> we all know how long a time *Perfumes* hold their *Scent*, if wrapt up in proper Coverings. And it is very remarkable, that the strongest of these, like the *Matter* we are treating of, are most *Animal* Juices, as *Mosch, Civet*, &c. (Mead 17)

Like civet, contagion stuck to commodities in a durable fashion.

Ironically, one recommendation for testing the quality of true civet was to rub it on paper. If the paper could be written on afterwards, then the civet was genuine (Milburn 72). Sniffing paper as a test of quality was not unusual. Testing powder for fireworks involved placing it on white paper, firing it, and then seeing whether it left "sooty" marks and a "noisesome" smell. If it did then the powder was no good (Howelett 39). The civet-cats that appeared on perfumer's trade cards performed a similar function in asserting quality. The animals had been imported to London to be farmed for their civet since the seventeenth century. Alternatively, some druggists and perfumers imported ready-made civet from the Netherlands, Africa, and Asia (Plumb 92; Hill 557). Taking pride of place on many trade cards, the presence of the civet cat was a reminder of the live animals from which the perfume had been obtained and therefore the quality, freshness, and authenticity of the products sold. It gestured to the live presence of civets in London itself – as producers and exotic pets – and the trade card formed one part of the civet's extended journey from its native soil to perfumer's shop and, thereafter, into the homes and hands of consumers (Newton 10; "Living Curiosities").

It is entirely possible that the trade card itself might have contained the scent of the shop – or the products which it rubbed against – and that, in some cases, the scent of civet accompanied its image. Print and paper both materially and metaphorically soaked up smell. The transfer of scent onto different forms of paper was no doubt aided by the reuse of ephemeral print in wrapping potentially odorous purchases. Vendors of quack medicines produced puffs to trumpet their products, but if people refused to accept such pamphlets then they might be "old to the Chandler's shop" (Turner 87). Here they might be used to wrap potentially pungent tallow candles or buttery pastries, soaking up their scent (*Politicks* 17). In the eighteenth century scenting letters was not uncommon among those that could afford it – described as evidence of aristocratic affectation or romantic refinement (Swift 3: 34; Holloway 85). When contagion reared its head on the continent, letters back home were frequently fumigated, smoking them before sending with the smell of tar, vinegar, and aromatics (Browne 53; Howard 427). It-narratives also meditated on the tendency of the "particles" of paper and print to be "blended" with the scents of tobacco, tallow, sweat, and perfume (Bridges 95, 138, 185). Sat with highly perfumed products, the trade card would have retained its scent.

Trade cards had multiple uses – announcement, invoice, receipt, demand for payment, wrapping paper, list of wares and services, or a way of advertising processes of production and the origins of products (Raven, *Publishing*, 61; Berg and Clifford 145). These ephemeral items have been described as part of the "economy of persuasion"(Berg 273). However, they were also much more than this. Erica Fudge has discussed the way in which civet, as the animal-made-object, continued to enact agency through its products (Fudge 86). Retaining the scent of the shop, a visual reminder of the perfumer's animal assistants, the exotic civet cat circulated as a pocket-sized presence – an indicator of the living, material, origins of the consumer product.

The endurance of civet on trade cards also symbolised the historical roots of the perfumer's profession. For example, a 1730s trade card from William Trunkett – a London perfumer – was dominated by a wood-block print of a civet cat and a later trade card from the 1750s for Trunkett's sister (who had carried on the business) likewise featured the same illustration (Trunkett 1732; Sister 1750). Various historians have pointed to the declining fashion for civet in the eighteenth century (Corbin 73; Dugan 19; Tullett, *Smell*, 35). In the second half of the eighteenth-century recipe books advised that "there are many to whom the scent of musk and civet are very disagreeable" (Dossie 2: 42). By the 1780s natural historians could write that civet was "as a perfume, some years back... in high estimation" (Catton 15). The animal origins and overpowering scent of civet were problematic in the eighteenth-century's new spaces of sociability.

Yet the civet cat did not disappear. It maintained its status as a symbol of the perfumer on trade cards and shop signs well into the nineteenth century. From the 1750s onwards fashions changed with greater rapidity and the press began to periodise the trends of the recent past. Consumers therefore exhibited a growing interest in the historicity of products (Campbell 27). In this context civet's decline in popularity made it even more useful to the perfumer, who could use it on trade cards and signage to symbolise the historical roots of their profession and therefore their reliability (Schober 65). The civet was, by the late eighteenth and early nineteenth century, a heritage scent. It therefore moved from encapsulating the materials of the perfumer's trade to promoting the historical origins of the perfumer's art. The civet cat now took those who handled trade cards on a historical and temporal journey rather than a commercial and geographical one.

A Voyage around the World in a Single Trade-Card

Yet perfumers' trade cards did not just rely on the civet cat to try and encapsulate the resonance of eighteenth-century perfume. Biblical tales of scent were still important in discussions of perfume in this period, especially when they were tied to descriptions of voyages. Three particular trade cards, with receipts for purchases made between February and April 1772 from the perfumers Peter Woulfe and Richard Warren, offer us a glimpse beyond the domestic consumption of perfume. These three receipts included purchases of essence of lavender, essence of citron, eau de luce, damask rose hair powder, storax, frankincense, windsor soap, and a selection of smelling and scent bottles. Their chief interest comes from the fact that they were made out to the naturalist, explorer, and man of science Joseph Banks and were part of the preparation for Banks' role, later aborted, in the second pacific voyage with Captain James Cook ("Voluntiers").

Banks himself was no stranger to fashion and was later labelled an effeminate Macaroni in prints by Mathew and Mary Darly (Fara 9). Perhaps some of these perfumes were meant for personal use, although Banks never recorded the use of any of such scents whilst on voyages. The frankincense was "to burn" and burnt perfumes had been advertised for use in fumigating ships ("Richard Warren and Co"). Yet by the 1770s such aromatics were falling into disuse in the context of ship-born fumigation as they were replaced by more thorough cleaning, policies of ventilation, and the use of other commodities such as vinegar (Corbin, 47–49). It seems far more likely that the perfumes were intended for use not on the ship but once the crew set foot ashore on the islands of the South Seas. In 1776, the Tahitian Mai, known as Omai in English texts, returned to Tahiti after spending two years in England. Mai had come to England with Cook on the return from the explorer's second pacific voyage (Fullerton). After spending time as an object of much curiosity and interest in fashionable society, he returned to Tahiti with gifts from his English hosts. On the list of those presents "to be sent out with Omai" we find, next to handkerchiefs, an entry for "14 perfum'd waters & oils" (Banks). The perfumes that Banks had intended to take with him on the second voyage may have been intended to be earlier, similar, scented gifts for the inhabitants of Tahiti and the other islands Banks had planned to visit on the expedition.

The receipts for Banks' perfumes present interesting intertextual references that serve to link together the exploration of exotic climes and the odours of perfumes. On the top of one of Richard Warren's trade cards, he advertised "Small Caskets of Rich Essences and Waters, adapted for the Country or long Voyages" ("Richard Warren and Co."). Warren's trade cards were also elaborate affairs, as the examples that recorded Banks' purchases show. This version of Warren's trade card, which exists in other copies in the British Museum, portrays the biblical scene in which the magi convey their gifts of myrrh and frankincense to the Christ child, whilst underneath a short poem describes the use of perfumes in "Jewish Temples," "Christian Churches," and by "Eastern Princes" ("Voluntiers"). This testifies to the resonance in English culture of associations between incense, here conflated with perfume, and both geographically "other" exotic contemporaries and a temporally "other" Judeo-Christian past. The British Museum examples also include lines from John Milton's *Paradise Lost,* describing the approach to Eden and comparing its "sabian odours" to those of Arabia:

> Now the gentle GALES
> Fanning their Odoriferous Wings Dispense
> Native Perfumes and Whisper when they stole
> Those balmy SPOILS (Warren, "Trade Card")

This trope, of the seductive perfumed gales of exotic lands, is one that recurs in eighteenth-century travel writing. It served to enfold the temporally and geographically other together, describing a fragrant scent characteristic both of a prelapsarian era before the decay concomitant with the fall and a contemporary Arabia and New World (Dugan 158–75). These descriptions were recycled in travel literature throughout the eighteenth century, where smell also functioned as an aid to navigation (Keate 92; Ovington 55; Morton). John Hawkesworth's account of the Pacific voyages described how when off the coast of New South Wales the voyagers experienced "a light breeze from the shore, which was so strongly impregnated with the fragrance of the trees, shrubs, and herbages that cover it, the smell being something like that of Gum Benjamin" (Hawkesworth 2: 655). Benjamin, in modern terminology benzoin, has a vanilla-like smell, is often used as a fixative, and was a popular ingredient in eighteenth-century perfumery. Describing the scent as redolent of benjamin served to associate the island with perfumery and the trade in exotic goods. Sydney Parkinson, for example, described the country about one bay where Cook, Banks, and their company set anchor, from which emanated a "most grateful perfume," as "a kind of second Paradise" (Parkinson 134). The invocation of Miltonic verse on Warren's trade card thus connected perfumery, travel, and the exotic in a way that mirrored the tropes used by travel writers.

The elaborate visual and poetic invocation of perfume's Biblical heritage and exotic fragrance of the east on Richard Warren's trade card enabled consumers to go on their own imaginary voyage across the world. We have proof that such imaginary voyages through time and space did in fact occur as a result of perfumers' trade cards. In 1770 an anonymous correspondent wrote to the *Lady's Magazine*. He had visited Warren's shop and brought away his "bill of the shop". Back at home he "revolved over and over" in his mind as he browsed the contents of the card. The letter followed the journey of his mind as he reflected on the "different fashions of the different parts of the world" and the historical cosmetic practices of "our old forefathers, the Picts," all set off by a perusal of Warren's lists. It also set off a train of imperial anxieties that the "milky Mr Warren" – whose signature product was his "milk of roses" – might "soften the rugged dispositions and hands of Englishmen." What, the author ruminated, would "old Admirable Benbow, Shovel, or Raleigh say?" ("To the editor" 81–83). The correspondent's close study of the trade card was clearly informed by contemporary anxieties about gender and empire that were rife in the metropolis (Wilson 41). But they also testified to the temporal and geographical journeys on which perfumers' trade cards aimed to take people. That perfumers had been successful in promoting themselves through the sign of the civet cat was also evident in the correspondent's suggestion that they should have:

> a statue erected in honour of all perfumers, and cosmetic geniuses; and as an emblem of their ingenuity, vigilance and sweetness, I would have the figure seated upon a golden civet cat, with a washball in one hand and a role of pomatum in the other. There is nothing extravagant in this thought; many statues in former times have been set up in honour of less deserving Greeks and Romans. ("To the editor" 83)

The long lists of products on perfumer's paper advertisements offered an explosive encyclopaedic potential for creative minds to travel into the past and across oceans. The scent and image of the civet cat on trade cards turned an exotic animal from beyond England's shores into a pocket-sized presence, took consumers on a trip through the history of perfumery, and was a potent and long-lasting marker of the journey perfume made from production, through retail, to consumption. The biblical and orientalising language of Richard Warren's trade card offered a trip not just into the Christian past but throughout the expanding geography of Britain's empire. As this suggests, trade cards could indeed take their readers on journeys through time and space. In this sense, they were extensive ephemera.

Conclusion

By tracking eighteenth-century trade cards from their origins in urban shops out into the journeys – real or imagined, historical or geographical – on which they took those that handled them, we gain a better understanding of just how extensive they could be. Situating ephemera in the daily sensory environment of its use and consumption helps us comprehend the cultural and material patina that objects might accrue in their circulation. But this multisensory materialisation of ephemera also reveals how important the eighteenth-century's particular understanding of the senses – how the senses worked and how sensory stimuli acted on bodies and on objects – was in comprehending ephemera not just as a category of print but as a daily experience. The corpuscular material imaginary in which eighteenth-century urban dwellers found themselves, surrounded by particulate matter that impinged on all five senses, produced an ephemeral environment in which the boundaries of bodies, objects, and spaces were blurred by the continual exchange of atoms. Fungible bodies and things circulated through a city that was in a constant state of going off. As these objects circulated through and imbibed the scented effluvia of their environments, they became a kind of archive of urban life. They therefore illustrated an eighteenth-century understanding of the ecological, chemical, and biological facets of the printed archive emphasised in Callan Davies's essay in this collection. But this atmosphere of atoms also had immense imaginative power. The mnemonic capacities of scent are often cited by scholars interested in both the psychology and cultural life of smell. Smelling provides a "powerful thread of connection to histories, like Hansel and Gretel's trail of breadcrumbs," and studies have shown that the journeys that it sets off are frequently spatial as well as temporal in their logic: journeying outwards from the intimate, personal, or domestic that connect them to the world at large (Marks 114; Groes and Mercer 64). The smell of the perfumer's trade card offered a similar narrative trip-wire, sending its users on journeys into the past and voyages across oceans.

Works cited

"The Advantages of Maternal Nurture." *The Lady's Monthly Magazine* 3 (1799): 183–185.

"A l'Etoile orientale. Varia aromata. London. Raibaud et Louis marchands-parfumeurs." Print. Cup.21.g.41/14. London, 1775. British Library, London.

Arndt, Ava. "Touching London: Contact, Sensibility and the City." *The City and the Senses: Urban Culture Since 1500.* Eds Alexander Cowan and Jill Steward. Routledge, 2007. 95–104.

"The Art of Being Pretty." *The Lady's Monthly Museum* 1.10 (1806): 150.

"Arthur Rothwell, Perfumer, at the Civet-cat and Rose." Print. Cup.21.g.41/12. London. 1740. British Library, London.

Banks, Joseph. "Accounts of Presents to be Sent Out with Omai." MS. MS.9, Papers of Sir Joseph Banks, Item 5-5b, sheet 2 of 3. National Library of Australia. Online. Accessed 15 Dec. 2021.

"Barnard's Old Perfume-Shop." Print. Heal 93.1. London, 1696. British Museum, London.

Berg, Maxine. *Luxury and Pleasure in Eighteenth-Century Britain.* Oxford UP, 2005.

Berg, Maxine and Helen Clifford. "Selling Consumption in the Eighteenth Century: Advertising and the Trade Card in Britain and France." *Cultural and Social History* 40.2 (2007): 145–70.

Boehrer, Bruce. "Time's Flies: Ephemerality in the Early Modern Insect World." *Practices of Ephemera in Early Modern England.* Eds Callan Davies, Hannah Lilley, and Catherine Richardson. Routledge, 2023. 44–64.

Boyle, Robert. *The Philosophical Works of the Honourable Robert Boyle Esq,* 3 vols. London, 1738.

"Brachygraphy." Advertisement. May 1760.*Old Bailey Proceedings Online.* a17600521-1. Online. Accessed 25 Jan. 2021.

Bridges, Thomas. *The Adventures of a Bank Note,* 4 vols. London, 1770.

Browne, Joseph. *A Practical Treatise of the Plague, and All Pestilential Infections.* London, 1710.

Campbell, Timothy. *Historical Style.* Pennsylvania UP, 2016.

Catton, Charles. *Animals Drawn from Nature.* London, 1788.

Chamberlen, Paul. *A Philosophical Essay upon the celebrated Anodyne Necklace.* London, 1717.

Cockayne, Emily. *Hubbub: Filth, Noise, and Stench in England 1600–1770.* Yale UP, 2007.

Corbin, Alain. *The Foul and the Fragrant.* Berg, 1986.

Corfield, Penelope J. "Walking the City Streets: The Urban Odyssey in Eighteenth-Century England." *Journal of Urban History,* 16.2 (1990): 132–74.

Cowper, William. *Poems: by William Cowper, of the Inner Temple, Esq.* London, 1782.

Crabbe, George. *Poems.* London, 1807.

"D. Rigge, perfumer, (from Mr. Warren's) Begs Leave to Inform the Nobility and Gentry." Print. 12330.k.12(1). British Library, London, 1780.

de Bolla, Peter. *The Education of the Eye.* Stanford UP, 2003.

Defoe, Daniel. *A Journal of the Plague Year.* London, 1722.

Doherty, Francis. "The Anodyne Necklace: A Quack Remedy and its Promotion." *Medical History,* 34.3 (1990): 268–93.

Dossie, Robert. *The Handmaid to the Arts,* 2 vols. London, 1764.

Dublin, A Society of Gentlemen in. *Essays and Observations on the Following Subjects.* Dublin, 1740.

Dugan, Holly. *The Ephemeral History of Perfume*. John Hopkins UP, 2011.

Dyer, Serena. "Shopping and the Senses: Retail, Browsing, and Consumption in 18thC England." *History Compass*, 12.9 (2014): 694–703.

Ellis, Markman. "The Buzz of Business: Soundscapes of Urbanization in Eighteenth-century London." *Sound, Space, and Civility in the British World*. Eds David Ellison and Peter Denney. Routledge, 2018. 83–105.

Fara, Patricia. *Sex, Botany and Empire: The Story of Carl Linnaeus and Joseph Banks*. Icon, 2003.

Fox, Adam. *Oral and Literate Culture in England, 1500–1700*. Oxford UP, 2000.

Fudge, Erica. "Renaissance animal Things." *New Formations*, 76 (2012): 86–100.

Fullerton, Jan. *Cook & Omai*. National Library of Australia, 2001.

Gay, John. "Trivia: Or, the Art of Walking the Streets of London." *Walking the Streets of Eighteenth-Century London*. Eds Clare Brant and Susan Whyman. Oxford UP, 2007. 169–218.

Groes, Sebastian and Tom Mercer. "Smell and Memory in the Black Country: The Snidge-Scrumpin Experiments." *Smell, Memory, and Literature in the Black Country*. Eds Sebastian Groes and R. M. Francis. Palgrave Macmillan, 2021. 59–79.

Harris, Michael. "Printed Ephemera." *The Book: A Global History*. Eds Michael F. Saurez and H. R. Woudhuysen. Oxford UP, 2013. 205–19.

Hawkesworth, John. *Account of the Voyages*, 3 vols. London, 1773.

Haywood, Elizabeth. *Present for a Servant Maid*. London, 1743.

Hicks, William. *Oxford Jests, Refined and Enlarged*. London, 1740.

Hill, John. *A General Natural History*. London, 1752.

Holloway, Sally. *The Game of Love in Georgian England*. Oxford UP, 2019.

Howard, John. "Venice Lazaretto, October 24th 1786." *The European Magazine and London Review* 19 (1791): 427.

Howelett, Robert. *The School of Recreation*. London, 1710.

Hunt, Lynn. *Writing History in the Global Era*. Norton, 2015.

Iter Oxoniense. London, 1681.

Johnson, Mary. *The Young Woman's Companion*. Dublin, 1770.

Keate, George. *An Account of the Pelew Islands*. London, 1789.

Keill, John. *An Introduction to natural philosophy*. London, 1726.

Lake, Crystal B. *Artifacts*. John Hopkins UP, 2020.

Laporte, Dominique. *History of Shit*. Trans Nadia Benabid and Rodolphe el-Koury. MIT P, 2000.

"Living Curiosities." Print. Bodleian Library Animals on Show 1 (65). Bodleian Library, University of Oxford, Oxford.

Mackarill, Diana R. "A History of Bellman's Verses." *Journal of the Printing Historical Society* 26 (1997): 14–32.

Marbecke, Roger. *A Defence of Tabacco*. London, 1602.

Marks, Laura U. *Touch*. U of Minnesota P, 2002.

Maxwell, Catherine. *Scents and Sensibility*. Oxford UP, 2017.

Mead, Richard. *A Short Discourse Concerning Pestilential Contagion*. London, 1720.

Moffett, Thomas. *Health's Improvement*. London, 1746.

Morton, Adam. "Intensive Ephemera: *The Catholick Gamesters* and the Visual Culture of News in Restoration London." *News in Early Modern Europe.* Eds Simon Davies and Puck Fletcher. Brill, 2014. 115–40.

Morton, Timothy. *The Poetics of Spice.* Cambridge UP, 2006.

Newton, Theodore F. M. "The Civet-Cats of Newington Green: New Light on Defoe." *Review of English Studies* 13.49 (1937): 10–19.

Nicholson, William. *A Dictionary of Chemistry.* London, 1796.

Nieuwentyt, Bernard. *The Religious Philosopher.* Trans. John Chamberlayne. 4 vols. London, 1719.

"Of the SMELL." *Universal Magazine of Knowledge and Pleasure* 10.4 (1752): 170–72.

"On Critics." *The Weekly Entertainer* 48 (1808): 465.

Ovington, John. *A Voyage to Surratt.* London, 1696.

Parkinson, Sydney. *Journal of a Voyage to the South Seas.* London, 1773.

Phillips, Edward. *The New World of Words.* London, 1720.

Phillips, Natalie M. *Problems of Attention in Eighteenth-Century Literature.* John Hopkins UP, 2016.

Plumb, Christopher. *The Georgian Menagerie.* I. B Tauris, 2015.

Politicks in Miniature. London, 1742.

Ramazzini, Bernadino. *A Treatise of the Diseases of Tradesmen.* London, 1705.

Raven, James. *Publishing Business in Eighteenth-Century England.* Boydell and Brewer, 2014.

Raven, James. "Why Ephemera Were Not Ephemeral: The Effectiveness of Innovative Print in the Eighteenth Century." *The Yearbook of English Studie* 45 (2015): 56–73.

Reid, Thomas. *An Inquiry Into the Human Mind, on the Principles of Common Sense.* London, 1764.

"Review of the Spirit of the Public Journals for 1804." *The European Magazine and Review* April 1805: 281–82.

"Richard Warren and Co. perfumers, at the Golden Fleece." Print. Cup.21.g.38/55. London, 1780, British Library, London.

Riley, James C. *The Eighteenth-Century Campaign to Avoid Disease.* Macmillan, 1987.

Rimmel, Eugene. *The Book of Perfumes.* London, 1865.

Robinson, Katelynn. *The Sense of Smell in the Middle Ages.* Routledge, 2019.

Russell, Gilliam. *The Ephemeral Eighteenth Century.* Cambridge UP, 2020.

Rusticus. "Adventures of a Quire of Paper." *The Weekly Magazine* 17 Nov. 1779: 172–73.

Schober, Sarah-Maria. "Zibet und Zeit. Timescapes eines frühneuzeitlichen Geruchs." *Zeitschrift für historische Forschung* 47.1 (2020): 41–78.

The School of Politicks. London, 1690.

Shadwell, Charles. *The Fair Quaker of Deal.* London, 1761.

Shakespeare, William. *The Merry Wives of Windsor.* Ed. Giorgio Melchiori. Bloomsbury, 1999.

"A short DISSERTATION upon PUFFS." *The Grub-Street Journal* 12 June 1735: 1.

Sister [of Mr William Trunkett]. "At the Young Civet Cat." Print. Heal 93.33. London. c. 1750. British Museum, London.

Smart, Christopher. "The Genuine Memoirs and Most Surprising Adventures of a Very Unfortunate Tye-Wig." *Morsels for Merry and Melancholy Mortals*. London, 1815. 83–88.

Smith, Kate. "Sensing Design and Workmanship: The Haptic Skills of Shoppers in Eighteenth-Century London." *Journal of Design History* 25.1 (2012): 1–10.

Smith, Pamela H. et al. "The Matter of Ephemeral Art: Craft, Spectacle, and Power in Early Modern Europe." *Renaissance Quarterly* 73.1 (2020): 78–131.

Strother, Edward. *Prælectiones Pharmaco-mathicæ & Medico-practicæ*. London, 1732.

Sweet, Rosemary H. "Topographies of Politeness." *Transactions of the Royal Historical Society* 12 (2002): 335–74.

Swift, Jonathan. *The Correspondence of Jonathan Swift*. Ed. Harold Williams. 3 vols. Clarendon, 1963.

Thompson, C. J. S. *The Mystery and Lure of Perfume*. John Lane, 1927.

"To the Editor of the Lady's Magazine, on the Effeminacy of the Male Sex." *The Lady's Magazine* 1 (1770): 81–83.

The Tricks of the Town laid open. London, 1746.

Trunkett, William. "At the Young Civet Cat." Print. H. P. 1239. London, 1732. Chetham's Library, Manchester.

Tullett, William. "The Macaroni's 'Ambrosial Essences': Perfume, Identity, and Public Space in Eighteenth-Century England." *Journal for Eighteenth-Century Studies* 38.2 (2015): 163–80.

Tullett, William. *Smell in Eighteenth-Century England: A Social Sense*. Oxford UP, 2019.

Turner, Daniel. *The Modern Quack; Or, Medicinal Impostor*. London, 1724.

"Voluntiers, Instructions, Provision for 2d. Voyage", being papers concerning Joseph Banks' preparations for the second pacific Voyage in HM Ships *Resolution* and *Adventure*. Print. State Library New South Wales. Online. Collections, Series 06. Accessed 15 Dec. 2021.

Ward, Ned. *The London Spy Compleat, in Eighteen-Parts*. London, 1703.

Warren, Richard. "Trade Card." Print. Trade cards Banks 93.45. London. c. 1768–1770. British Museum, London.

Wilson, Kathleen. *The Island Race: Englishness, Empire, and Gender in the Eighteenth Century*. Routledge, 2003.

Wooley, Hannah. *The Complete Servant-maid*. London, 1704.

Index